Colors of Truth

About the Author

Sonali Bhatt Marwaha, PhD, acquired her training in Clinical Psychology from S. N. D. T. Women's University, Bombay. An M. A. and M. Phil. in clinical psychology, with a focus in neuropsychology, She was awarded a PhD by the Andhra University. Her areas of interest are in the interface between philosophy, religion, and psychology, and in the study of religio-cultural aspects of self and identity. Her most recent publication is *Towards a Spiritual Psychology* co-edited with Prof. K. Ramakrishna Rao. Currently she is Director, Center for Empowerment of Women at the Institute for Human Science & Service, Visakhapatnam, India.

Colors of Truth

Religion, Self and Emotions

Perspectives of Hinduism, Buddhism, Jainism, Zoroastrianism, Islam, Sikhism and Contemporary Psychology

Sonali Bhatt Marwaha, *Ph.D.*

CONCEPT PUBLISHING COMPANY, NEW DELHI-110 059

Cataloging in Publication Data—DK
Courtesy: D.K. Agencies (P) Ltd. <docinfo@dkagencies.com>

Marwaha, Sonali Bhatt, 1963-
   Colors of truth : religion, self and emotions : perspectives of Hinduism, Buddhism, Jainism, Zoroastrianism, Islam, Sikhism and contemporary psychology / Sonali Bhatt Marwaha.
   p. cm.
   Includes bibliographical references (p.   )
   Includes indexes.
   ISBN 818069268X

   1. Psychology and religion. 2. Self—Religious aspects. 3. Emotions—Religious aspects.   I. Title.

DDC 201.615   22

All rights reserved. No part of this work may be reproduced, stored in a retrieval system, or transmitted in any form or by any means electronic, mechanical, photocopying, micro-filming recording or otherwise, without the prior written permission of the copyright owner and the publisher.

ISBN 81-8069-268-X

First Published 2006

© Sonali Bhatt Marwaha (*b.* 1963)

Published and Printed by
Ashok Kumar Mittal
Concept Publishing Company
A-15/16, Commercial Block, Mohan Garden
New Delhi (INDIA)

Phones : 25351460, 25351794
Fas : 091-11-25357103
Email : publishing@conceptpub.com

Dedicated to
Life,
Alisha and **Rohit**

The truths are truths for man
And the values are values for man;
Man becomes the center of reference for all.

P. T. Raju
The Concept of Man

Foreword

Understanding self, the deepest part of human existence, has been a challenge since antiquity. *Atmanam viddhi* (Know thyself) stands as a goal since Upanishadic period. It also forms one of the core concerns of contemporary psychological discourse and has significant implications for personal, social, and spiritual development of the people. Interestingly enough the functioning of self is often loaded by affect or emotion. This is not surprising as self is the dearest feature of our experiential world. Dr. Sonali Bhatt Marwah has tried to capture the relationship between the self and emotions in a variety of thought systems. Her analysis encompasses a critical appraisal of various perspectives. This work is a welcome addition to the growing field of self psychology. Being multi-disciplinary in its orientation it informs the reader about many unattended issues.

The questions pertaining to self and emotions raised in this volume constitute the core of the play of human life. The emotions are often involved in pursuing goals that we cherish. As persons endowed with capacity to reflect everyone of us holds a view of "self" that organizes our thoughts, feelings, and actions oriented towards self and others. We value self, nourish it, and try to sustain a positive view of it. People present self to others and try to defend it, in case there is any threat to its existence. It is very dear to us, and as *Upanishadic* story goes we love others because we love our own self. It is, therefore, important to know and realize self. Within this ethos it is not surprising to see self-realization as the highest goal. As Sankaracarya says: if one knows Self other learnings are meaningless and if one does not know it, still other learnings are meaningless. Here the references are for higher self and spiritual experience. But it argues that there is no duality and whatever exists, exists in the form of Brahman. This great identity is not easy to realize. Its realization is characterized to lead to salvation or *Moksha*. The person becomes *Jivanmukta* and achieves *Kaivalya*. By expanding the identity this goal, opens the possibilities of an authentic and responsible life. The spiritual self is common to all the perspectives discussed in the present volume.

The linkages between self and emotion in Indian thought have been expressed in many ways. At a mundane level during everyday functioning we are very sensitive about bodily self and *Ahamkar* (egoity) and our thoughts about it remain emotionally coloured. Perhaps we never approach or appreciate self in a neutral way. That's why Lord Krishna had to propound the ideal of *Sthitaprajya* that maintains equanimity. Such a person views pleasure and pain as equal pieces of information. This needs effective emotional regulation. The Yoga system also talks about *Yama* and *Niyama*. They also draw attention to emotional regulation of self. Emotions often lead to suffering (*Kleshas*) and in order to overcome the resulting suffering we have to take recourse to the path of devotion (*Bhakti*), action (*Karma*) or knowledge (*Jyana*).

The intimate relationship between self and emotion is best exemplified in the notion of *Sat Chit Anand*. Being is consciousness and blissful. The state of *Samadhi* too is described to result in the experience of immense pleasure or bliss. In the *Rasa* theory the aesthetic rapture/sap (*Rasa*) is also treated as a form of Brahman (*Raso Vai Sah*). The pleasure in aesthetic experience is like one that is comparable with experiencing Brahman (*Brahmanad Sahodar*). The devotional emotions change the lives of people in a positive way and perform emancipatory functions.

In the domain of psychology we find that early developments in this discipline did pay attention to self processes. However, with the advent of scientific spirit founded on a physicalist model self was marginalized. Majority of the modern psychologists, adopting an objective, reductionistic, quantitative, and mechanistic stance to the study of psychological phenomena were preoccupied with developing a framework in which all the psychological processes (e.g. learning, memory, perception, motivation etc.) are supposed to be entities in their own right subject to all the operations that are performed with respect to physical objects. These themes are dealt with and explored without any serious concern for a conscious being having self. Not only the cognitive processes are conceptualized in terms of a computational metaphor but also other aspects including social processes are examined within the same framework. The idea of self as knower, experiencer, sufferer and enjoyer became redundant in this framework. This, however, has shaped the approach, vocabulary, and vision of the mainstream psychology. As a consequence a peculiarly limited perspective that undermines the diversity in approaches to psychological phenomena and their situatedness in the cultural context has taken shape.

The phenomenon of self was confined to soft areas of personality research and clinical work. In this tradition emotions occupied an important place. The psychodynamic theories and subsequent developments in this tradition have tried to focus on emotions as site for deciphering the turbulence in the intra psychic world of the people. The clinical interventions are primarily aimed to mould the emotions. Also, being considered as evolutionarily primitive, emotions were treated as irrational, biologically given, and relatively more natural. They reflected changes in basic neuro-physiological functioning. The scene, however, has started changing in recent years. Now we find the recognition of complex interactions between culture and emotions as far as their appraisal, display rules, expression, and vocabulary are concerned. Researchers are showing active interest in these aspects of emotions.

Recent years have also witnessed revival of interest in the study of self processes. It coincides with changes in conceptualization of science, increase in qualitative studies, and rethinking about the role of culture in conceptualizing psychological functions. As a result respect for diverse perspectives is gaining ground. Also, multidisciplinary approaches are being used to address the different problems and issues. The emerging post-modernist position is open to the multiplicity of views and allows space for dialogue across diverse traditions of thought.

Against this backdrop the effort of Dr. (Ms.) Sonali Bhatt Marwah to relate self and emotions is refreshing. By contextualizing her endeavour in the diverse perspectives she has created a bridge between major thought traditions and contemporary psychology. As such the volume fulfils a major gap in the field of cultural psychological inquiry. Past attempts by the scholars like Akhilanand, J.N. Sinha, Ramchandra Rao, Raghunath Safaya, B. Kuppuswamy, and Anand C. Paranjpe have addressed such issues in a limited way by focusing on the Hindu /Indian thought systems only. This volume may be looked at a major initiative to encompass a larger spectrum of thought systems in a manner informed by diverse perspectives.

Dr. Marwah takes the reader on a trip to a terrain covering major traditions that are continuing to inform the world views of the people in the modern period. Also, she presents the perspectives from psychology. In doing so she adopts the strategy of appreciating the position of a particular system of thought with respect to the twin concepts of self and emotion and then critically analyzing it. She thinks that the biological self, the one devoid of any colour is the real self. It is true that the conceptual history of self is not secular or neutral. But there is little possibility of having a view from nowhere. Biological self does not represent the totality of self experience. It is a part truth. Upanishads say: the face of truth is veiled (*Satyasyapihitam mukham*). Humans are perhaps destined to have only the partial truth (or multiple truths!). I think the search for truth is an unending journey and not a destination. It's true that the societies have pathologies and negative experiences are greater than positive ones. But it cannot be attributed to the diversity of views. Adopting biological self as ultimate cannot solve the problems. The biological self has another connotation. It leaves no scope for change. Also, it cannot account for the variety that we find in construing self. It will close the possibility for growth and change. We need to struggle with the situation and have to evolve towards a higher level of consciousness.

Also, biological self in terms of neural circuitry or physiological processes in itself cannot do the job that the colourful self does. We need self to perform various functions (social, communicative) and, therefore, we add to it various qualities (*upadhis*). It is in terms of the social self or identities that we act towards each other. The biological self, however, is certainly an important aspect of selfhood. It also reminds us about our common or shared nature. But treating it as the self shall be a misidentification. It is only by expanding the boundaries of self that can solve the problems of hatred and prejudice. The colours as misidentifications need to be examined and taken care of if we seek the experience of a positive feeling or bliss for self as well as others.

I congratulate Dr. Marwah for undertaking the commendable job of putting the diverse traditions of thought on self in a meaningful manner. I hope the present volume shall contribute to the domain of self studies and encourage readers to learn more about the complexities of the phenomena of self and emotion.

Girishwar Misra
Professor of Psychology
University of Delhi
Delhi

Preface

Living in a multicultural multireligious society like India, it is difficult to escape from the glimpse of different worldviews. Like most people brought up in such environs, I too grew up with the idea of 'that is their way and this is mine'. Unlike most, I dare say, I have not been able to accept the notion of an absolute truth based on any particular religious doctrine. As I look around me, I find too many examples of truth believers who perceive the truth in different ways, as also considering the truth of another as a fallacy. With truth itself a victim in this process, and human lives slaughtered in defending this truth, like many others I asked the question, what is it that makes me believe in a particular truth? The most obvious reason that appeared to me was a belief in a particular doctrine, a religion that we were accidentally born in to. In this train of thought, I asked myself, had I been born in a different community having different beliefs or following a different religion, would I be 'me', with the identity and uniqueness that I attribute to myself right now? Without a doubt I would have been different, as all of us would have been were we born into a culture with different religious beliefs and values. Our religion is the single most influential factor that influences our self, our identity, our worldview, and just about everything that we call our own. This shows up in subtle ways such as in body language, vocabulary, and social attitudes. Understanding religion as a cultural entity thus becomes essential in understanding self and personal identity.

As a naive explorer, I entered into chartered territories and walked the well-worn roads looking for answers in truths that were proclaimed thousands of years ago. This first leg of my journey has taken me through the religions of Hinduism, Buddhism, Jainism, Zoroastrianism, Islam, and Sikhism. In this book, I present a glimpse of these masterpieces of human creativity and angst that have sought to find some meaning in this chaotic world. I have presented these worldviews in the backdrop of contemporary psychology and the perspectives that it assigns to the concept of self. At this point, I may be accused of deviating from the perspectives of the ancient cultures or worldview, and diluting it with perceptions of the new world. However, I believe if it is truth we are seeking, neither the west nor the east has the prerogative of having found the truth.

Having passed through this spectrum of colors, I grow firm in my belief that the only way to end inter-religious prejudice and hatred is an exposure to different worldviews, which will enable us to realize that we all have truths of our own; the foremost *truth* being, we all belong to the species *homo sapien*.

In making acknowledgements, I express my gratitude to all the thinkers, known and unknown, named and unnamed, who have stimulated and influenced my thoughts through the years. Echoes of their perspectives are seen throughout this work, in critique and in agreement. I consider myself fortunate to have had close family and friends as fellow travelers on this journey.

Sonali Bhatt Marwaha

Truth

I met a man ten feet tall with silver spurs at his feet.
Dressed in black, he rode a golden stallion
With wings of flaming red.
He held out his hand and gathered me up
Not a word he spoke, as we rode into blue skies.
Soft white clouds floated by,
Caressing my skin with their moistened feel.
At the gate of heavens door we stopped,
He held out his hands, gently helped me down,
And eased my anxious mien.
With each light step I could feel
The force of life rise within me,
As through the portals we walked
For a mile and some.

On a throne of crystal in the open she sat,
Dressed in the vibrant force of life.
Without a word he sat me down,
On a cloud of disbelief,
And washed my feet with his gentle hands.
He sat across on a cloud of faith
Looked at her as if to speak.
Not a word passed their sublime lips,
But I could feel the language of the soul
Pass through their eyes.
Suddenly I found myself addressed without a sound,
And I could hear the voice of the soul,
As they spoke to me in silent words.

"My friend, She asked,
"You bow not your head in obeisance
As you sit by my side?"
"To the truth I give my soul,
To a doubt I bow not my head,
With unshaken lips, said I.
A peaceful smile crossed her lips,
She looked in me, and I could feel she new
Every thought hidden in the crevices of my mind.
Yet she deigned to ask me,
"My friend, what is this truth that you speak of,
Truth of your flesh or truth of your soul,
Truth of the life you live or the truth of theirs,
Truth of words spoken with belief or
Truth of words spoken in different faiths,
Truth of words of your fellow beings
Or truth of the visions in your soul.
What is this truth that you speak of?"

"My faith, my beliefs and my life are the truth", said I.
"But the world you live in flesh is different than
The world you live in your dreams,
Which then is the truth of your life?"
I sank further into the cloud of disbelief,
As she asked me this in silent words.
Not a place had I to hide
To find the answers to her words.
Seeing my discomfort, the man in black walked across,
Reached out to me, held my hand and walked me up.
Thank the Lord, said I, for this savior.
Their eyes danced a merry smile, as to my chagrin,
He sat me down on
A cloud of doubt.
They stood there by my side,
For how long I know not,
As I sat there confused
With my head bowed down low.

What is the Truth?
The question ran around in my mind.
The life I lead in flesh is true,
I can feel it with my senses.
The life I lead is real,
My kin can feel it through their senses.
But the world that lays hidden within my dreams,
Is just mine to behold.
I sank further into the cloud of doubt
As this question gnawed me through.
I pictured my life as I had lived,
Felt the marks that were left behind,
Yes, that is The Truth.
And the world that rests in my dreams
Is The Truth of my soul.

Ere the doubt could ease,
She questioned me again.
"They walked a road you have not tread,
Nor visioned in your mind,
They feel the scars of the life they've lead,
Not a speck has touched your senses.
Is that the truth?"
"That is their truth and this is mine,"
Shouted I in exasperation.
"I bear not scars in life,
Does that negate the marks of my life?"
The river of life flowed gently within
As She touched my eyes with her slender hands.
To ease my mind they walked me through
Clouds of sublime peace.
For a moment I did think, the test of life was past.

Endless time did pass,
Before they spoke to me again.
"What is your truth? She asked,
As the colors of truth were passing by.

*"My truth lies within my soul
And the life I lead is true."
"What is the truth? Asked he.
Said I,
"In life there is no truth, and
The truth is, all is the truth."
As I spoke these words,
The cloud of my faith dispersed.
I found myself in the midst of
The cloud of truth.
The man in black held me close,
Walked me to the gate of being.
There stood a black stallion
With wings of sheer light.
She touched my soul
With the force of Life
And helped me on the stallion.
As I journeyed to my life,
I could see
The true colors of our worlds.*

Contents

	*Foreword by **Shri Girishwar Misra***	7
	Preface	13
	Truth	15
1.	Introduction	21
2.	Hinduism	39
3.	Buddhism	77
4.	Jainism	97
5.	Zoroastrianism	131
6.	Islam	154
7.	Sikhism	183
8.	Contemporary Psychology on Self and Emotions	215
9.	Understanding the Colors	256
	References	287
	Subject Index	311
	Author Index	316

1
Introduction

The historical time-space of our species is dotted with internecine battles—be it a war of words or a war with armaments. The events of September 11, 2001—the destruction of the World Trade Centers and the attack on the Pentagon in the USA, and the consequent attacks on Afghanistan and the protracted war with Iraq, since 2003; 13 December 2001, attack on the Indian Parliament; 27 February 2002, burning alive of fifty-eight people in a train, and subsequent continuing interfaith riots in Gujarat; the ongoing war in Kashmir, and the unending hatred between the Jews and Palestinians, killing thousands in its wake; the innumerable acts of individual violence carried out against one's kith and kin. Such events continue to unfold, and are endless. These are just the most current in the long series of such unending battles. What motivates our species to violence against its own kind? They are acts unseen in any other species of the wild animal kingdom. Our species seems to be in a constant struggle with its own kind, of "we" against "they"—be it at an individual need based level or at a larger ideological level. Who is this "we" and who are "they"? Persons within who have developed for themselves an identity—an "I." What motivates "I"? Who is this "I"? Is he different from the others—a species created out of God's benevolence in his own image? How has he developed this sense of "I" that sets him apart from the others, and at the same time inextricably links him to the "other"? Answers to such questions seem to be related to the identity of the individuals, their belief systems, and their emotions.

Through the ages, different philosophical systems have evolved around the basic question of our identity. Creationists believe that the mind sprang suddenly into existence fully formed. In their view, it is a product of divine creation. Humanity's egotistic perception as the central point of the universe and all life forms has largely colored our ideas of our place in the scheme of life. According to the evolutionists, the mind has a long evolutionary history and can be explained without recourse to supernatural powers. The recent science of genetics has amply disproved our centrality. Every animal, plant, bug, or blob, if it is alive, it will use the same three-letter word of the genetic code. We all use exactly the same language. All living things are certainly descended from a single ancestor (Dawkins, 1995, Ridley, 1999). What, then, is the history of man? What constitutes, defines, and influences his "self" and its expression in emotions?

The Pre-History of Man

The pre-history of modern man extends beyond in time to the 4.5-million-year-old ancestor known as australopithecus ramidus; the 2 million year old homo habilis, among the first of our ancestors to make stone tools; homo erectus, the first to leave Africa 1.8 million years ago, bringing about the revolution of fire and hunting. The Homo erectus manufactured quite sophisticated stone tools, devised long-distance hunting strategies, and migrated out of Africa over much of the Eurasian landmass. Homo neanderthalensis (the Neanderthals), who survived in Europe until less than 30,000 years ago; and finally our own species, homo sapiens, appearing 100,000 years ago; emerging with them, the revolution of language (Mithen, 1996; McCrone, 1991).

According to Leakey (1994), there was nothing inevitable about the evolution of the homo sapien, as natural selection operates according to immediate circumstances and not toward a predetermined, long-term goal. Thus, from our present status, we are not going to move towards a logical "higher" status of evolution[1]. Evolution is not progress. The popular notion that evolution can be represented as a series of improvements from simple cells, through more complex life forms, to humans (the pinnacle of evolution), is incorrect.

According to Colby (1996), all species have descended from a common ancestor. Different species of organisms modified to adapt to their environments. Thus, evolution is best viewed as a branching tree or bush, with the tips of each branch representing currently living species. No living organisms today are our ancestors. Every living species is as fully modern as we are with its own unique evolutionary history. No extant species are "lower life forms," atavistic stepping stones paving the road to humanity.

Several anthropologists have contributed to the view that instead of being the product of an evolutionary trend throughout the old-world, modern humans have arisen out of a single geographical location. Bands of modern Homo sapiens would have migrated from this location and expanded into the rest of the old-world, replacing existing pre-modern populations. This is known as the "Out of Africa" hypothesis, because sub-Saharan Africa has been identified as the most likely place where the first modern humans evolved (Stringer, 1990). This hypothesis is supported by the "mitochondrial eve" or the "African Eve" hypothesis of contemporary population geneticists (Margulis & Sagan, 1986; Rouhani, 1989; Wilson & Cann, 1992). According to this analysis, modern humans can trace their genetic ancestry to a female who lived in Africa perhaps 150,000 years ago. This one female was part of a population of as many as 10,000 individuals; she was not a lonely Eve with a lonely Adam (Leakey, 1994).

---

1. According to the philosophies, the expansion of our consciousness to a "higher consciousness" is the next phase of evolution for humankind. Will this evolution be that of a population requiring genetic variation, which would then qualify it as "evolution" and would be inheritable; or would it be the "evolution" of a single organism or individual, which would then qualify it as the "development" of an indivdual?

With the advance in our understanding of the behavior and evolutionary relationships of our ancestors, many archaeologists now feel confident that the time is ripe to move beyond the questions about how these ancestors looked and behaved, to a 'cognitive archaeology'—asking what was going on within their minds. The field of 'evolutionary psychology' developed as psychologists realized that we could understand the modern mind only by understanding the process of evolution. This inter-disciplinary approach is essential for a holistic understanding of the evolution and development of the human mind (Mithen, 1996).

Donald (1991) integrated data and ideas from psychology, evolutionary biology and archaeology, and proposed that the mind has passed through three major changes: an 'episodic culture' associated with homo australopithecines, earliest homo and living apes. Donald agrees with Olton's (1984) suggestion that apes have episodic memory that is the ability to store their perceptions of specific episodes. However, they have very poor episodic recall, because they cannot self-trigger their memories: that is, they have great difficulty in gaining voluntarily access to the contents of their own episodic memories independently of environmental cues. Thus, they are largely environmentally driven, or conditioned, in their behavior and show very little independent thought that is not directly related to specific episodes. Donald calls this style of thought and culture "episodic". The second major change was the 'mimetic culture' associated with homo erectus. The form of the adaptation was a revolutionary, supramodal improvement in motor control called "mimetic skill." The development of motor skills enabled hominids to use the whole body as a representational/communication device, that lead to the development of a "proto-language" or non-verbal skills. This provided hominids with a new means of representing reality; this set the stage for the later evolution of language. The last of these, 'mythic culture' associated with homo sapiens involved the ability to construct conceptual models and was closely related to the evolution of language.

He believes that with this third stage the 'mind' became extended in the sense of beginning to use external storage devices i.e. material symbols.

The dominant view within the social sciences of the mind was that of a general purpose learning mechanism. Evolutionary psychologists Cosmides and Tooby (1992) adopted an explicitly evolutionary approach to their work, challenging many of the conventional notions about the mind. They reason that we can only understand the nature of the modern mind by viewing it as a product of biological evolution. The starting point for this argument is that the mind is a complex, functional structure that could not have arisen by chance. In this regard, they treat the mind as one treats any other organ of the body. They argue that the human mind evolved under the selective pressures faced by our ancestors as they lived by hunting and gathering in Paleistocene environments. As that lifestyle ended no more than a fraction of time ago in evolutionary terms, our minds remain adapted to that way of life. Thus, the mind is viewed as a series of specialized 'modules', or 'cognitive domains' or intelligences, each of which are dedicated to some specific type of behavior (Fodor, 1983; Cosmides & Tooby, 1987, 1992, 1994; Greenfield, 1991; Karmiloff-Smith, 1992; Sperber, 1994). Although there are differences of specificities between the theorists, the fundamental concept of modularity is common. Mithen (1996) views the evolution of the mind in three phases: Phase I—Minds dominated by a central nave of general intelligence. Phase II—Minds in which isolated chapels of specialized intelligences are built. In this phase there are likely to have been at least three dominant intelligences. Intuitive psychology, implying social intelligence; intuitive biology as natural history intelligence; intuitive physics as technical intelligence. And, Phase III—minds in which the chapels have been connected, resulting in a 'cognitive fluidity'.

The British anthropologist Kenneth Oakley was among the first to suggest, in 1951, that modern human behavior was associated with the first appearance of fully modern language.

Christopher Willis (1994), a biologist, sees in the emergence of language the possibility of an accelerating pace of evolution. The reason why the ability to speak is such a sharply defined boundary goes deeper than the mere existence of a method of communication. Language paved the way for all the special human abilities that we so value—abilities such as self-awareness, higher emotion, and personal memories. Individuals could now become introspective about their non-social thought processes and knowledge. Consequently, the whole of human behavior was pervaded with the flexibility and creativity that is characteristic of modern humans. Once established, language quickly bred new habits of thought that allowed man mentally to break free of his surroundings. Man became an active thinker about life rather than a passive reactor to the events of the world around him. Chomsky (1957) concluded that there were underlying similarities to all languages that bore witness to a universal human grammar. We all know how to use it, though we are rarely conscious of that ability. Although language may not be the source of the self, it certainly is the source of the 'I'. Ironically, language has proved to be as much a bind to an individuals "personhood," as it has freed humankind from its animal like existence (McCrone, 1991; Damasio, 1994; Leaky, 1994; Mithen, 1996; Ridley, 1999).

The Self

What is the "self"? Why is there a need to relate the "self" with "emotions"? Why is there a need to look at cultural differences, especially at a time of human history where we, as a global community, have never been as close as we are today? According to current perspectives on emotion, culture can penetrate deeply into virtually every component process of emotion. Not only cognitive or linguistic elements that are directly provided by the culturally shared pool of knowledge, but also physiological and neurochemical elements, which need to be adjusted or tuned for the individual to accomplish a reasonable degree of adaptation and adjustment to the pertinent cultural environment (Kitayama & Markus, 1994, p. 5).

According to Paranjpe (1988), social constructionists have repeatedly pointed out, communities tend to share constructions of reality that help guide their collective life; religious constructs, political constructs such as Marxism, autocracy, and other such views of human nature are instances of constructions shared widely in different cultures. We are different because we *think* we are different. As a cultural group or community, our thought processes, combined with our unique experiences has led us to different points within the circumference of the plateau of our unified existence, teasing us into believing that we have arrived at our own exclusive truth.

As a species are we same or are we different from each other? An overwhelming response would be in favor of our individual ethnic differences. In the light of our shared evolutionary history and the human genome project, what, then, contributes to these perceived differences? Our unique genetic structure, our unique geographical position, our unique experiences, or our unique philosophy and culture?

In the absence of a commonality of thought, where does the individual stand? Is he a by-product of his environment or is there a core element that constitutes his self? Like the contaminated waters of the world, does he need to cleanse himself to find his "true" self? Are there basic attributes that form his expression or are they colored by the landscape against which he finds himself?

Irrespective of the philosophical and academic deliberations on the definition of the self, these are truisms we all live by:

> *"I" am body and mind*: From the perspective of a psychologist, the philosophical issue, whether the "I" is a fact or fiction or whether it is a hypothetical construct, accepted as a "fact", based on language, is

inconsequential, as the fact that "I" exist, and "I" act, and am acting now, is a reality.

"I" feel: An attribute and expression of the self, experienced through physiological sensations. Psychologically experienced feelings such as joy, sadness, grief, are as real, as the sensation of pain caused by inflamed nerve endings.

"I" think: An attribute and cognitive expression of the self experienced in the process of acquiring a language, memory, learning new tasks, and utilizing these through the process of thinking. These are basic processes of our self, which aids in forming our identity.

"I" will die: What remain are memories, the existence of which also disappears with the death of the person who remembers. In this sense, "I" cease to totally exist after the last person who remembers "me" ceases to exist. There is considerable debate on this depending on an individual's belief system. However, in the absence of sufficient evidence to support the view of the beliefs of our philosophical systems, be it rebirth or an after life in heaven or hell, we take a pragmatic approach to this issue.

There are as many definitions of the self as there are theories of human nature and behavior. To capture the essence of the individual, I use a simple mode of defining the self, to enable us to make an adequate analysis of all the viewpoints under review.

As the self is a fluid, dynamic organism, we cannot compartmentalize it. Each aspect is dependent on and influenced by the others. It is the knower, the subject, content, and the process of its knowledge. These are the attributes of the self. After a point, it is impossible to identify which aspect of the total personality emerges from which "self."

The self exists at different levels of awareness, forming different aspects of the self. I have identified three primary levels of the self: the biological, social, and private self. These are interdependent self-divisions, viewed as such for theoretical analysis. Each self-division has distinctive, interdependent attributes. The integration of these is the totality "I". Elaborations of these perspectives are dealt with in Chapter 8 on 'Contemporary Psychology on Self and Emotions'.

The superstructure of the self rests on the foundation of the biological or organismic self. It comprises of inherent instincts, traits, and needs formed out of its genetic, biochemical, neurological, and physiological structure. In this rests our cognitive and emotional abilities. Various scientists have approached its study from different angles. It has variously been described as the 'Embodied self' (Marcel, 1949; Sartre, 1956; Merleau-Ponty, 1962, 1963; Byrne & Maziarz, 1969; Neisser, 1991); 'Organismic self' (Williams, 1970; Maturana & Varella, 1975; Blasi, 1976; Ryan, 1991; Unger, 1991; Fisher, 1995a, 1995b); 'Core self' (deCharms, 1968); 'Genetic self' (Dawkins, 1989, 1995, 1998); 'Immune self or the Body's self', (Varela, 1997); and the 'Neural self' (Stuss, 1991; Damasio, 1994, 1999; Brown, 1999).

The social self is the second tier of the self. It comprises the persona of the individual. The roles he plays based on his status within the group, and the internalized norms, which dictate his behavior, that eventually translate into the identity that he assigns himself. There are two aspects of the social self: the Collective self, and the Projected self. The Collective self represents learnt behavior, acquired through the acculturation process, representing typical cognitive styles, prescribed norms of behavior, beliefs of the culture and subculture. It represents internalized roles and group goals, and is largely "other" defined. The Projected self is based on the Collective self, implemented in the process of social interactions. It is self and other defined. It is essentially a combination of the Biological and Collective self. It varies with the role that the individual is playing within a group. It is the persona or functional behavior of an individual in social interactions.

Although referring to the same identity, theorists have taken different positions in describing and highlighting different aspects of the social self. Harré, (1991) and Shotter (1995) emphasize the social constructionist theory of the self; Burkitt (1994) speaks of social differences in the construction of the self. (Kant (1724–1804), Baldwin (1897/1968), Cooley (1902), Mead (1934), Heidegger (1962), Erikson (1968), refer to the self in relation to world. Theorists such as Klein (1976), Trevarthan (1979), refer to "we" identities or intersubjectivity. Rogers (1951) and Sullivan (1953), emphasize the influence of social expectations on self-concept; Greenwald (1982) refers to it as "the public self", and Neisser (1991) as "the extended self". Kaplan (1984), Stiver (1984) and Gergen (1995), identify the "interacting sense of self" or, according to Jordan (1984) and Surrey (1985), the "relational self". The feminist approach emphasizes a different paradigm of the self as "being in relation" (Miller, 1976; Gilligan 1982), or the need for ongoing relationships in shaping self-image (Kohut, 1984).

The private self grows from the biological self and the social self. Although greatly influenced by the social self, it is primarily self-defined. It gives rise to various forms of self-referencing, such as self-love, self-knowledge, self-esteem, self-alienation, self-perception, self-deception, self-appraisal, self-image etc. It is the subjectively derived identity that the individual claims as "real me". Theorists have variously defined it as the 'True or Spontaneous self' (Fromm, 1964; Jung, 1939; Winnicott, 1986; Bergmann, 1991), the 'Real self' (Horney, 1950; Rogers, 1951), the 'Autonomous self' (Van Kamm, 1966), the 'Transparent self' (Jourard, 1964)', the 'Authentic self' (Wild, 1965), or the 'private self' (Fenigstein, Scheier, & Buss, 1975; Greenwald, 1982; Greenwald & Pratkanis, 1984; Neisser, 1991).

Each individual develops varying blends of the different selves and functions from them. This, combined with his individual experience, gives rise to a unique "self"—an individual with his own "personhood." The aim of each aspect of the self is to function in a unified manner, to emerge as a holistic individual.

The Emotions

The emotions are an integral part of the self. They find their roots in the biological self, and are expressive of the private self, and are expressed through the biological and social self. Cognitive appraisal of the environment and emotions play the intermediary role between the Collective, Projected, and Private self.

Emotions arise from, and influence the body, mind, memories, learning, perceptions, interactions with the environment, and the selves. Their expressions are influenced by social and cultural norms. The emotions play an intermediary and interdependent role between the biological, social, and private self. They are the expressions of the self. They influence the relationship between the biological, social, and private self. Their primary goal is to preserve the biological self, as in the welfare of the biological self, rests the life of the individual. In expressing the voice of the self, they strive to bring about harmony between the selves. The experienced emotion is an indicator of the dissonance or consonance between the selves, and between the self and its environment.

The origins of emotions are in the biological self. They are the physiological expression and experience of feelings that occur at a primary unconscious level before they come forth to the conscious level. These are experienced as instinct, intuition, gut feel, sixth sense, and are essential for the welfare of the individual. A pleasant experience and/or safety to the self make it a positive emotion; an unpleasant experience and/or danger to the self make it a negative emotion. The pleasantness/unpleasantness has to be experienced at both the physiological and psychological levels to be truly at consonance or dissonance with the self. For instance, if the social self expresses a positive affect, but this is not experienced by the biological self, the expressed emotion is self-deceptive and in dissonance with the self.

Emotions are cognitive expressions of the self. Different

emotions arise from the different selves. The five basic emotions are fear, anger, love, joy, and grief. The finer nuances of each emotional expression and their culture specific expressions are dependent on language but find their basis in the primary emotions. Emotions are innate; their *expression* is learnt through the acculturation process.

According to Ellsworth (1994b), although the basic emotions are universal, cultures differ in their beliefs about the meaning of these emotions and about the appropriateness of emotional expressions and emotional behaviors in different social contexts. It is not only a matter of visible behaviors; cultures also differ in their beliefs about the appropriateness of even feeling certain emotions in certain contexts. A point to be considered now is that no culture is isolated. There is a far greater exposure of the mass to different cultures today than at any other point of time in history. Finding a 'pure' culture, without any influence from externals, is a rarity. Differences that exist are in the norms and belief systems of a people rather than their propensity for experiencing emotions. The idea that emotions are not purely natural or biological events, but are influenced and shaped through social and cultural processes, has received considerable attention in recent years (e.g., Campos, Campos, & Barret, 1989; Frijda, 1986; Lutz, 1988; Ortony & Turner, 1990; Rosaldo, 1984).

The Self and Emotions

The biological, social, and private selves are in constant dialogue with each other. The level of awareness of these states varies for each individual. An individual strives to maintain or achieve a sense of well-being by the gratification of his needs that are physiological and psychological, primary and secondary, simple and complex.

All needs are necessary to some degree or the other: The biological self seeks gratification of bodily and instinctual needs that are essential for its survival. The social self seeks gratification of needs arising out of social contact, that maintain his membership within his group. The private self seeks gratification of psychological needs necessary for the preservation of his personhood. Thus, emotions serve as the expressive link between the self and its needs. This triad of self, emotions, and needs are the motivation that propels behavior. This is the individual.

As culture plays an important role in the formation of group and personal identity, we need to see how a culture defines self and emotions. Whether the cultural norms take cognizance of the needs of the individual, even within the framework of a collective society. As is largely observed, there is a discrepancy between ideals, norms, and behavior. The evidence for this is observed in social disorder that exists everywhere. Why does this discrepancy exist?

The disciplines of philosophy, psychology, and sociology may choose to debate on the construct of the self, depending on the current trend of thought. However, the issue is a palpable living entity with each individual, who is not even remotely connected with the formal disciplines. His definition of himself, his psycho-social reality, is a reflection of society's perceptions, and expectations, of his role within it. Ironically, the definition of self is greatly dependent on the governing philosophy of the society. To view these concepts from any one perspective—philosophical, psychological, or sociological, would present a monochromatic picture. Where one ends and the other begins is a moot point, and at best, it can be viewed as on a continuum of thought.

To consider that an aboriginal of Australia has the same worldview and perception of himself, as a follower of Islam or Hinduism, is the same as saying that all the waters of the world are same. Though the basic elements of which it is constituted is the same, each has it's own peculiarity depending on the source of its flow, the parts of the world that it traverses, its purity, its contamination, the flora, fauna, and weeds that grow in it. These change its manifest characteristics.

In the absence of a commonality of thought, where does the individual stand? Like the contaminated waters of the world, does he need to cleanse himself to find his "true self"? Are there basic attributes that form his expression or are they colored by the landscape against which he finds himself?

In understanding the underlying psychological framework of a society and its people, it is imperative to look at the values and belief systems of that society. These values and belief systems have their basis in the philosophical traditions and myths of that culture. These traditions have grown out of the critical dialogue of the thinkers of that society in the developmental stages of its growth span. At this point, it is essential to bear in mind that the philosophers themselves are a product of the society in which they have grown. Consequently, their concepts may be a reflection of the prevailing conditions. We can also assume, that a few thinkers, not reflecting the then existing social realities, developed the philosophical system. Their philosophies developing from their own life experiences and idiosyncratic intra-psychic dynamics. However, they do have their moorings in the masses. In essence, there exist two (and more) sets of realities, and truths, at any given time in a society.

In the words of Fernández-Armesto (1998), "We are followers of ill-glimpsed guides. Most of the early thinkers whose influence has helped to form the world left scarce and sketchy indications of their teachings. That is part of their remarkable enduring attraction: unrecorded or poorly recorded thoughts can be reinterpreted to the taste of every generation, without the discipline of fidelity to an unknown questionable text" (p. 101).

The philosophy that defines a society is the *ideal* upheld by them—a perpetuated social myth. Although influenced by these, the psychosocial reality of the individual is different from the ideal. Then how does one attribute a philosophy as being representative of a people? The factor of power (and hence fear), individual and state, largely governs the rules that a group of people live by. For instance, an uninformed and ignorant audience, who cannot really comprehend the nuances of the concepts, would consider the perceptions of a physicist or a "god man," as the absolute. That he wields the power of knowledge or he has the ability to present his views in a convincing manner, are sufficient to assure his audience of the truism of his words. Thus, making them believers. Concepts thus acquired through the force of power—physical, intellectual, and emotional—are internalized and transmitted to each successive generation, constituting our belief systems.

To try to trace back in time the development of a people would indeed be an onerous task. One route is to look at the historical literature. But for an ancient society like India, with its vast source of mythology, folklore, and verbal tradition, it may become difficult to separate fact from fiction; the reality as it existed, from the imagination and internal dynamics of the authors of the mythology and folklore, and the politics of writing history. Moreover, for a society as ancient as India, where myths are considered a reality of history, it becomes all the more difficult to understand the root of social behavior. This, in fact, would hold true for studying any civilization.

In the light of contemporary state of the evolution of our thoughts and knowledge, with the free flow of information in this global village, interpretation of our guiding philosophies would yield a better understanding of the truism of their perceptions. A retrospective analysis of a situation does clear the cloud of confusion that prevailed at that time, when based on limited information and maturity, we believed that that was the truth. This does not negate the experiences or knowledge of our past, nor does it necessarily imply a level of immaturity. Just as we have evolved from the invention of the wheel, from the geocentric, flat-earth perception of our world, we also need to, and have, evolved in our cognitive abilities. Hence, it is worth a thought that our reference point to our present day behavior is still our ancient past.

The literature of each culture developed around the prevailing school of philosophy. These texts have been the guiding force of our social history. They have formed the values, mores, and traditions of social life. They have influenced every sphere of our activity in society and within our self. So much so that our response to the question "Who am I?" is inadvertently, the name of our faith—"I am a Hindu", "I am a Catholic," "I am a Parsi", "I am a Muslim", "I am a Sikh" (even the sub-sect within these). How we view the world and ourselves, our expressions of our self—the most intimate aspects of our life, arise from our identification with our faith. This gives each society its cultural identity. It is the single most influential factor in our life. Whether we choose to be just believers, dogmatists, or renegades, this influence is immeasurable.

Presenting an Indian perspective is an exacting task. There is no single pan Indian identity that can be identified as natively Indian. In this kaleidoscopic social matrix where all faiths are alive, it is indeed difficult to understand how each has influenced the other. Hence, the person of a particular belief system in India is quite different from a person following the same in a different part of the world.

In this book, I do not aim at looking into the "enigma of the self." Nor do I aim at looking at the self through issues of duality/non-duality, subjectivity/objectivity, and permanence/impermanence. Rather, I aim to look at the self as an intra-dependent, interdependent, systemic whole. In this sense, I look at the "person," whom we have verbalized as "I" or "me." Towards this end, I review the predominant and influential philosophies in India—the Hindu, Buddhist, Jaina, Zoroastrian, Islamic, and Sikh philosophies and belief systems—for their perspectives on the concept of self and its expression in emotions. The primary hypothesis of this review is that the percepts of our guiding philosophies influence our self-construal. I have undertaken this theoretical inquiry to understand our "lived reality." A lifelong participation in, and observation of, the Indian culture has formed the basis of this analysis.

The scriptures of each belief system are referred to widely by its members, as indoctrination into their faith. Our clergy preach us the word of our God. From our early years, we learn and internalize the concepts and words of our respective faiths. These tenets are believed and strictly adhered to, as it is the word of our God or Gods.

The word of our "God" is interpreted to suit the specific needs of the prevalent religio-socio-political forces at the helm of society. Norms of conduct are formed, taking refuge in the blind faith of the people. These are further reinforced through the mass media. Alongside, differing views are also expressed. At such points we, as ordinary people, opt for our unique selective vision, which permits us to see only that which we want to see and that which fits within our belief system, bringing forth our prejudiced view of life. The psychodynamics of this is complex and simplistic at the same time, setting up a conflict cycle within the society and individual at the same time. New vistas open up, creating a fear of the unknown, a fear of abandonment by our long held beliefs. Thus, pushing some to opt for a greater dogmatic stance, some to start thinking anew, and some to choose an escapist route from this chaos. Reflections of these reactions are abundant in our global village.

The antecedents of the development of each system is beyond the scope of this work, as is looking into all the finer nuances of its philosophy. The sheer volume of literature and thinkers contributing their perspectives in each of these systems on the concept of self and emotions makes it impossible to do justice to all viewpoints in this work. However, a brief overview of the history of each system is presented in order to gain a better understanding of the concepts under question.

Each philosophical system is looked into independently, along with the implications of its view on contemporary society and individual. Following which an overview of contemporary western psychological perspectives on the self and emotions are presented. The exposition of the concepts under study in each system is by no means exhaustive, or extensive. As much as this writing does not cover in depth the concepts under review, it covers in breadth. For it is only from a panoramic view, that a pragmatic picture can emerge, the ultimate aim being to raise more questions than can be answered here. In this, I hope to find an answer to what the self encompasses, devoid of the colors of a faith, and in the process gain a better understanding of this eternal question "Who am I?"

2

Hinduism

The origins of Hinduism lie in the distant past. A conventional history of Hinduism has been formed and is divided nowadays into three broad but distinct stages, namely, the vedic, the ancient, and the modern. There is no absolute consensus on the dates, which can be taken as broad estimations. However, there is consensus that the primitive foundations of Hinduism are in part of Indo-European origin. The time of the composition of the *Vedas* has been variously placed at 2500 BC, to 2000 BC, to 1500 BC.

The word "hindu" was originally only a geographical term. It is derived from the River Sindhu (the Indus), for the Persians referred to India as the land beyond the Sindhu. The words 'India' and 'Indian' are only Greek and Latin adaptations of the Persian word. But since the inhabitants could never, in any aspect of their life, be separated from their religion, the word "Hindu" became religious, and the national identity became the same as the adherence to a religion (Chaudhri, 1979, p.24). Hinduism would thus appear to be a generic term meaning the religions of the people of India.

The fabric of India has been greatly influenced by the stream of humanity that has made her their home. From the early Aryans, to the Muslim settlers, to the influence of Christianity and the West, all of whom have had a great impact on the beliefs of Hinduism. The materialistic perspective in the form of the Lokayatas and Carvakas[1] are as much a part of the ancient Indian philosophy as the spiritual perspective. The influence of the West brought about a revival of rationalism in Hindu thought. Raja Ram Mohun Roy (1772–1883) founded the Brahmo Samaj movement, under the aegis of which *sati* was abolished, scientific education was encouraged, idol worship and the caste system were denounced. The Arya Samaj movement founded by Swami Dayanand Saraswati (1824–1883), became the spearhead of a dynamic type of hinduism trying to unify all sections of Hindu society, reclaiming those who had gone out of its fold, making new converts, and fighting all enemies who made inroads into the vedic religion. It based its guiding principles on the vedas alone. In the renaissance of modern Hinduism, Mrs. Annie Besant (1847–1933), an English woman, translated and popularized the *Gita*. Her Hinduism was colored, especially in the later years, by occultism and the teachings of the Theosophical society[2]. The true renaissance of Hinduism began with the teachings of Sri Ramakrishna (1836–1886). The religion that he lived and taught was not mere absolutism or theism, not mere *jnana* (knowledge), or *bhakti* (devotion), or *yoga*, not mere vedism or vedantism or *saktism* or puranic Hinduism, not even entire Hinduism, but the universal religion of which all the historical religions of the world are only certain aspects. Yet, he never cut himself off from the Hindu tradition and authority. He handed on the torch to his favorite disciple Swami Vivekanand (1863–1902), who pointed out in a thousand ways how the Vedanta was the steel frame within that vast structure which goes by the name of Hinduism. Sri Aurobindo (1872–1950) reinterpreted the concepts of *moksha*, *yoga*, and *jivanmukti*. He taught that by means of a new type of integral yoga the higher consciousness might not only be realized but also brought down to irradiate the mind and the body of the individual. Mahatma Gandhi (1869–1948), though essentially a political figure, espoused the Hindu way of life, contributing to the interpretation of Hindu thought. The impact of his words having a significant influence over contemporary Hindu world. In the present times, Sri Sai Baba, Maharishi Mahesh Yogi, Sri Satya Sai Baba, Sri Rajneesh, have expounded various aspects of Hinduism (Morgan, 1953).

Hinduism

The *Vedas* (of which there are essentially four—the *Rig Veda, Sama Veda, Atharva Veda and Yajur Veda*)[3] offered the basis on which Hinduism developed. On its foundation developed the mythology, the rites and rituals, the philosophical systems, and all that is relevant to Hindu thought.

The beliefs and practices of the religion have remained substantially unchanged from the fifth century to the present day. Although new features have been added and some old ones modified, nothing that existed at the beginning has become obsolete. The mythology has remained virtually unchanged, for it is the same in classical Sanskrit literature and in the literature in the modern Indian languages. In spite of the various reform movements through its history, the mindset of Hindu social thought has not changed. At the smaller group and community level, in the cities, towns, and villages, the Hindu religious and social doctrines continue to guide individual and social behavior. The basic principles of Hinduism have not been affected by any subsequent changes and continue to exist in the post-modern era.

What is Hinduism?

Hinduism defies description. It is a philosophy, a way of life. None can claim to be the founder of Hinduism, nor is there an exclusive text, nor are there well-defined, dogmatic, and rigid principles of faith or practice. An enormous corpus of literature is associated with Hinduism, to which one can refer for its beliefs, principles, and philosophies. However, none can claim exclusive authority to its authorship. Some of the important texts of Hinduism are—the *Vedas*, the *Upanishads*, the *Purānas*[4], the *Dharma Sūtras* and the *Dharma Śāstras*, the *Rāmāyana*, the *Mahābhārata*, and the *Bhagavad-Gītā*. This list is also not exhaustive. Of these, the *Vedas* are the oldest. They are regarded by Hindu tradition, as begeningless and in a way exert the highest authority. *Veda* means "knowledge" and the *vedānta* means "the end of knowledge." *Vedānta* is another name of the *Upanishads*. The *Upanishads* are the later part of the *Vedas*. There are one hundred and eight prominent *Upanishads*, eleven of which are considered as pre-eminent. The *Upanishads* are the greatest source of Hindu philosophical thought, and all the systems of Hindu philosophy can be found, in their latent but potential form, in these works. The theories of the *Vedas* take on an explicit form in the *Upanishads*. Faith in texts such as the *Rāmāyana*, *Mahābhārata* and the *Bhagavad-Gītā* have held the Hindus together despite their varying beliefs and practices.

There are no basic tenets of Hinduism. There are basic principles on the way to live life, the concept, and nature of God, the varying paths to reach God, a system of social organization, a system of social principles that govern social and individual life. It characterizes society as a whole. The caste system and the various "stages" of life is part of Hinduism. Religion, philosophy and social life all function within a comprehensive system as an integrated whole. Varying beliefs can be found within the framework of Hinduism. A polytheist is as much a Hindu as a monotheist or a monist or even an atheist. All the features of primitive religions, animism, magic, fetishism, shamanism, etc., may be found in their undisguised forms in the current religious life of the Hindus. The Hindus always were, and in their overwhelming majority still are, firm in their conviction that everything in their mundane existence is determined and controlled by the planets and stars. Even today, nothing is undertaken without finding out whether the hour is propitious, and to deny the influence of stars is to provoke derisive contempt (Chaudhri, 1979, Tiwari, 1983).

Monier-Willams (1877), who wrote his book on Hinduism from his knowledge of the Sanskrit texts as well as from information derived from Hindu pundits and reformers, described the diversity in Hinduism as a religion in the European sense very vividly. He wrote: "It is all tolerant, all compliant, all comprehensive, all-absorbing. It has its spiritual and its material aspect, its esoteric and exoteric, its subjective and its objective, its rational and its irrational, its pure and its impure. It may be compared to a huge polygon, or irregular multilateral figure. It has one side for the practical, another for the severely moral, another for the devotional and imaginative, another for the sensuous and sensual, and another for the philosophical and speculative. Those who rest in ceremonial observances find it all sufficient; those who deny the efficacy of works, and make faith the one requisite, need not wander far from its pale; those who are addicted to sensual objects may have their tastes gratified; those who delight in meditating on the nature of God and Man, the relation of matter and spirit, the mystery of separate existence, and the origin of evil, may here indulge their love of speculation. And this capacity for almost endless expansion causes sectarian divisions even among the followers of any particular line of doctrine".

As all aspects of Hindu life, religious, philosophical, social, and individual, is based on the numerous texts, it is essential for our understanding to refer to these. However, the difficulty arises in understanding the Sanskrit lexicography. The meaning of words in ancient Sanskrit was never clear, and the modern is very unsatisfactory. This has lead to numerous interpretations of the texts, based on personal beliefs and orientation of the authors.[5]

The feat of closing the gap between the mundane and the concrete on the one side and the ideal and the abstract on the other was accomplished by the epics and the *Purānas*, a genre of writing considered 'mythology' from the western point. Unlike the *Vedas* and the *Upanishads*, access to the *Purānas* is not restricted by the caste bar. The *Vedas* and the *Upanishads* were cloistered within the confines of demanding and rigorous rules of Sanskrit grammar; unraveling their meaning required the knowledge of the rules of logic spelled out by the *Nyāya* system. Their niceties were shrouded in the complicated arguments and controversies among the various schools of *Upanishadic* and Buddhist thought. By sharp contrast, the epics were made accessible in many Indian languages; the stories in the epics and the *Purānas* were open to be told, retold and endlessly modified into regional and individual variations, and were immensely popularized through the means of classical and folk art (Paranjpe, 1998). That is how the intellectual elite or the Brahmins spread their hegemony over the people. Thus, they subjugated the people through the worldview that they propounded, denying liberty, fraternity, and equality to the vast majority of the folk.

Śankara and traditional *Advaita Vedānta* were vigorous in their position on the exclusion of sudras from the study of the *Vedas*. Śankara presupposes that the *varna* system is based upon birth and physical family membership, and he makes it clear that the metaphysical unity of the "real" cannot in any way be taken as a premise of social and religious equality in an empirical sense (Halbfass, 1991).

Basic Principles of Hindu Philosophy

There are six main systems of Hindu philosophy. The *Nyāya, Vaiśesika, Sāmkhya, Yoga, Mimāmsā,* and *Vedānta.* Of these, the *Nyāya* and the *Vaiśesika* form one group, the *Sāmkhya* and the *Yoga* have much in common, and the *Mimāmsā* and the *Vedānta* are related to each other. They trace their origins to the philosophical expositions of the Vedas and the Upanishads. The vedic literature contains all the seeds from which sprouted the various schools of philosophy, each with its own particular emphasis and style.

The Nyāya—Vaiśesika System

The Nyāya system of philosophy was founded by Sage Gotama (200 BC) and developed by Vatsayana (400 A.D.), Uddyotakara (600 A.D.), Jayanta Bhatta (1000 A.D.), Udayana (1050 A.D.). The Vaiśesika system of philosophy was founded by Sage Kanada (300 BC), and developed by Prasatapada (400 A.D.) Samkara Misra (1500 A.D.), Jayanarayana (1700 A.D.), Mahadeva Pandita.

The Nyāya-Vaiśesika is predominantly based on logic and reasoning. This philosophy asserts that obtaining valid knowledge of the external world and its relationship with the mind and self is the only way to attain liberation. If one masters the logical techniques of reasoning and carefully applies these in daily life, he will rid himself of all suffering. This method is just a means to the ultimate goal of the self-liberation (Tigunait, 1983, pp. 70-71).

The Sāmkhya-Yoga System

The Sāmkhya philosophy is considered the most ancient of all the philosophical schools. It was systematized by the great sage Kapila. The Sāmkhya-karikā of Isvarakrsna is the earliest available Sāmkhya text. Among its well-known commentators are Gaudapada, Vaēaspati Misra, and Vijnānbhiksu. The uniqueness of this system lies in its summing up of all the categories of reality as described in the Nyāya-Vaiśesika into two categories—*purusha* and *prakriti*—and thereby introducing a dualistic philosophy (Tigunait, 1983).

According to the Samkhya theory of causation, an effect, *parinamavada* or manifestation is already existent in unmanifested form in its cause. This is essential to Samkhya philosophy and forms the foundation for its other theories (Tigunait, 1983).

The Samkhya system holds that the entire world—including the body, mind, and senses—is dependent upon, limited by, and produced by the combination of certain effects. Material atoms cannot produce the subtler forms of nature such as mind, intellect, and ego. The ultimate cause from which gross objects and their subtler aspects are derived is called *prakriti*. Prakriti is neither atomic substance nor consciousness, but it possesses the three gunas of *sattva, rajas*, and *tamas*. These *gunas* are intrinsic nature of *prakriti*. They are the root cause from which the entire universe is derived. They cannot be perceived, but can only be inferred. This state of natural equilibrium of all things is called *prakriti*, and when the balance is disturbed, they are said to be in *vikrti*, the heterogeneous state. *Sattva* is weightlessness and light (*laghu*); *rajas* is motion or activity (*calam*); and *tamas* is heaviness, darkness, inertia, or concealment (*avarna*). The *gunas* are formless and omnipresent when in a state of balance, having given up their specific characteristics when submerged in each other. In a state of imbalance, *rajas*, is said to be in the center of *sattva* and *tamas*, thus resulting in creation (Tigunait, 1983).

The Mimamsa-Vedanta System

The Mimamsa emphasizes the teachings of the Vedas and developed out of the ritualistic teachings of the Veda; the Vedanta is the culmination of vedantic thought, and emphasizes them the teachings of the Vedas in the light of knowledge.

The word *"mimamsa"* means to analyze and understand thoroughly. Traditionally the Mimamsa system is called the Purvamimamsa, which means the earlier or initial teachings of the Veda, and the Vedanta is called the Uttara-mimamsa, which means the later or higher teachings of the veda. The main goal of the Mimamsa philosophy is to provide a practical methodology for interpreting the teachings of the veda. In so doing, it also provides a philosophical justification for rituals and explains the meanings behind them. It also discusses the science of sound and the science of *mantra*, but the major concern of the Mimamsa system is to emphasize the use of meditation with rituals (Tigunait, 1983, pp. 183–184).

The major teachings of the Mimamsa-Vedanta system are that of selfless action, as selfish action serves as a rope of bondage; by loving all, one loves the life force itself. One should learn to express love through mind, action and speech; of these, actions is the most important. No one can help a person who is not committed to self-improvement. To attain this, the Mimamsa emphasizes importance of well-organized daily schedule, which does not interfere with one's external or internal life well organized daily schedule, social awareness. When one becomes self-controlled and self-disciplined, he gradually becomes socially aware and eventually finds himself in perfect resonance with society.

Different commentators have explained the *sutras* of the Vedanta philosophy, each commentator trying to justify his position through profound reasoning and argument. In this way over the course of centuries, many schools have developed the most famous ones being those developed by Sankara, Ramanuja, Madhava, Vallabha and Nimbarka.

There are four basic principles of Hindu thought which are common across all the sects of Hinduism, which unifies it as a singular system. These are belief in the supremacy of the Vedas, belief in the supreme consciousness *Brahman* and the immortality of the soul, the law of *karma* and rebirth, and the possibility of *moksha.*

"The Upanishads center around the doctrine of the Brahman and the atman. By Brahman is meant the all pervading God. Atman means self. The Upanishads point out that the Brahman and the atman are the same. The supreme has manifested Himself in every soul. In the Upanishads the student of religion is told 'Thou art That' (*tat tvam asi*). This idea provides the core of most Hindu religious thought. This is a monistic doctrine, which denies the existence of the world as separate from God. The meaning of Brahman is not easy to grasp. He is described as the one Divine Being 'hidden in all beings, all-pervading, the self within all beings, watching over all works, dwelling in all beings, the witness, the perceiver, the only one, free from all qualities. He is the one ruler of many who (seem to act, but really) do not act; he makes the one seem manifold' (Svetasvatara Upanishad, VI, 11–12). The supreme has manifested itself in every soul. Through the cycle of births, man approaches his final end—the realization of his self. Thus the individual soul is immortal (Sen, 1961, p.19).

Karma is the consequence of action. *Samsāra* is the cycle of indefinite transmigration of living beings. These are elements at an esoteric level, which most resemble religious dogmas. They are postulates based on a conviction, which is not open to discussion. Man suffers passively the necessity of death in order that he may be born and die again, and again. This retributive accountability is the basis of Hindu pessimism. However, by his actions man can, to a certain extent, direct his destiny. Actions that determine later stages can create results in exact proportion to the original action. The non-liberated man is subject to a common destiny. Enslaved by his actions that follow him indefinitely, he is condemned to be reborn; and as most human actions are tainted by malice, the risk of being reborn in a lower condition, ultimately as an animal, is greater than the possibility of achieving an exalted state (Renou, 1961, pp. 43–44).

Moksha or liberation is the freedom from the cycle of birth and death and merging with *Brahma*. In principle, this is seen as the ultimate aim of life, and an ideal. However, the means of achieving this are arduous, and even after many cycles of birth and rebirth, make the possibility quite remote. Hinduism speaks of four roads to the ideal of *moksha*. The *jñāna mārga* (the way of knowledge), *karma mārga* (the way of works), *bhakti mārga* (the way of devotion), and the *yoga mārga* (the way through psychophysical exercises). According to Tiwari (1983, p. 9), "anyone according to his temperament may adopt any of these ways and attain salvation. Thus, Hinduism in its very temperament is against any rigid rules of religion. It is very liberal and broad hearted in its approach and outlook." However, in practice, this liberality is within narrow confines of a tradition bound system. The ancient lawgivers were averse to the idea of permitting freethinking. "By this they mean thinking outside the general structure of faith, or, in the way in which they put it, reasoning not in strict conformity to what is declared in the scriptures.

This would have suited their social and political purpose" (Chattopadhyaya, 1976, p. 172).

The philosophy is one aspect of the Hindu religion. Another is its moral code of behavior. There are "approaches" to the spiritual life; and there is "*dharma*", which is at once norm or law, virtue and meritorious action, the order of things transformed into moral obligation—a principle which governs all manifestations of Indian life. These in totality form the *sanātana dharma* or the eternal law (Renou, 1961).

The ultimate source of all the rules is the sacred law, or *Dharma Shāstras*, in the ancient texts like the *Manu Smriti* and the *Parasāra Samhitā*. For the greater part, rules are so well established that they have become customs, so that even when no authority for a practice can be found in any text it is binding if it has been customary for a long time. It is a matter of pride for all Hindus to follow these rules. They describe this as having *'achāra'* (observance, good conduct) and *'vichāra'* (discriminating between actions). In addition to the *Dharma Shāstras*, the ideal of Hindu social behavior is drawn from other texts such as the *Rāmāyana* and the *Mahābhārata*. These ideals are upheld more for the Hindu women, coercing them to function within the confines of these ideals. These socio-religious customs are well entrenched in Hindu society governing all aspects of social, personal, and intimate life. Obedience to the inhibitions and taboos is as much a part of the Way of Works (*karma Mārg*) of the Hindus as is the scrupulous performance of the rites of the religion (Chaudhri, 1979, pp. 188–189).

In this chapter, I look at the *Upanishadic* philosophy along with the *Bhagavad-Gītā*, the most popular rendering of this position. Along with it the popular epics, the *Mahābhārata* and the *Rāmāyana* are alluded to, as they represent the popularization of the principles of *Upanishadic* thought. For the social aspects of this philosophical tradition, I refer to the *Manu Smriti* as it prescribes the laws that govern Hindu society.

The Self in Hindu Thought

Different commentators have explained the *sūtras* of the Vedānta philosophy each trying to justify his position through profound reasoning and argument. All comment on and try to resolve the following questions: what is the ultimate reality? From where do all physical and mental phenomena originate? What is the nature of the state in which all phenomena dissolve? What is that reality through which everything is known? What is the means for attaining immortality? What is the nature of the self? What happens after death? What is the importance of the body, mind, and senses? (Tigunait, 1983).

"(i) They unanimously maintain the existence of an all pervasive reality, called Brahmā or Ātman. (ii) They analyze the self as distinguished from the body, breath, mind, and intellect, which cover the self like veils or sheaths (kosha). (iii) The pain and pleasure one experiences are considered to be the passing and changing modes of the body, senses, and mind, born of ignorance and not ultimately real. (iv) The self is considered to be eternal and to have the essential nature of bliss and knowledge. (v) Whatever seems to be pleasant is so because of the existence of the pure self in that object; the pure self is the ultimate source of all joy. (vi) This self is to be realized with the help of a sharp and penetrating intellect. (vii) This self-realization is the highest goal of life. (viii) To achieve this goal, the Upanishads do not encourage external rituals but instead emphasize the internalization of awareness" (Tigunait, 1983, p. 215)

A human being is a combined state of self, mind, *prāna*, and body. The body is the dwelling place of the self. The self is hidden in the innermost chamber of the heart, and five sheaths veil it. Human life is a composite of these five sheaths and the self. The five sheaths are the physical sheath, the energy sheath, the mental sheath, the sheath of wisdom, and the sheath of bliss. The physical sheath, which includes the skin, blood, flesh, bone, marrow, and ligaments, is composed of five gross elements. This is the grossest and outermost veil

Hinduism

of the soul. The next sheath the energy or *prāna* sheath is subtler. The gross manifestations of the energy sheath in a human being, is the breath. There are ten subtle levels of prāna sheath, on which human biochemical functioning depends. Subtler than the energy sheath is the mental sheath. It comprises four inner instruments of cognition: lower mind (*manas*), ego (*ahankāra*), intellect (*buddhi*), and mind stuff (*chitta*). Beyond this sheath is the sheath of wisdom, through which knowledge from eternity transmits into the intellect. The last sheath is the sheath of bliss. This sheath should not be confused with *Brahmā*, whose essential nature is pure bliss. Compared with this bliss, this sheath is merely pseudo-bliss predominated by ignorance. The self at this level is very close to realization of its essential nature but is not yet free to see its glory and perfection (Tigunait, 1983).

"The self has a body, but the body is not the self. The self becomes a slave of the senses and their objects because of its identification with the body, senses, mind, and the other sheaths. The moment the self remembers its real nature and understands that the five sheaths are provided for its enjoyment, it detaches itself from them and is no longer affected by the charms and temptations of the world. The Vedānta system does not deny the importance of the sheaths, but it makes one aware that he should not identify himself with them, that he should go beyond them to enjoy eternal life" (Tigunait, 1983, p. 236).

"In Vedānta, the mind is divided into four parts or functions: lower mind, ego, mind-stuff, and intellect. "The lower mind (*manas*) is the importer exporter of feelings and sensations from the external world through the intellect to the self. Ego (*ahankāra*) is the faculty that is responsible for the sense of 'I-ness'. It relates dualistically to the external world, identifying with the objects of the world and developing attachment or aversion to them. Mind-stuff (*citta*) is that faculty in which all memories—whatever passes through the lower mind, ego, and intellect—are stored and are occasionally recalled to the surface of the lower mind. Intellect (*buddhi*) is the decision-making faculty. It is the aspect of mind nearest to the self and is predominated by *sattva*, the quality of brightness and lightness" (Tigunait, 1983, p. 239).

The Upanishad looks upon the development of the self as the aim of the human being and the human society. The mature and well-integrated self is the goal so that the mind and the ten organs are under firm control, of the intellect, which is under the control of the self. Here the self is equated with individual consciousness, and ultimately with the pure consciousness, the individual, and absolute. The individual self is the highest reality among finite objects. It comes nearest to the absolute. The self exists but cannot be objectively represented, it can only be realized; the self can neither be perceived nor conceived. Self-realization is the supreme aim of man (Kriyananda, 1975; Kuppuswamy, 1990).

"To reach (the goal of man—the supreme treasure, the supreme bliss), the Upanishad asks us to renounce all selfish desires, the tyrannies of lust and greed. The mere striving to satisfy the instinctive cravings and social needs, they declare boldly, is not the goal of human life. They affirm values that are higher than the physical, biological, and social. They also affirm that it is the pursuit of those higher values which lead to an integrated and whole life" (Kuppuswamy, 1990, p. 27).

According to the Bhagavad Gītā, the body is mortal, but the self that is embodied in it is immortal. The body is born and dies. However, the self neither is born nor dies. It is unborn, eternal, inexhaustible, omnipresent, unmoving, and immutable. The self assumes a new body when its old body is worn out. The body, five cognitive organs, five motor organs, mind (*manas*), intellect, and egoism are composed of purity or essence (*sattva*), energy (*rajas*) and inertia (*tamas*), which are effects of *prakriti*. However, the self is devoid of these *gunas*. The objects of the world also are composed of these three *gunas*. The *gunas* act upon other *gunas*. There is determinism in the realm of nature. The sense organs are greater than their objects; mind is greater than the sense organs that are controlled by them; intellect (*buddhi*) is greater than mind; self (*ātman*) is greater than intellect. The mind-body complex is the not self (*ksetra*), while the self is its knower (*ksetrajña*). The knower is different from the known. The self is devoid of the *gunas*. However, it experiences through the mind-body-complex. The body is the organ of the self's action. Without it the self cannot act. The cognitive sense organs, mind, intellect, and egoism are the organs of knowledge. The self is the master of the body. When it departs from the gross body, it takes the sense organs, *manas, buddhi,* and *ahamkāra* along with it. It leaves the gross body, and departs with the subtle body. Until it realizes its disembodied and non-empirical nature, it cannot achieve liberation (Sinha, 1961, p. 3).

The *Mahābhārata* recognizes the influence of body and mind on each other. It asserts that bodily disease is produced by mental disease, and that mental disease is produced by bodily disease. It ascribes bodily diseases to the predominance of any of the bodily humors—flatulence, bile, and phlegm—over the other two. It traces bodily health to the equipoise of the bodily humors. The mind is composed of purity or essence (*sattva*), energy (*rajas*) and inertia (*tamas*). When these are in a state of equilibrium, the mind is in a healthy condition. However, when *rajas* and *tamas* predominate over *sattva*, it becomes diseased (Sinha, 1961, p. 4).

The Social Self in Hindu Thought

Hinduism addresses the social self through its treatises on social norms and behavior. The *Dharma Shāstras*, the *Manu Smriti*, the *Rāmāyana*, and the *Mahābhārata* address these through their specific laws or by implication as expressed through characters in the unfolding of the epics. It is important for us to refer to these texts, as they are the basis of the Hindu social identity and provides them norms of social conduct, which influence their perception of themselves. These norms provide stereotypes of gender identity and behavior. They are the basis on which the social self is formed and developed. The social self is our individual and collective reality. In this reality, it influences our self-construal.

The *Smritis* embody the laws formulated by saints and sages—Manu, *Yājñavalkya,* and others. No date can be definitely assigned to these scriptures, since scholars differ by as much as several centuries in their estimates. The *Manu Smriti,* for instance, is assigned by Sir William Jones to 1250 B.C., and by Sir Monier Williams, to as late as 500 B.C. We can be safe in asserting that the *Smritis* are post-Vedic, inasmuch as the code of laws found in them is traditionally supposed to be based on the Vedas (Prabhavananda, 1978, p. 134).

The Laws of Manu or the *Manu Smriti* is an extensive and detailed exposition on the rules of behavior that an individual has to follow. They record civil laws, social obligations, and ceremonies performed at the birth of a child, during initiation into Vedic *mantra,* at marriage, and at the moment of death. They comprise, in short, the daily duties, and customs to be observed by the several castes and by people in different stages of life; and their avowed purpose is to aid all men to attain the highest spiritual development. Among the duties and disciplines prescribed by the Laws of Manu are conquest of the senses, freedom from lust and greed, study of the sacred scriptures, and detachment from the world. One must speak only when necessary, honor old age, respect ones' parents, and injure no one, whether in thought, word, or deed. In the twelve books of Manu, there is an account of creation, and there are teachings regarding education, marriage, domestic life, and laws of the state, punishments, reincarnation, and ultimate freedom. The main purpose of the code was to preserve a fixed society, which it achieved through the caste system (Prabhavananda, 1978, pp. 134–135).

Although the rules for women are few, the impact of these has been profound on their selfhood. The *Manu Smriti* states, "By a girl, by a young woman, or even by an aged one, nothing must be done independently, even in her own house"

Hinduism

(M. S.: V, 147). "In childhood a female must be subject to her father, youth to her husband, when her lord is dead, to her son, a woman must never be independent" (M. S.: V, 148). "She must not seek to separate herself from her father, husband or sons; by leaving them she would make both (her own and her husband's) families contemptible' (M. S.: V, 149). "She must always be cheerful, clever in (the management of) household affairs, careful in cleaning her utensils, and economical in expenditure" (M. S.: V, 150). "Him to whom her father may give her or her brother with her father's permission, she shall obey as long as he lives, and when he is dead, she must not insult his memory" (M. S.: V, 151). "A virtuous wife who after the death of her husband constantly remains chaste reaches heaven, though she may have no son, just like those chaste men" (M. S.: V, 160). "But a woman who from a desire to have offspring violates her duty towards her (deceased) husband, brings on herself disgrace in this world, and loses her place with her husband (in heaven)" (M. S.: V 161). "Offspring begotten by another man is here not considered lawful, nor does (off spring begotten) on another man's wife (belong to the begetter), nor is a second husband anywhere prescribed for the virtuous women" (M. S.: V, 162). "By violating her duty towards her husband, a wife is disgraced in this world, (after death) she enters the womb of a jackal and is tormented by diseases (the punishment of) her sin" (M. S.: V, 164). He further states, "She who controlling her thoughts, words, and deeds, never slights her lord, resides (after death) with her husband (in heaven), and is called a virtuous (wife)" (M. S.: V, 165). "In reward of such conduct, a female who controls her thoughts, speech, and actions, gains in this life highest renown, and in the next world a place near her husband" (M. S.: V, 166). "Though destitute of virtue, or seeking pleasure elsewhere, or devoid of good qualities, (yet) a husband must be constantly worshipped as a god by a faithful wife" (M. S.: V, 154). "A faithful wife, who desires to dwell (after death) with her husband, must never do anything that might displease him who took her hand, whether he be alive or dead" (M. S.: V, 156). "At her pleasure let her emaciate her body by (living on) pure flowers, roots, and fruit; but she must never even mention the name of another man after her husband has died" (M. S.: V, 157). "A man is given the right to beat his erring wife" (M. S.: VIII, 299) (Buhler, 1990).

Manu asserts, the characteristics of man are more important than those of the woman. One of the important reasons for looking upon women as being inferior is that she has her monthly period. Even when a man is mad with desire, he should not approach his wife when her courses appear, nor should he sleep in the same bed. The wisdom, energy, strength, and sight of the man who approaches a woman in her periods utterly perish. If he avoids her during that period, his wisdom etc. will increase (M. S.: IV, 40–42). He should not even converse with a menstruating woman (M. S.: IV, 57). A menstruating woman becomes pure after the menstrual secretion has ceased to flow (M. S.: V, 66). The impurity of the woman in this period is clearly declared in another verse. 'A man becomes pure by bathing when he has touched a chandala, a menstruating woman, an outcaste, a corpse etc.' (M. S.: V, 85). Thus, the menstruating woman is equated in pollution to an outcaste and a corpse (Kuppuswamy, 1990).

Manu also declares that it is in the nature of women to seduce men. So, the wise should always be guarded in their company. Not only a fool, but even a learned man will be led astray by a woman and will be made a slave of desire and anger. This is why Manu recommends that one should not sit in a lonely place even with ones' mother, sister, or daughter! He, however, adds that this is because the senses are powerful. He puts the blame on the man's senses rather than on the wiles of the mother's life (M. S.: II, 213–214). The creator himself, it is asserted, made women to love their bed, their ornaments and hence impure desires, dishonesty, malice and bad conduct (M. S.: IX, 17) (Kuppuswamy, 1990).

Manu also asserts that women must be honored and adorned by fathers, brothers, husbands, and by brothers-in-law. "Where women are honored, there the Gods are pleased.

Hinduism

However, where they are not honored, no sacred rite yields rewards. Where the female relations live in grief, the family soon perishes. There is prosperity only where the women are not unhappy" (M. S.: III, 55–57) (Buhler, 1990).

The Emotions In Hindu Thought

The Vedantists have given us a detailed phenomenological analysis of emotions, emotional states, and the range of emotional nuances that are experienced by us. Emotions are described as differing effects of, *rajas* (energy), *tamas* (inertia), and *sattva* (purity or essence). Attachment, clinging, yearning, lust, detachment, non-greed, haughtiness, intolerance of excellence, self abasement, harshness, purity of motive, firmness, endurance, remorse, indifference, are some of seventy three different states described. These are based on observations and an acute awareness and understanding of human nature. However, emotions and emotional states are described as afflictions and perversions of the mind.

Sankara, (around 700 AD), maintains that negligence in the quest for ones' real nature produces delusion (*moha*). Delusion produces egoism (*ahamkāra*). Egoism produces bondage. Bondage produces suffering. Forgetfulness of the real nature of the self produces intellectual disorders in a person who pursues pleasures of the senses. Intellectual disorders are the causes of emotions. Rāmakantha asserts, all persons have their right knowledge eclipsed by their individual nascence, and cannot discriminate between reality and unreality, and are, consequently infected *by mental perversions like joy, sorrow and the like* (Sinha, 1961).

Sankara mentions desire—for self and 'not self'. Bodily desires, social desires and intellectual desires are of the 'not self'. Desire for immediate apprehension of the absolute or *Brahmā* is for the self. He treats all emotions—lust, anger, greed, delusion, fear, dejection, grief, joy, sorrow and the like as mental modes of *māyā* (illusion) which is the root cause of the phenomenal world. Delusion is destroyed by discriminative knowledge (*viveka*), which is due to the distinct knowledge of the self (*Ātman*) or *Brahmā* (Sinha, 1961).

Love, is defined by Śankara as a kind of attachment. He regards it as a feeling of identity of oneself with some other entities. Love is sympathetic identification of others emotions of happiness and misery with ones' own emotions. Attachment (*rāga*), clinging (*asanga*), desire/lust (*kāma*), compassion (*dayā, karunā*), friendship (*maitrī*) are some of the nuances of love, which are described as independent emotions (Sinha, 1961).

Buddhaghosa defines joy (*harsa*) as an emotion, which is manifested as mental enjoyment that has the characteristic of experiencing a desirable object. Its function is to exploit the desirable aspect of an object in one-way or another. Joy is further described as an exaltation (*utkara*) of the mind, elation of the mind, joy as mental happiness and not bodily pleasure; felicity which is evoked by the attainment of a desired object (Sinha, 1961).

Anger is defined as aversion for hostile objects that are perceived or remembered and painful to the self. It arises from the obstruction of a desire by an agent, conscious or unconscious. Ānandagiri defines anger as a mental mode, which arises from subjection or oppression by another person and which gives rise to a desire to inflict injury on oneself and the wrongdoer. Vallabha defines anger as intolerance of the non-attainment of an object of desire (Sinha, 1961).

Sankara regards grief as mental agony due to the advent of a calamity or the loss of a cherished object or a beloved person. It is aroused by the frustration of ones' endeavors for the realization of an end. Rāmakantha describes grief as a mental perversion due to non-discrimination between self and not self, which overwhelms the heart and causes utter bewilderment of the mind (Sinha, 1961).

Rāmānuja (1017–1137 AD) describes fear as a painful emotion that arises from the perception of a cause of the loss of a cherished object or the advent of an evil. Ānandagiri describes fear as a learnt behavior, as he observes that fear is

Hinduism

experienced by a person to whom harm has been done. He observes that unless a person has suffered injury, he cannot apprehend evil and feel an emotion of fear. Anxiety is described as mental agitation that is generated by fear (Sinha, 1961).

The *Mahābhārata* traces all emotions to essence or purity (*sattva*), energy (*rajas*) and inertia (*tamas*) of the *manas*. *Sattva* produces pleasure, *rajas*, pain, and *tamas*, delusion or false knowledge. *Sattva* gives rise to cheerfulness, joy, and equanimity. Lust, anger, greed, fear, fatigue, dejection, grief, vanity, conceit, and infatuation arise from *rajas* and *tamas*. Excessive joy, delight, bliss, pleasure, and mental equilibrium arise from *sattva*. Discontent, mental agony, grief, greed, and intolerance are due to *rajas*. Non-discrimination, delusion, and languor are due to *tamas*. Physical and mental pleasures are due to *sattva*; physical and mental pain, to *rajas*. Whatever is perceived with a pleasant feeling tone is an effect of *sattva*. Tranquility and purity of mind also are its effects. What is perceived with an unpleasant feeling tone is an effect of *rajas*. What is perceived with a neutral feeling tone and cannot be definitely ascertained is an effect of *tamas*. Concentration of the mind (*citta*) on the self in its essential state, dispassion, forgiveness, nobility, and the like are modes of *sattva*. Egoism, mendacity, lust, anger, and enterprise for the attainment of objects of desire, pride, vanity, and hatred are modes of *rajas*. Delusion, indolence, oversight, and the like are the modes of *tamas* (Sinha, 1961).

The *Mahābhārata* describes the origin, interrelation, and control of emotions. Anger springs from greed, is increased by others' faults, and suppressed by forgiveness. Lust springs from desire, is increased by indulgence, and suppressed by abstinence from sex-gratification due to wisdom. Greed always springs from false knowledge, and is suppressed by true knowledge of the transitoriness of all objects of enjoyment. Delusion springs from false knowledge, and leads a person to commit sinful acts through habit. It quickly disappears when it arises in a wise persons' mind because it cannot stand the light of reason. Pride springs from the possession of noble lineage, learning, wealth, and the like, and it is quickly suppressed when it is known. Jealousy springs from sex-desire and joy, and it is suppressed by wisdom. Deep resentment is felt by a person who is powerless to retaliate on a powerful enemy who has inflicted injury upon him, and is suppressed by compassion. Grief springs from the loss of an object of love, and is quickly suppressed by the knowledge of its antidote. Lust and anger are suppressed when desire and aversion are suppressed. Anger springs from delusion or intellectual confusion and generates a desire. Desire produces greed and infatuation, which generate pride and arrogance. They give rise to egoism, which leads to action. Egoism is the main spring of action. Anger, joy, and dejection, spring from one another. Attachment and aversion are due to ignorance of the transitoriness of their objects. Anger is suppressed by forgiveness. Love and hatred are suppressed by the transitoriness of their objects. Lust is suppressed by abstinence from sex desire. Fear is suppressed by vigilance. Desire, aversion, and yearning are suppressed by firmness. Greed and delusion are suppressed by contentment. Conjecture is suppressed by definite knowledge. A person who has controlled his sense organs is not subject to lust, anger, greed, vanity, haughtiness, self-glorification, wrath, envy, and disparagement of others (Sinha, 1961).

Through The Prism

The central figure in the personality pattern, in the Hindu sense, is the 'concept of self', 'self-consciousness' or 'self-awareness' or the 'impression' of the individual about himself, his capacities, his characteristics, his worth, and his abilities *in relation to* the 'universal self'. According to Hinduism, just as the identification of the self with reality is a delusion, the emotions are a consequence of the delusion, and perpetuate this delusion. They are variously considered as intellectual disorders or afflictions of the mind, preventing the self from seeking the ultimate goal of merging with the supreme self, *Brahman*. This forms the basis of Hindu philosophy. Thus, all aspects of the philosophy and social laws are directed towards attaining this goal of merging with the Ultimate Reality. Life as is lived is "*māyā*"—an illusion, which deviates one from the path towards seeking liberation. This conceptualization creates an inseparable bond between "religion" and the "way of life."

Saksena (1944), surveying the literature on the psychological nature of consciousness in Hindu philosophy, has derived four possible theories of "self-consciousness": (a) self as a mental perception; (b) self not by perception but by inference; (c) self as a higher and supernormal perception; (d) self as self-luminosity. He has further categorized the first two theories as realistic and the last two theories as idealistic. The realists make the self as essentially unconsciousness, and impose upon the process of self-consciousness the status of an object and derive the self-subsisting reality of consciousness. The idealists on the other hand insist upon its transcendental, unchanging, and distinction-less nature.

Thus, for the Hindu, the "I" is neither self, which is the object of "I" nor ego, a psychic agency. "I" is pure consciousness whose only counter player is *Brahman*. Thus, "I" as an individual am negated, and "my" reality is denied, as just an illusion. At one level, there may be a blind acceptance of this ideal, as it has a strong religio-cultural backing, but at the level of the individual person, what are the consequences on his personal development and self-concept? When the self, as one knows oneself, is constantly measured against a higher ideal of the 'universal self', it may generate a sense of discomfort with oneself, as a 'lesser being'. In addition, as Kakar (1981) states, "the Hindu is taught that his perception of himself, of the outside world and others around him, remains *māyā*: a fragment, an apparent reality which, even if it is socially shared and sanctioned as *mātam* (opinion about reality), is not *tatvam*, the ultimate, true reality known only to the liberated man". The consequences of this are likely to be a lack of confidence in the wholeness and naturalness of our individual self.

According to the Upanishadic view, the self is considered to be eternal and to have the essential nature of bliss and knowledge (of the 'universal self'). Matter rests in the state of its essential nature. However, the Upanishadic concept of "I" is an abstraction, not based in the realm of our experiences and lives. This "ideal", especially an unknown ideal, is a concept which is primarily derived out of the thought processes or thinking patterns of philosophers. As Lin Yutang states, "ideals are caricatures of thought."

A counter point to this may be that this mode of thought arises out of ignorance of the scriptures, and ignorance of the true nature of the self, as one has not attained the requisite higher level of consciousness. Why does the 'self' rest within us, in a state that is not in its essential nature? This absence of bliss is the state of the self as observed in all individuals around us. In which case, should not this contrary state be the norm, and the state of bliss a deviation from the norm, or a factor existing—and achievable—within the realms of normal existence? Hence, should we not learn to live in this "non-bliss" state, rather than consider it an abnormality and yearn for an illusive "bliss" state? In accepting this state of "bliss" as the true state, are we not discounting reality as it exists? As a group of people sharing common beliefs, does this become a socially sanctioned shared delusion?

"The *Maitri Upanishad* declared, '*indrajalamiva mayamayam svapna ive mithyadarsanam*": The experience of this false world, is a mere illusion, like that of the magic show, it is like a dream. This brief formulation determined in an important sense the subsequent course of the development of Indian idealism for over two thousand years. Practically all the Indian idealists follow the Upanishadic suggestion and try to explain away the reality of the material world by reducing our normal experience of it to the status of a dream and illusory experience" (Chattopadhyaya, 1976, p. 309).

Hinduism

In Chattopadhyaya's (1976, p. 300) analysis, "Indian idealism, since its inception in the Upanishads, persistently draws its sanction from the condemnation of normal knowledge and the sources thereof." According to Kakar (1981), "reality, according to Hindu belief, can be apprehended or known only through those archaic, unconscious, preverbal processes of sensing and feeling (like intuition, or extra sensory perception), which are thought to be in touch with the fundamental rhythms and harmonies of the universe. The Hindu conception of ego-oriented reality as "*māyā*" or illusion helps to explain the average Hindu's fascination and respect for the occult and its practitioners. Astrologers, soothsayers, clairvoyants, sadhus, fakirs and other shamanic individuals who abound in Indian society are profoundly esteemed, for they are thought to have begun to transcend the bonds of *māyā*" (p. 20).

There have been dissenting voices against the idealist position of Vedic thought. The *Lokāyatas* or *Cārvākas*, the Indian materialists, hold the rationalistic position in Indian philosophy. "Our knowledge of these materialists is incomplete. Their writings are presumably destroyed, their personality tenaciously depicted as devilish and monstrous, their philosophical position distorted beyond recognition, and their mode of arguments depicted as mere bluff. The very name, Lokāyatas or Cārvākas becomes in Indian philosophy a mark of monstrosity, vulgarity, impiety, and evil. Still, since the idealists find it necessary to illustrate how very impious and detestable these materialists are, some of the old and authentic popular verses of the materialists are quoted in the writings of the idealists themselves" (Chattopadhyaya, 1976, p. 213).

From the surviving scraps of what the Lokāyatas actually argue, it is evident that, as outspoken materialists, they reject idealism along with all its accessories, religious orientation, and faith in the scriptures and superstitions in most of its major forms. The main point on which the Lokāyatas arguments hinge is based on hard common sense of practical life. From the Lokāyatas standpoint, the *vyāvaharika-satyā* (the truth of practical life) is the only *satyā*: that alone is true which proves itself so, in practical life. Any truth-claim outside the verdict of practice is only a fiction. From the point of view of the ultimate truth, the proofs of arguments with which the idealists demonstrate the unreality of the material world are as unreal as the material world itself. With the dawn of the ultimate metaphysical wisdom, one realizes that the demonstration of the unreality of the world is itself as unreal as the world that is demonstrated to be unreal (Chattopadhyaya, 1976).

The Jaina philosopher Haribhadra, in his compendium of Indian philosophy, describes the position of the Lokāyatas as follows: The Lokāyatas say that there is nothing called soul, liberation, virtue, and vice resulting from pious and impious actions. That which is past can never return. The body is just a combination of the four material elements, which are earth, water, fire, and air. These are the basis of consciousness. Perception alone is the valid source of knowledge. The combination of the material elements like earth etc. results in the body; just as from the ingredients of preparing alcoholic drink originates the intoxicating power, so also originates the soul (i.e. consciousness) from the material elements combined to form the body. Therefore, the Cārvākas claim, that it is a folly to renounce what is actually observed (like the pleasures of the world) for running after what is never observed (like heavenly pleasure) (Chattopadhyaya, 1976, p. 429).

In Brandon's (1962) analysis, "the interpretations of human nature and destiny (seem to) rest upon certain basic assumptions made about the significance of life, that life, as it manifested itself here, was to be feared and not accepted at its face-value. Consciousness of the tragedies of life, whether accidental or inherent, seems to have outweighed appreciation, which was indeed lively and real, of its blessings. Hence, fear concerning the price at which individual life is lived seems to have guided the development of the philosophy. This fear is manifest in the teaching that consciousness of individuality is the root of all evil, being the basic illusion that produced all the evils of human experience. In *bhakti-marga* (path of devotion) a like fear manifests, for herein the individual seeks to flee from his own self-consciousness of living in a universe in which the twin process of creation and destruction pursues inexorably its awful way; salvation for him lies in the virtual oblivion of ecstatic union with his divine lord" (p. 333).

Although the concept of the supreme soul being manifest in all life forms does imply an underlying unity of life, finer nuances and details of the philosophy diverges from this point. This brings us to the basic contradiction within the philosophy—between *Brahman* the ultimate reality, the self, and the social aspect of Hinduism. If all is *Brahman*, then why is there a need to stratify society? This stratification becomes *the* reality of a Hindu—that which affects his self-perception, his existence and daily life. Because of this, it influences the reality and self-construal of persons on the fringes of Hindu society, and those lying outside its fold.

In Halbfass' (1991) analysis, "in Hindu philosophy, there is no tradition of explicit and thematic thought about man as man. There is no tradition of trying to define his essence and to distinguish it from other forms of life. The ideas of historical progress, of cultural and technological development, of mans' growing mastery of nature, of a man-made dignity of man seem to be conspicuously absent from traditional Hindu thought. Traditional Hindu thought is preoccupied with the *ātman*, that "self" and immortal principle *in* man, which it also finds in animals and other forms of life. *Manushya*, man as a particular species of living beings, seems to be insignificant compared to this self *in* man and other beings. This topic has not yet met with the scholarly interest that it deserves. It has often been noticed that there is a worldlier earthly temporal atmosphere in the older Vedic texts than in later Indian thought; this has obvious implications for the understanding of man. In fact, man as an earthly, temporal being plays a more significant role in these texts. Words like *ātman* or *purusa*, which in later thought are commonly associated with the absolute self, are in their Vedic usage often closer to the embodied person, to man in his concrete individuality. Moreover, there are explicit attempts to define man as man and to draw that borderline between man and animal that seems to be so much less important in later philosophical literature. In a basic and general sense, the Vedic texts, in particular, the *Brāhmanas* classify man (*manushya, purusa*) as a *paśu*, a domesticated animal; he appears frequently in a five-fold group together with cows, horses, goats, and sheep. He appears as a very special and distinguished animal" (p. 266).

Halbfass (1991) further states, "The most explicit, coherent and emphatic Vedic statements on the uniqueness of man are found in the *Aitareya Āranyaka* (11, 3, 2): In man (*purusa*) we are told, the self (*Ātman*) exists in a more manifest manner (*āvistarām*) than elsewhere. He is almost endowed with intelligence (*prajñā*); he alone understands, discerns (*vijānāti*) what he sees; and he knows how to express what he understands. The intelligence, the cognitive power (*abhivijñāna*) of the animals is bound by or coincides with their hunger and thirst; they are unable to plan for the future. Man, on the other hand, knows the tomorrow (*veda śvastanam*), the "world and the non-world" and "by the mortal he desires the immortal" (p. 269). However, the idea of man as planning, intelligent, future-oriented creature has remained ephemeral. It was dismissed by Sankara and his followers, and disregarded by the majority of philosophical schools. In a sense, it simply evaporated in the climate of Indian ritual and soteriological thought. (p. 281)

Sankara presupposes that the *varna* system is based upon birth and physical family membership. He makes it clear that the metaphysical unity of the real cannot in anyway be taken as a premise of social and religious equality in any empirical sense. From within the Indian tradition, Rāmānuja, Sankara's great rival, expressed the discrepancy between the metaphysics of an all-encompassing unity and the insistence upon strict hereditary barriers in the social domain and even in religious and sorteriological matters. The Advaita Vedāntist, got around these and similar problems by means of a conception that Rāmānuja could not accept. Their doctrine of the "twofold truth" posits a distinction between truth in its absolute sense (*paramārtha*) and truth in the conventional, relative sense of empirical life (*vyavahāra*), juxtaposing the two without mediation or mutual adjustment. For this reason, they did not consider it necessary to "adjust" or reconcile the absolute (i.e. the unity of *Brahman*) with the relative and ultimately unreal world of spatio-temporal particulars and interpersonal relations" (Halbfass, 1991). Those who present themselves as the most orthodox and uncompromising guardians of the sanctity and authority of the Vedas are not necessarily closest to its spirit. Here, as in other areas of Hindu thought, the role of the Vedas is ambiguous and elusive.

The "hierarchical supremacy" of man over other life forms, including women and other "lower" groups, governs Indian social organization. This has its implications on self-construal and well being at an individual and societal level. This seems to be the most influential dichotomy, between theory and practice, of Hindu thought. The impact of this, probably due to imitation of the "higher castes," has permeated through every section of Indian society. Thus, it has become an "Indian" way of thought. What are the implications of this on self-construal? Low self-confidence, low self-esteem, and negation of the self as an individual with personal rights. Here we see rights not as aggressive assertion, but, to start with, just an acceptance of the value and worth of the individual. The lack of these rights to individuation and self-respect can be seen as the outcome of this dichotomy.

Referring to passages such as IV, 13, of the *Bhagavad-Gītā*, which state that the institution of the four *varna* follows the distribution of the *guna* and works (*karma*), and speaking of the role of the *guna* theory in the *Bhagavad-Gītā* in general, modern Hinduism has often advanced the thesis that the hereditary view of the caste system has here given way to an ethical or characterological view. The manner in which the term *karma* was applied to the four castes is revealingly ambivalent: while "works" in the sense of ethically relevant behavior (*ācāra*) is ascribed to the two higher *varna* (*Brāhmin, Ksatriya*); "works" in the sense of types of livelihood or employment are associated with the two lower *varna* (*Vaiśya, Śūdra*). The reasons behind this practice are easy to understand: since ancient times, the status of the *Brāhmin*, and to a lesser extent that of the *Ksatriya*, has been associated with such characteristic virtues as wisdom, honesty, and self-discipline. These values were reserved for the higher castes, and could not be assigned to the lower castes as their appropriate norms (*svadharma*). The lower castes, especially the *Śūdra*, were associated with such ethically negative attributes as an impure way of life, licentiousness, and dullness—attributes hardly suitable to be assigned or recommended as norms or duties. Accordingly, the only alternative was to refer to the means of occupation, whose faithful fulfillment could open up the dimensions of "ethical" values, to give meaning to the concept of *svadharma* for the lower castes. For this reason, while a *Śūdra* could indeed be a good *Śūdra*, his caste-bound achievements could not help him to attain the peculiar ethical potential that belongs (i.e., is 'innate') to the *Brāhmin* (Halbfass, 1991).

Kakar (1981) further analyses, "Hindu culture has consistently emphasized that as long as a person stays true to the ground-plan of his life and fulfils his own particular life task, his *svadharma*, he is traveling on the path to *moksha*. However, how does an individual acquire the knowledge of his *svadharma*? Hindu philosophy and ethics teach that 'right action' for an individual depends on "*desa*", the culture in which he is born, on "*kāla*", the period of historical time in which he lives, on "*srama*" the efforts required by him at different stages of life, and on *guna* the innate psychobiological traits, which are the heritage of an individual's previous life. Thus, 'right' and 'wrong' are relative. The individual can never know in any absolute sense, nor even significantly influence this configuration. It is given. One of the psychosocial consequences of this ethical relativism, or uncertainty, is the generation in the individual Hindu, from earliest childhood, of a pervasive doubt as to the wisdom or efficacy of individual initiative. To size up a situation for oneself and proceed to act upon ones' momentary judgment is to take an enormous cultural as well as a personal risk. For most Hindus such independent voluntary action is unthinkable. Right action and individual *svadharma* thus increasingly come to mean traditional action and *jāti* (caste) *dharma*, in the sense that an individual's occupational activity and social acts are right or 'good', if they conform to the traditional pattern prevalent in his kinship and caste groups. Suspicion of innovation and unconscious avoidance of activities not charted in traditional maps are the consequences (pp. 37–38)."

In Kakar's (1981) analysis, the *karma* theory assures the individual that none of his efforts has been wasted, for he will start the next life with the balance of *guna* attained at the close of his previous existence. For many, in spite of their best efforts during a lifetime to tilt this balance in the direction of *sattva*, the initial handicap of innate dispositions (*samskāras*) that shape the unconscious at the beginning of life, may prove to be insurmountable. The unconscious, then, occupies a central place in the Hindu world image and theory and of the meaning of human life; the origin and constitution of the unconscious are not biological but metaphysical, its nature depending upon the actions of a previous birth. *Karma* is not just a doctrine of 'reincarnation', 'fatalism', or 'predestination'; it is a promise of hope. This tendency to stress the *samskāras*, the innate constitutional dispositions, rather than acknowledging and 'working through' conflicting emotions, thoughts, and actions in the context of ones' life history is a culturally specific form of resistance in dealing with the problems of life, with the Hindu. With the cultural acceptance of the notion of *samskāra*, there is little social pressure to foster the belief that if only the caretakers were good enough, and constantly on their toes, a child's potentialities would be boundlessly fulfilled. The concept of *samskāra* can be the proverbial noose, as the components of this *samskāra* is, again, defined by the culture. Hence anything different from the culturally defined is easily put across as 'bad *samskāra*, resulting in guilt for not following or living up to expectations, thereby denying the person his individuality. The preconscious system of beliefs and values associated with the concepts of *moksha*, *dharma*, and *karma* forms a meta-reality for Hindus.

In addition to the universal self, the factors of *karma*, caste etc., the Hindu also contends with gender strictures and stereotypes that influence his identity. The consistent dichotomy of Hindu thought, between the essential philosophy and the social laws, are glaring in the *Manu Smriti*. To present day, these laws govern the Hindu. Although the shade of the law may have changed a bit, the color remains the same. It is deeply entrenched within the socializing system, and derives its identity from it.

Although the *Manu Smriti* is primarily a rulebook for the upper caste male members, by implication, the norms of behavior and identity of the lower castes and women are also laid down. The rules of behavior laid down by the *Manu Smriti* have, over the centuries, become norms of behavior and guided the personality of individuals within Hindu society. The injunctions in these are what ultimately affect the social self. This social self is the self in the real, tangible world—and is what we need focus on.

The message of this has been widely propagated through the epic *Rāmāyana*, where the ideal woman, is personified in the form of *Sitā*. *Sitā*, the epitome of womanhood as expected in the *Smriti*, is docile, pure, chaste, tender, gentle, and has a singular faithfulness, which cannot be destroyed or even disturbed by her husbands' rejections, slights or thoughtlessness. Being deified, this "*Sitā* ideal" forms a split in the identity of women. The "good" of the *Sitā* ideal, being in direct opposition to the state of a 'natural' woman—in touch with her thoughts, emotions, senses, and sexuality.

In contrast to this is the portrayal of *Draupadi*, in the *Mahābhārata*—an assertive, sensuous, strong willed woman in charge of her emotions, and her self. As if to highlight the non-acceptance of these traits in a woman, the epic provides her with five husbands, which is against the laws of Manu. The result of this is the destruction of the family. Though not stated as such, the meaning of it is quite implicit.

The *Manu Smriti* has denied women an access to her individuality. Making a suppression of her thoughts, needs, and desires a norm. The consequences of this, is the lack of individuality that is expected and experienced by Hindu women. Her physical, sexual, personal, and social identity is denied her. Paradoxically, as much as the philosophy speaks of non-attachment, these laws are framed in a manner that sanctifies the 'attachment' of the woman to her man, and the 'possession' of the woman by her man—be it father, brother, husband, or son. She is thus identified by her social role, or her borrowed identity. Her individuality is denied her. As she is encultured in these traditions and norms, she identifies herself with her social role alone. May be in the silence of her thoughts she may be in touch with her individual identity and has learnt to accept and deal with this enormous discrepancy in her socialization.

In the discussion of Hindu social thought, the *Manu Smriti* has invariably been highlighted for its portrayal of women and its impact on the identity and status of women in Indian society. However, the majority of the *Manu Smriti* is directed towards rules, regulations, and rites for the Hindu male. He is as much governed by these laws as the woman in Hindu society. He too bears the burden of, accidentally or willfully, not abiding by these rules. He too pays the price for such neglect by losing his place in heaven. However, he does have recourse to penance, which can negate the influence of his misdeeds. He too has to deal with guilt and fear for dealing with himself as a mortal, with basic instincts, needs, and frailties. The Hindu male, too, is socialized in a fear bound environment. He is raised in a dichotomous environment, where he is considered superior (to women and individuals of the lower castes), but is not permitted to develop himself, as he has no permission to think, in deference to the wishes of elders and his religious training. He too has to follow the elaborate laws of Manu that are primarily set out for him. In relation to women, he may also be acting against his better judgment and feelings. Being in a patriarchal society, the dice is cast in his favor. However, looking at the matter dispassionately, the Hindu man does not have a right to assert his individuality and freedom of thought and affect. He is as much bounded by the scriptural injunctions, as the woman is by the negativistic attitude towards her gender, in all its natural, realistic forms. As far as his personal, individual freedom and sense of personhood is concerned, he runs the risk of depleting his intellect and wisdom, losing his vitality and the coveted place in heaven. The attending fear and grief can be quite imaginable. The *Rāmāyana* also gives us a glimpse into the Hindu imagery of manliness. *Rāmā* may have all the traits of a god like hero, yet he is also fragile, mistrustful and jealous, and very much a conformist, both to his parents' wishes and to social opinion. The "*Rāmā* ideal" is what he is encultured to live by.

Expressions of joy, too, are denied him by Manu. "Let him not dance, nor sing, nor play musical instruments, nor slap (his limbs), nor grind his teeth, nor let him make uncouth noises, though he be in passion" (M. S.: IV, 64). He is also denied the freedom of sharing simple moments of delight, "..a wise man, if he sees a rainbow in the sky must not point it out to anybody." (M.S.: IV, 59). He has to follow elaborate rituals for purifying himself due to various lapses on his part. All his normal bodily functions are considered impure, requiring purification. His sexuality is also suppressed, although he has greater freedom, than the woman does. Sexuality for him at an older age is also looked at derisively, celibacy being the ideal state. He is reared in an environment where emotional expressions are denied him—or at least not considered appropriate. As his primary social aim is deference to his parents, developing strong bonds with his wife and children are discouraged. Parenthood for him is meant to be a means to a selfish end—a son to light his funeral pyre to facilitate his passage into heaven. It is indeed ironical, that the Hindu man may find his freedom in the freedom of women.

"To reach the goal of man—the supreme treasure, the supreme bliss, the Upanishad asks us to renounce all selfish desires, the tyrannies of lust and greed. The mere striving to satisfy the instinctive cravings and social needs, they declare boldly, is not the goal of human life. They affirm values that are higher than the physical, the biological, and the social. They also affirm that it is the pursuit of those higher values which lead to an integrated and whole life" (Kuppuswamy, 1990, p. 27). This constant referencing to these negative traits of human nature do imply the naturalness of these characteristics, even from the time of the Vedas and the Upanishads.

Although recognizing all the emotions and emotional states, including providing a good genesis of each state, the ancient philosophers have chosen to deny these, rather than accept them as human nature and work towards dealing with the cause (from within, and from the environment) giving rise to such states. Discounting the emotions as essential to the individuals' repertoire of behavior, in search of an illusive ideal, is the mainstay of Hindu philosophy and thought. In denying our emotions, the philosophy denies our human characteristics. This is in congruence with the basic difference in perception of the self.

The concept of "control" and hence "denial" of the emotions and the self, is a basic theme of Hindu philosophy. The ideals being of far greater importance than reality. Is there a primary rift between the guiding philosophy and the reality of human nature? The Hindu does behave in a manner natural to our species, despite the religophilosophical tradition and indoctrination. How does this chasm reflect in behavior? A denial in accepting his emotions? More guilt proneness, in experiencing emotions? Alternatively, is there a wiser recognition of this rift in the Hindu mind that reconciles to these dichotomies by living in a world of dualities—the material world and the spiritual path?

Emotions are considered a result of greed. Is this where the Hindu sense of discomfort in taking pride of his personal identity and not only the rich heritage of his culture, which lies in the distant past come from? As pride is a negative attitude, is this where concepts such as—beauty as a lure, shame in wealth, shame in achievement attitude instead of acceptance of ones' strengths and achievements arise from? Within these beliefs lies the key to the Indian attitude of subservience. The repercussions of it extend to all spheres of individual and group life. This attitude may not lie in the history of successive foreign rule, but may instead be a cause of it. Here too, there is a dichotomy between observed behaviors and the philosophy, for the Hindu is as much a slave of power and wealth as any other.

Hindu philosophy is freedom oriented. Every fiber of it is a protest against bondage. However, this freedom is sought from the real world, to attain the idealized freedom of *mukti* or *moksha*. Ironically, in the life of the mortal Hindu, he is far from being free. He is shackled by a history of thought which prevents him the freedom to think and make choices. He is shackled by the narrow confines of a social order in which he is born. He is shackled by the scriptural promise of "eternal bliss" that prevents him from living life to its hilt. Ancient social laws bound him and modes of thought which govern his negativistic views of his sensuality. He is shackled by narrow perceptions of gender identity. He is shackled by the dichotomies of his experiences and emotions, and norms of society. This bondage occurs from the time he is born.

His identity is that of the self (*ātman*), that he shares with all creatures and which is neither the subject, nor the object of planning and reasoning. In trying to discover this self, man has to abandon his humanity; he has to discard himself as a rational emotive animal. Here too we see the dichotomy in Hindu philosophy and practice. At one level, the self is that which pervades all living creatures. On the other hand, the hereditary social hierarchy does not permit equality. Ironically, it is from the same scriptures and reference points that both these sets of rules emerge. How does one reconcile to these differences? Lack of respect for other life forms, aside from the attitude towards the holy cow, is also evident in the attitude towards conservation of animals in the present context. The non-rational mode of thought and preoccupation with spirituality has prevented the Hindu from taking practical steps and even considering these as a priority. The lack of respect for all life is also evident in the attitude towards the handicapped, which is one of disdain. At the crux of it then, the absolute timeless self (*ātman*) that we find at the center of traditional Hindu thought does appear to be an abstraction.

As P. T. Raju (1995) states: "The main aim of almost all the Indian systems is to show the way to salvation; and they were written after the ideal of renunciation (*sannyasa*) took definite shape. Not even one out of ten thousand take to renunciation; so the philosophical literature of the systems cannot be said to represent the whole of life of every Indian, although the life of renunciation is presented as an ideal for everyone" (p. 207)

NOTES

1. Lokayata, also called Charvaka system is considered as the concerted materialist philosophical thought in ancient India. Krishna Mishra, a contemporary of Gautama Buddha, states the essence of Lokayata Darshana as follows: "In it only perceptual evidence is authority. The elements are earth, water, fire, and air. Matter can think. There is no other world. Death is the end of all."
2. Theosophical Society, a religious group formed by Helena Petrovna Blavatsky in New York City in 1875. The group's major beliefs center on the nature of the soul and its ability to know God and the universe through mystical intuition. Annie Besant was born in London, where she became a member of the society and subsequently came to India.

She became a leader of the Hindu nationalist movement. She lectured frequently on theosophy and in 1926 traveled widely with her Indian protégé Jiddu Krishnamurti.

3. The hymns of the *Rig Veda* are considered the oldest and most important of the *Vedas*, having been composed between 1500 BC and about 900 BC. The *Rig Veda* is dominated by hymns praising the Aryan gods for giving them victories and wealth plundered from the local Dasas through warfare. Generally, the hymns of the *Rig Veda* praise the gods and ask them for worldly benefits such as wealth, health, long life, protection, and victory. The *Sama Veda* contains the melodies or music for the chants used from the *Rig Veda* for the sacrifices. These are considered the origin of Indian music. The *Sama Veda* helped to train the musicians and functioned as a hymnal for the religious rites. The *Yajur Veda* are a collection of the ritual formulas for the priests to use in the sacrifices, which is what *yaja* means. It explains how to construct the altars for new and full-moon sacrifices and other ceremonies. The *Atharva Veda* is much longer than the *Sama* and *Yajur* and only about a sixth of it is from the *Rig Veda*. much of it draws from the customs and beliefs of pre-Aryan or pre-Vedic India. The *Atharva Veda* is primarily magical spells and incantations for healing and cures using herbs

4. The Puranas are a class of 18 literary texts, all written in Sanskrit verse, whose composition dates from the 4th century BC to about 1,000 A.D. The special subject of the Puranas is the powers and works of the gods. The Puranas deal with five characteristic topics, or *panchalaksana*: (1) The creation of the universe; (2) Its destruction and renovation; (3) The genealogy of gods and patriarchs; (4) The reigns of the Manus, forming the periods called Manwantaras; (5) the history of the Solar and Lunar races of kings." No one purana can be described as exhibiting in fine (or even coarse) detail all five of these distinguishing traits.

5. The complexity of interpreting and understanding the meaning of the ancient written word is well explaind by P. T. Raju (1995, p. 232). He states, "in philosophical discussions atman means the self, But the Upanishads use the word to mean sevearal things; the physical body, the vital principle, mind, reason, the bliss body, and the metaphysical principle as well as the Brahman. In popular literaure, it means also one's own nature, striving, and steadfastness."

3

Buddhism

The man who was to become the Buddha was born about 563 BC of Kshatriya stock at a place called Lumbini, situated in the Terai region of what today is the kingdom of Nepal. He was given the name Siddhārtha and took the clan name Gautama. His father Suddhodana has been variously described as the king or leader of a local people known as the Shakyas—or even just as a prominent citizen of Kapilavasthu, the Shakyan capital. The Shakyas were in fact just one of a number of more or less independent peoples then inhabiting this part of northern India which were politically organized into tribal republics ruled by elected aristocracies (Snelling, 1987).

At the time when Gautama took *parivarāj* (renunciation), there was great intellectual ferment in the country. Besides the Brāhmanic philosophy, there were as many as sixty-two different schools of philosophy, all opposed to the Brāhmanic philosophy. Of them, at least six were worthy of attention. The school of the *'Akriyavāda'* doctrine, headed by Purana Kassappa maintained that, the soul was not affected in any way by *karma*. An act, however licentious, does not affect the soul with sin. An act, however good does not bring merit to the soul. When a person dies, all the elements of which he is made join in their originals. Nothing survives after death, neither body, nor soul. Buddha rejected this doctrine on the grounds, that if this were true then one can do evil or any harm; or one may even go to the length of killing another without involving any social responsibility or social consequences. The doctrine of the *'Niyativāda'* school of

Mikhali Gosala was a kind of fatalism or determinism. He taught that no one could do anything or undo anything. Things happen. No one can make them happen. No one can remove happiness, increase it, or diminish it. One must undergo ones' share of the experiences of the world. Buddha rejected this doctrine on the grounds that man becomes a slave of destiny, and cannot liberate himself. The "*Vikshepavāda*" school of philosophy headed by Sanjaya Bellaputta was a kind of skepticism, denying the existence of the soul, rebirth, heaven, and hell. Gautama rejected this doctrine too, as man would then float about and live without a positive philosophy of life. The philosophy of '*Chaturyamsamvarvād*', which later developed into Jainism, preached the existence of the soul, rebirth, *karma*. According to Gautama, if the teachings of Mahāvīra were true then mans' life must be subjected to asceticism and *tapaschārya*, a complete subjugation and uprooting of mans' instincts and desires. Thus, none of the paths of life suggested by the philosophers appealed to the Buddha. He thought they were the thoughts of men who had become hopeless, helpless, and reckless. He therefore decided to seek light elsewhere (Ambedkar, 1991).

Buddhism was a revolution. Though it began as a religious revolution, it became a social and political revolution. Because of the new rational and sensitive tenets as propounded by Buddha, which made man and not faith and belief as the center of the picture, a clash between Buddhism and Brāhmanism was inevitable. Brāhmanism was shaken to the foundation by Buddhism, which thrived until the end of the 1st century AD, when Brāhmanism again started to recover its poise. The earliest *Purānas* like *Agni*, *Vishnu*, *Vāyu* and *Matsya* mentioned the Buddha as one who deluded people to ruin, but the later *Purānas* like the *Garuda* reconciled themselves with the fading Buddhism after the 6th century and invoked the Buddha as an incarnation of Vishnu. The loss of royal patronage, the intolerance of Brāhmanism to the Buddhist doctrines, the foreign attacks on India all contributed to the decline of Buddhism. This continued to the 10th century with

Buddhism

a small respite during the reign of the Pala kings at Magadha but in about the year 1000, the Muslim conquerors of India dealt a final deathblow to Buddhism in India (Bhole, 1991; Ambedkar, 1987, 1991).

Since the sixth century B.C., Buddhist beliefs and practices, literature, and institutions have been spreading, developing, and adjusting to diverse cultural environments in more than thirty countries in Asia and, in turn, influencing their cultures and religious ways of life. Since the nineteenth century, Buddhist ideas have also been of interest to western philosophy and literature. In these and other respects, Buddhist historical developments are so complex and ramified that it is difficult to view them comprehensively (Gard, 1962). For this chapter I have drawn mainly from Dr. B. R. Ambedkar's interpretation of Buddhism.

What is Buddhism?

Buddhism in its original form is an atheistic doctrine, and therefore no ritualistic practices find a place in it. It is a practical doctrine of pure ethical discipline. It is out and entirely a man centered religion, totally humanistic in its outlook, approach and aim whose sole concern was the liberation of the suffering man. It concerns itself with human life as it stands here and now, and puts forth ways and means to tide over the present problems of conditioned existence. Mans' only religious obligation is to free himself from the bonds of worldly suffering by following the eight fold path. The center of his *dharma* is man and the relation of man to man, in his life on earth. In its essence therefore, Buddhism gives us a way of life intended not for persons belonging to any particular caste or nationality but universally for all. Later Buddhism however accepts Buddha himself as a god and believes in his various incarnations. Thus, modern Buddhism has a place for various Buddhist temples in which there are images of Buddha, which are worshipped and adored more or less in the fashion of the Hindu gods (Tiwari, 1983; Chitkara, 1997, Gard, 1962).

The Buddha never claimed that he was a prophet or a messenger of God. He rejected any such description. Rather than a religion of 'revelation', his religion is a discovery. It is the result of inquiry and investigation into the conditions of human life on earth and understanding of the working of human instincts with which man is born, the molding of his instincts and dispositions that man has formed as a result of history and tradition and which are working to his detriment. All prophets have promised salvation. The *Buddha* is the one teacher who did not make any such promise. He made a sharp distinction between a, "*moksha dātā*"—one who gives salvation, and a "*mārga dātā*" one who shows the way. He was only a *mārga dātā*. Each for himself must seek salvation, by his own effort. With Mohammed and Jesus salvation meant saving the soul from being sent to hell by the intercession of the prophet. With the Buddha salvation means *nirvāna*, which means control of passions. He claimed that he was one of the many human beings and his message to the people was the message of man to man. He never claimed infallibility for his message. The only claim he made was that his message was the only true way to salvation, as *he* understood it. It was based on universal human experience of life in the world. He said that it was open to anyone to question it, test it, and find what truth it contained (Ambedkar, 1991).

In Ambedkar's (1991) analysis, in formulating the principles of his philosophy, the Buddha dealt with the prevailing stock of ideas in his own way. The following are the ideas that he rejected: (i) He condemned indulging in speculation as to the origins of man and the question 'what am I'? (ii) He discarded heresies about the soul and refrained from identifying it with the body, sensations, volitions, or consciousness. (iii) He discarded all nihilistic views that were promulgated by certain religious teachers. (iv) He condemned such views as were held by heretics. (v) He repudiated the theory that a god created man or that he came out of the body of *Brahmā*. (vii) The existence of the soul he either ignored or denied. The Buddha could find no proof in support of the thesis of the Upanishads, therefore, he had no difficulty in rejecting it as being based on pure imagination.

He modified and accepted the law of cause and effect with its consequences. He repudiated the fatalistic view of life and that the destiny of man was laid out by God. He discarded the theory that all deeds committed in some former birth have the potency to produce suffering, making present activity impotent. He denied the fatalistic view of *karma*, and replaced it with a different view. He replaced the doctrine of the transmigration of the soul with the doctrine of re-birth. He replaced the doctrine of *moksha* or salvation of the soul with the doctrine of '*nirvāna*' (Ambedkar, 1991).

The first distinguishing feature of his teachings lay in the recognition of the mind as the center of everything. The mind precedes things, dominates them, and creates them. If mind is comprehended, all things are comprehended. The second distinguishing feature of his teachings is that mind is the fount of all the good and evil that arises within and befalls us from without. The third distinguishing feature of his teachings is the avoidance of all sin-full acts. The fourth distinguishing feature of his teachings is that real religion lies not in the books of religion but in the observance of the tenets of the religion. It does not demand that anyone accepts its teachings on trust. The practitioner is instead invited to try them out, to experiment with them. If he finds that they work in practice, then he can take them on board. However, there is no compulsion. If he happens to find the truth elsewhere or otherwise, he is free to pursue it there. When the Buddha was requested by his followers to appoint a successor, he refused. His answer was, 'The *dharma* must be its own successor. Principle must live by itself, and not by the authority of man. If principle needs the authority of man, it is no principle. It is not *dharma*, if every time it becomes necessary to invoke the name of the founder to enforce the authority of *dharma* (Ambedkar, 1991; Snelling, 1987).

The Dalai Lama (1999) interprets the distinction between the *Hīnayāna* and the *Mahāyāna* sects of Buddhism based on motivation. The motivation of the *Hīnayāna* sect is concerned mainly with ones' own *moksha* or salvation through the practice of moral conduct and the convergence of mind and wisdom. The motivation of the *Mahāyāna* sect (which is the ritualistic sect) is not to think only of oneself, but to have concern for all living beings and pursue the practices of the six or ten *pāramitās* (perfections) to ultimately achieve Buddha hood. This is *Bodhisattvayana*. Based on philosophical tenets there are four different schools of thought—the *Vaibhāsika, Sautrāntika, Cittamātra* and *Mādhyamika*. The essence of Buddhist conduct according to these schools is *ahimsā* or non-violence. *Ahimsā* is important because of the law of interdependence. The theory of interdependence is interpreted differently according to the various tenets. According to one, the meaning of interdependence is that all conditioned phenomena depend on causes. This implies that there is no creator; things depend only on their own causes and those causes in turn have their own causes, with no beginning. Everything changes because of these causes and conditions. New circumstances produce new events; these in turn, act as causes and produce something different and new. This is the process of dependent arising: *pratityasamutpāda*. The concept of interdependence is accepted by all schools of Buddhist tenets.

The Buddha's original teachings were collected chiefly in three major scriptures called *Tripitakās*, which means "the three baskets of knowledge". These three scriptures are *Vinayapitakā*, which deals chiefly with the codes of conduct for the general population; *Sutrapitaka*, which contains the ceremonies and dialogues related to ethics, morality, and spirituality; and *Abhidhammapitakā*, which contains an exposition of Buddha's philosophical theories. As is the case with other doctrines, the oral tradition of communication, the later dates at which the teachings were recorded and the difficulties in translating from an archaic language have opened the views to varied interpretations, through the centuries.

Basic Principles of Buddhist Philosophy

The Doctrine of *Karma*: The Buddhist doctrine of *karma* has created much confusion, as there are many diverse perspectives on it. In Ambedkar's (1991) analysis, the Buddha's law of *karma* is not the same as the Brāhmanic law. The Hindu law of *karma* is based on the soul. Buddhism is not, as there is no soul in the Buddhist belief system. The Brāhmanic law is hereditary because of the transmigration of the soul. The Hindu law is based on the soul, which is distinct from the body. When the body dies, the soul does not die. The soul flies away. This is inconsistent with the Buddhist no-soul theory. The Law of *Karma* or the Law of Causality as enunciated by the Buddha was that our future depends on today's actions. The Buddhist doctrine applied only to *karma* and its effect on present life. Gautama did not believe in the inheritance of past *karma*. Secondly, he asserts that the status of a man be governed not so much by heredity as by his environment.

The Doctrine of Impermanence/transitoriness, or the Theory of Universal Change: This doctrine has three aspects. There is the impermanence of composite things, impermanence of the individual, impermanence of the self. In short, a human being is always changing, always growing. He is not the same at two different moments of his life. It is on the impermanence of the nature of all things that the possibility of all other things depends. The Buddhist *sūnyatā* or *sūnyavada* does not mean nihilism. It only means the perpetual changes occurring at every moment in the phenomenal world (Ambedkar, 1991).

The Theory of the Law of Kamma: Belief in the supernatural does not find a place in Buddhist philosophy, as every event must be the result of mans' action or of an act of nature. In repudiating supernaturalism, the Buddha had three objects. His first object was to lead man to the path of rationalism. His second object was to free man to go in search of truth. His third object was to remove the most potent source of superstition, the result of which is to kill the spirit of inquiry. This is called the law of *Kamma* or Causation. *Kamma* means mans' action and *vipakā* is its effect. The moral order in the universe is maintained by "*Kamma Niyam*" and not by an illusory God. If the moral order is bad, it is because man does *akusala* (bad) *kamma*. If the moral order is good, it is because man does *kusala* (good) *kamma*. It may be that, there is a time interval between the moment when the *kamma* is done and the moment when the effect is felt. It is so, often enough. From this point of view, *kamma* is either *ditthadamma vedaniya kamma* (immediately effective *kamma*); *upapajjavedaniya kamma* (remotely effective *kamma*); and *apoapariya vedaniya kamma* (indefinitely effective *kamma*). Kamma may also fall into the category of *ahosi kamma*, i.e., *kamma* that is non-effective. This comprises all such *kammas*, which are too weak to operate, or which are counteracted by a more potent *kamma*, at the time when it should have worked. The law of *kamma* has to do only with the question of general moral order. It has nothing to do with the fortunes or misfortunes of an individual (Ambedkar, 1991).

The Theory of Rebirth: The Buddha believed in the regeneration of matter and not in the rebirth of the soul. According to this theory, there are four elements: earth, water, fire, and air. When the four elements from this floating mass join, a new birth takes place. The elements need not and are not necessarily from the same body that is dead. They may be drawn from different dead bodies. It must be noted that the body dies. However, the elements are ever living. This is the kind of rebirth in which the Buddha believed. Annihilation has therefore a two-fold aspect. In one of its aspects, it means cessation of production of energy. In another aspect, it means as new addition to the stock of general floating mass of energy. The Buddha was an annihilationist as far as the soul was concerned and not an annihilationist so far as matter was concerned (Ambedkar, 1991).

Since the Buddhist point of view begins with the "here and now", Buddhist thought fundamentally concerns the nature of existence. A person begins to think Buddhistically when he becomes aware, physically and mentally, of himself in his natural and social environment. He experiences something because he "is there in relationship." This "something" is life, conditioned, ever changing, and not yet fully known. However, in Buddhism life is meant to be rightly comprehended, and fully realized as freedom in perfect existence. For this purpose, the Buddha taught four essential principles according to *his own experience and insight*. They are characteristic of the Buddhist way but not peculiar to it and are in common with many other approaches to life. These four principles in Buddhism are collectively called *Cattari-ariya-saccani / Catvāri-ārya-satyāni*. In essence, these four principles in Buddhism are stages of progress in the realization of the Buddhist way of life (the epistemological-psychical aspect) and states of existence in the attainment of ultimate freedom (the metaphysical–existential aspect). These truths are that suffering exists; that there is a cause for suffering; that suffering can be stopped; and that there is a method for stopping it (Gard, 1962).

The First Principle : The Nature of Existence is initially perceived and experienced as dukkha (dukha satya). There are three aspects or states to this: (1) *dukkha-dukkhatā* as that state of quasi-physical pain and mental anguish, viz ordinary suffering; (2) *parināma-dukkhatā* as that state caused by change (for the worse); and (3) *samskāra-dukhatā* as that state of conditioned-ness (not being free). Thus, suffering as phenomenal existence is imperfect and to be transcended. It has three interdependent characteristics—impermanence, imperfection, and essentially unsubstantial, non-independent. Buddha came to realize that suffering results from old age, disease, and death, and that life itself is suffering. Birth, wishes, despair, frustrations, dejections, emotions, and failures in desired attempts are all sources of suffering (Gard, 1962; Tigunait, 1983).

The Second Principle: Samudaya Satya, concerns the cause of suffering as the imperfect condition of existence.

According to this principle, the cause of suffering can be described as a chain with no end and no beginning. Nothing is unconditional. The existence of everything depends upon certain conditions. Therefore, the existence of suffering and misery also depends on something. This series of cause and effect of suffering is described as the twelve-linked chain of causation. The links in the chain are: ignorance (*avidyā*); past impressions (*samskāras*); initial consciousness (*vijñāna*); the body / mind organism (*nāmarūpa*); the five cognitive senses and the mind (*sadāyatana*); contact of the senses with objects (*sparsa*); previous sense experience (*vedanā*); thirst to enjoy (*trsnā*); mental clinging (*upādanā*); will to become (*bhava*); birth (*jātti*); old age and death (*jarāmarana*). Existence in ignorance is suffering and that the clinging to a false individuality, as something real and permanent, is the root of this ignorance. *Buddha* declares that only life as we know it, and as we live it in ignorance, is painful (Gard, 1962; Tigunait, 1983).

The Third Principle: is that of the Ultimate Freedom in Perfect Existence. This principle (*nirodha-satya*) concerns the cessation of the suffering (*samudaya-satya*), (the Second Principle) and thus the disappearance of *dukkha-satya* (the First Principle) whereupon freedom in perfect existence may be attained. *Nirodha* therefore has a twofold meaning: stopping or eliminating causation and, correlatively, realizing freedom. This two-fold task of *nirodha* is undertaken by means of *mārga-satya* (The Fourth Principle). Conditioned by the *karma*-formations is consciousness; conditioned by consciousness is psycho-physicality; conditioned by the psycho-physicality are the six (sensory) spheres; conditioned by the six (sensory) spheres is sensory impingement; conditioned by sensory impingement is feeling; conditioned by feeling is craving; conditioned by craving is grasping; conditioned by grasping is becoming; conditioned by becoming is birth; conditioned by birth, ageing and dying, grief, suffering, sorrow, lamentation, and despair come into being. Such is the arising of this entire mass of anguish (*dukkha*). But from the utter fading away and stopping (*nirodha*) of this very ignorance is the stopping of the *karma*-formations; from the stopping of the *karma*-formations the stopping of consciousness; from the stopping of consciousness the stopping of psycho-physicality; from the stopping of psycho-physicality the stopping of the six (sensory) spheres; from the stopping of the six (sensory) spheres the stopping of sensory impingement; from the stopping of sensory impingement the stopping of feeling; from the stopping of feeling the stopping of craving; from the stopping of craving the stopping of grasping; from the stopping of grasping the stopping of becoming; from the stopping of becoming the stopping of birth; from the stopping of birth, old age and dying, grief, sorrow, suffering, lamentation and despair are stopped. Such is the stopping of this entire mass of anguish. This third truth affirms the second truth. All suffering is because of the twelve links of the causal chain, and their effective power results from ones' own involvement in them. If one keeps oneself away from the conditions that invite suffering, then there will be no suffering any more. The state that is free from conditions is called *nirvāna* (Gard, 1962; Tigunait, 1983).

The Fourth Principle: The Middle Way and the Eightfold Path as the means to cease suffering (mārga-satya).—This is the means whereby the First Principle (*dukkha-satya*) is recognized and realized, the Second (*samudaya-satya*) is known and understood, and the Third Principle (*nirodha-satya*) is actualized and thereby *nirvāna* attained. It is therefore called the Noble Way. The way by which one may become a Buddha is also the path on which one progresses toward enlightenment. Hence, in principle it is the Middle Way and in practice the Eightfold Path (Gard, 1962; Tigunait, 1983).

The Eightfold Path consists of eight interdependent categories or aspects of proper Buddhist practice, both mental and physical:

Right Views: Ignorance can be termed as misunderstanding of or wrong views regarding ones' relationship with the objects of the worldly things or persons and preoccupations with the expectations of them are the main cause of all misery and pain. Here 'right view' is used in the sense of correct knowledge about the Four Noble Truths. Knowledge here does not imply any theoretical speculation regarding the nature of the self, but rather refers to an awareness of the imperfection and impermanence of the world and of a persons' relationship with it.

Right Resolve: This means firm determination to reform ones' life in the light of truth, so in practicing this second rung of the eight fold path to liberation a student has to renounce all attachments to the world, give up ill feelings towards others, and desist from doing harm to anyone. This mental reformation calms down the mind's fluctuations and makes the mind turn inward.

Right Speech: Abstaining from slander, abuse, and idle talk. Right resolve followed by right speech is a systematic way to practice non-violence and truthfulness.

Right Conduct: This includes the five vows of non-violence, truthfulness, non-stealing, non-sensuality (celibacy), and non-possessiveness. These five vows are to be practiced with right resolve, right speech, and right conduct.

Right Livelihood: One must earn a living to meet the needs of the body. This essential livelihood earned by improper means makes a person a victim of guilt feelings, which deteriorate inner strength and invite suicidal tendencies. Therefore Buddha emphasizes right (honest) livelihood that does not harm or interfere with others' lives and does not disturb social harmony.

Right Effort: This consists in making sincere efforts to give up evil habits and cultivate the good ones. It comprises of the following four constant efforts: (a) The effort to prevent the arising of evil which has not yet arisen, (b) The effort to eradicate that evil which has already accumulated, (c) The effort to induce good which has not yet arisen, and (d) The effort to cultivate that good which is already present.

Right Mindfulness—According to Buddha, right mindfulness means a constant remembrance of the perishable nature of things. This is essential for keeping ones' mind away from attachments to worldly things and their charms.

Right Meditation—One who lives his life in the light of the first seven steps and thereby gradually frees himself from all passions and misunderstandings gains emotional maturity. He has prepared himself step-by-step for the inward journey by trying to understand and bring into operation in his own life the moral and ethical laws that teach one how to live in the world and yet remain above it. These inner explorations of consciousness constitute the final step of the Eightfold Path.

Buddhist ethics are not codified into a rigid moral code; nor are they about making judgments and arousing sin and guilt, though every willed action produces consequences. Buddhists try to be aware of any particular failing to live up to any ethical principle and resolve to do better next time. They also note in such cases that they still have a long way to go towards finally overcoming their faults, which builds a healthy humility. The *dharma* was aimed at reconstructing society as distinct from the religious purpose of explaining the origin of the world. Buddhism sought to outgrow the religious myth of other worldliness and fatalism. It was rooted in the world, in the human being. Thus, eternal damnation is a concept unknown in Buddhism, where every being is ultimately destined for *nirvāna*, even the most foul-hearted degenerate (Snelling, 1987; Tigunait, 1983; Tiwari, 1983, Chitkara, 1997).

The Self in Buddhist Thought

It is evident that much of early Buddhist thought about the self or soul was certainly conditioned by way of reaction against many of the traditional Vedic concepts that were accepted in Indian culture when the Sakyan mission began. After a thorough analysis of the different constituents of human personality, Buddha shows that nothing permanent and blissful is to be found in any or all of these various constituents which we hold as our true 'I' or the 'self' saying 'this is mine, I am this or this is myself'. It is only due to our clinging to or grasping of the five constituents that we develop this erroneous notion of 'I' or the 'self' (David, 1936/1978; Brandon, 1962; Kuppuswamy, 1990).

"Man according to Buddhism is neither a purely physical being, as the *Cārvāka* system would say; neither is he a being with a permanent soul within him, as the other systems insist. He is rather a combination of physical and mental forces. According to the *Hinayāna*, man is a *sanghāta* (aggregate) of five *skandhans*—*rūpa* (matter), *vedanā* (sensation or feeling), *samjñā* (perception), *samskāra* (disposition) and *vijñāna* (consciousness). Buddhism thus does not deny a spiritual element in man as the *Cārvāka* does, but then it also does not believe in the reality of a permanent soul in man. According to its theory of momentariness, it does not believe in anything permanent. The soul is just a passing stream in a moment of thought or consciousness" (Tiwari, 1983, p. 52).

The Buddhist Theory of Man / The Theory of Nāma Rūpa: According to Buddhist thought it is the mind that exists. The Buddhist theory against the existence of the soul as a separate entity is called *nāma rūpa*. It is a collective name for a sentient being. A sentient being is a compound thing consisting of certain physical mental elements. These elements are called *Khandas*—the *rūpa khanda* and *nāma khanda*. The *rūpa khanda* primarily consists of physical elements such as earth, water, fire and air. They constitute the body or *rupa*. The *nāma khanda* is called *viñāna*, or consciousness. It includes the three mental elements: *Vedanā* (sensation springing from contact of the six senses with the world), *sannā* (perception), *sankhahā* (states of mind), *chetanā* (consciousness) is the center of a sentient being. Once consciousness arises, man becomes a sentient being. Consciousness is therefore the chief thing in a mans' life. Consciousness is cognitive, emotional, and volitional. Consciousness is cognitive when it gives knowledge, information, as appreciating or apprehending internal or external events. Consciousness is emotional when it exists in certain subjective states, characterized by either pleasurable or painful tones, when emotional consciousness produces feeling. Consciousness in its volitional stage makes a being exert himself for the attainment of some end. Volitional consciousness gives rise to activity. The sentient being through and because of consciousness performs all the functions of a sentient being. Consciousness is certainly not a kind of pure omnipresent mind-substance that registers impressions while existing independently of them. When suitable sets of conditions have arisen, consciousness coincidentally arises. When all these aggregates come together, the fertile ground exists for the arising of a notion of "I" (Ambedkar, 1991; Snelling, 1987).

According to Buddhist thought, there are four classes of persons. Those who strive only for their own welfare; those who strive only for others welfare; those who strive neither for their own nor others welfare; and those who strive for their own welfare and that of others. This last person is deemed just and good. As indicated by the Dalai Lama (1999), the concept of Buddha nature, the concept of the preciousness of this life and this body are very important for developing self-confidence. There are two types of ego, just as there are two types of desire. Of the two types of feeling of "I", the feeling of 'strong I' that forgets about the rights of others' and in which one considers oneself more important than others, is wrong. The other type of ego that makes one feel 'I can do this, I can help, I can serve' is positive.

The Emotions in Buddhist Thought

The Buddhist recognize all the emotions that human nature is capable of experiencing. However, they regard these as the source of mans' sorrow. The Buddhist regards all as pain. The five *khandas*—body, feeling, perception, disposition, and self-consciousness are full of pain. Life is excruciating pain. Birth is attended with pain; decay is painful, disease is painful, painful is separation from the pleasant, and craving that is unsatisfied, that too is painful. In brief, the five aggregates that spring from attachment are painful. Sentient pleasure is transitory and attended with pain. It ought to be eschewed. There is no pleasure like peace. It is the supreme pleasure. The peace of dispassion or desirelessness ought to be pursued (Sinha, 1961).

The exercise of control of passions underlies their concept of *nirvāna*. These passions, according to Buddhist analysis, fall under three groups. First, that which refers to all degrees of craving or attachment—such as lust, infatuation and greed. Second, that which refers to all degrees of antipathy—hatred, anger, vexation, or repugnance. Third, that which refers to all degrees of ignorance—delusion, dullness and stupidity. This cause is *avidyā* (ignorance) of the real nature of man. This psychological explanation of human suffering, despite the variant versions that are found in many documents, is characteristic of Buddhism. It is also true to the tradition of Indian philosophical thought in making ignorance of what is held to constitute reality the fundamental cause of all ill, with the concomitant assumption that the cessation of this ignorance, which is regarded as synonymous with enlightenment, will achieve salvation (Ambedkar, 1991; Brandon, 1962).

The first and second relate to the emotions and over the whole scale of attitudes and feelings towards other beings, while the third is related to all ideas that are in any way removed from the truth. Complete annihilation is one extreme and "*pari-nirvāna*" is another extreme. *Nirvāna* is the middle way. This spirit of contentment is not to be understood to mean meekness or surrender to circumstances. The Buddha has not said that the sufferer should not try to change his condition. The necessity of controlling greed is emphasized. Thus, in Buddhist thought desires, feelings, and emotions play a significant role in the causation of sufferings and its control in preventing suffering. They cloud the intellect and lead him to thought, speech, and action, which ultimately harm others and harm himself. This can be overcome through self-control and vigilance. One should not allow oneself to be swayed by emotions and feelings. One should be conscious of them and thus control them (Ambedkar, 1991; Kuppuswamy, 1990).

According to the Buddha, there were two extremes, a life of pleasure, and a life of self-mortification. One says let us eat and drink, for tomorrow we die. The other says kill all *vāsnās* (desires) because they bring rebirth. He rejected both as unbecoming to man. He was a believer in the *Mādhyama Mārga*, the middle path, which is neither the path of pleasure nor the path of self-mortification. Celibacy is recognized as a healthy state, as it helps to simplify life. By freeing a person from the very large energy and time consuming duties of supporting and bringing up children, a celibate life affords them the opportunity of devoting themselves wholeheartedly to spiritual practice (Ambedkar, 1991; Snelling, 1987).

Buddhism recognizes mans' fear of death. In the words of the Dalai Lama (1999), the clear realization that it is part of ones' life and has come into existence due to ignorance and negative emotions makes a difference. From this perspective, the existence of the body is due mainly to attachment. The realization that ones' present life is based on ignorance and attachment, and the ability to see ones' present existence as something that is projected by ignorance and attachment will also make one realize that something that is a product of ignorance and attachment is bound to cause suffering; that is its nature.

The Buddhist recognizes neutral feeling as a distinct kind of feeling. He recognizes pleasure, pain, and neutral feeling as three kinds of feeling. "Pleasure arises from the experience of a desired object. Neutral feeling arises from the experience of an object that is neither desired nor undesired. Pleasure and pain are opposed to each other. Neutral feeling is the absence of pleasure and pain." It is different from equanimity, which is an emotion (Sinha, 1961).

The Dalai Lama (1999) elucidates the popular misconception regarding desires. There are two kinds of desire, just as there are two kinds of ego. One is desire with a purpose that is good. This desire leads to determination. According to Buddhists, we ultimately reach "Buddhahood" because of this desire. The other desire is without a reason—a mere 'I want'. This kind of desire without a proper basis very often leads to disaster and suffering, hence needs to be shunned.

Through The Prism

Buddhism provides man a rationale for comprehending his life, as it exists. According to Brandon (1962), "the road to attain the happiness that man craves for, even of those who were prepared to make the sacrifice of entering the Buddhist Order, the ideal was too high and demanded too great a measure of self-reliance. Consequently, it is not surprising that in process of time a fundamental change was wrought in Buddhism that had the effect of changing it from an austere philosophy of life to a religion characterized by an intense devotion to a personal savior."

Although the Buddha had admitted that women possessed the same spiritual potential as men, his attitude towards women did not follow the rationale and egalitarian mode of his larger philosophy. Although reflecting the prevalent status of women in Indian society, his prejudice betrayed his intense fear of life, suffering, and death. As the procreator of life, and therefore misery, as the seducer who lures men to desire and therefore sorrow, women had to be shunned. He was reluctant to ordain women into the *sangha*, but only if she would agree to submit to eight very stringent rules, one of which was that a nun (*bhikkuni*) of 100 years seniority would still be junior to a *bhikku* who had only been ordained that very day and must accord him respect (Gard, 1962; Snelling, 1987).

Although Buddhism is perceived as an individualistic religion, it had a greater social role, then and now. The *varnāshram dharma* (caste system) prevalent in India, then and now, was not based on justice, equality, and fraternity. The theory of *Chaturvarnā* (four castes), preached by the *brāhmins* was based on birth. The worth of a man according to the *brāhmins* was based on birth and nothing else. Concomitant to this was the excessive privileges granted to the upper castes, to the detriment of those on the lowest rung, and for those outside the pall of the caste system. Buddha's doctrine was just the opposite. It was his doctrine that worth and not birth was the measure of the man. In Ambedkar's (1991) analysis, in the Buddha's percept, the graded inequality in society might produce an ascending scale of hatred and a descending scale of contempt, and might be a source of perpetual conflict. The philosophic foundations on which the social order as reared by brāhmanism did not serve the interests or welfare of all. Rather, it was deliberately designed to make many serve the interests of few. In it, man was made to serve a class of self-styled supermen. It was calculated to suppress and exploit the weak and to keep them in a state of complete subjugation. The Law of *karma* as formulated by the *brāhmins*, was calculated to sap the spirit of revolt completely. No one was responsible for the suffering of man except he himself. Revolt could not alter the state of suffering; for suffering was fixed by his past *karma* as his lot in this life. The *Sudras* and women, the two classes whose humanity was most mutilated by Brāhmanism, had no power to rebel against the system. They were denied the right to knowledge with the result that due to their enforced ignorance, they could not realize what had made their condition so degraded. The *varnāshram dharma* leaves no room either for development of mans' individual, spiritual, and social progress. It degrades man to the level of a beast. For these reasons the Buddha rejected *brāhmanism* as being opposed to the true way of life.

In contemporary India, Dr. Ambedkar chose Buddhism, in 1956, with its democratic egalitarian ideal. His followers have embraced Buddhism, and thus it has again been revived in India. How much of the Buddhist doctrine is also embraced by the individual contemporary Indian Buddhist, in such circumstances, is a moot point. At one level, he would be immensely influenced by his traditional belief system, which may be the primary influencing factor on his self-construal. At another level, in the present scenario, the sociopolitical implications also influence his self-construal. The implication of these on his self-construal and emotionality may be far removed from the principles enunciated by the philosophy. In fact, the philosophy, aside from its egalitarian code, advocates that life is suffering, and the only way out is through *nirvāna* or a "no-life." This may induce the neo-Buddhist to opt for a passive, rather than a proactive approach to improve his lot. With the continued dominance of the caste concept, the Indian neo-Buddhist may still find himself in the quagmire of a restrictive, non-egalitarian, conflicting society, with its concomitant influence on his personhood.

4

Jainism

During the Vedic times there prevailed a stream of cultural thought that was quite independent of the *brāhmanical* or *vedic* system and, probably quite older than it. This system was the *'śramana'* system. The word *'Śramana'* is derived from *śram* to exert effort, but is mixed in meaning with *sam* a wanderer, recluse. This system was based on equality. According to it, a being is himself responsible for his own deeds. Salvation, therefore, can be obtained by anybody. The cycle of rebirth to which every individual was subjected was viewed as the cause and substratum of misery. The goal of every person was to evolve a way to escape from the cycle of rebirth. Each school of *śramana* preached its own way of salvation. However, they all agreed in one respect, namely, in discounting ritual means of emancipation and establishing a path of moral, mental, and spiritual development as the only means of escaping the misery of *samsāra*. The Vedic cultural system differed from the *śramana* cultural system in three respects, viz. (a) attitude to society, (b) goal of life, and (c) outlook towards living creatures (Bhaskar, 1972).

There are two principal theories concerning the origin of this cult: according to one, it is more or less a protest against orthodox vedic cult, and according to the other, it is of independent origin. The majority of Jaina scholars no longer accept the first theory, though supported by Winternitz (1933), Rhys David (1936/1978), etc. The *Śramana* System is considered to be led by the Jaina, existed before the Brāhmin cult and most of the leaders of different sects of that time were influenced by the Jaina dogmas. Thus, it appears that, Jaina ideas and practices must have been current at the time of Mahāvīra, and existed independently of him. Jainism is thus, believed to be a pre-vedic religion. Jainas are referred to in early Vedic literature by the name of *Vratyas*. Modern scholars appear to agree with the view that Jainism is the oldest of non-Aryan group and an independent and pre-Buddhist religion (Bhaskar, 1972).

The Jaina system exhibits archaic traits not found in other systems. Among these, we have the theory of the elementary particles (earth, water, fire, wind) possessing souls, and the names of *dharma* and *adharma* for the media of motion and stop. (The meaning for *dharma* and *adharma* is considerably different from the vedic meaning of these words). The former can be rubricated as animism, whereas in the latter there appears the conception of 'invisible fluids, which by contact cause sin and merit', a conception coming near to primitive sorcery (Schubring, 1962).

According to the Jaina belief, Jainism is both eternal and universal. It is open not only to human beings of all castes and classes, but even to animals, *devas*, and souls in hell. According to Jaina tradition, twenty-four *Tirthankaras'* appear in every *kalpa*. *Rsabhadeva* is said to be the first *Tirthankara* of the present era. The beginnings of human civilization are associated with him. *Jina* came to be used as the popular name of Rsabha and other *Tirthankara's* and their adherents came to be known as *Jainas* (Bhaskar, 1972).

Mahāvīra or the *Nigantha Nātaputta* was the reformer of the already existing sect. He was born near Vaisali, an important seat of the *Jnātri Kshatriyas*. He was the son of Siddhartha and Trislā, who belonged to the clan of *Jnātris* or *Nāta*. According to the tradition of the *Digambara* sect, he renounced worldly enjoyment at the age of thirty without getting married and became a *nigantha* ascetic. According to the *Śvetāmbara* sect, Mahāvīra married Yasoda, had a daughter from her, and then renounced the world. He then underwent a course of severe bodily mortification for the next twelve years and attained omniscience. He was called *Nigantha* in the sense that he was free from all bonds, and was called *Nataputta* because *Nāta* was the name of his clan. The death of Mahāvīra is placed somewhere between 468 and 482 or 527 and 546 BC (Bhaskar, 1972, Sangave, 1997).

The religious doctrines, principles, tenets as they were enunciated and taught by Mahāvīra were not committed to writing during his lifetime or immediately after his death. The religious teachings were memorized by his immediate successors, and were handed down through the generations until they were canonized at the Council of Pataliputra in the early part of the third century BC. Much of what was canonized was not acceptable to all; some vigorously maintained that the canon did not contain the actual teachings of Mahāvīra. Again, there was the question of interpreting what had been canonized. Various schisms arose in the Jaina community because of which Jainism was divided into several sects and sub-sects. It may also be stated that they arose as a revolt against the actions and policy of ruling priests or heads of the church. The schism of the Order into *Digambara* and *Śvetāmbara* seems to date from as early as the second century AD. There is considerable dispute on both sides regarding the origin of the sects. In order to prove their antiquity, both the sects have put forward their own theories regarding the origin of the other sect. Literally, *Digambara* means 'sky-clad' and *Śvetāmbara* means 'white robed'. The monks of the *Digambara's* are naked while those of the *Śvetāmbara's* wear white clothes. There is very little difference between the two branches as regards the essential doctrine (Schubring, 1962; Sangave, 1997).

What is Jainism?

Jainism is an atheistic religion believing in no creator God behind the world. The world according to it eternally exists, and works by its own inherent laws. It is a religion of moral and spiritual purity aiming at the elevation of man to the state of perfection and Godhood. Thus, man himself is God because potentially he is all-perfect. The *Tirthankaras, Kevalis* and the *Siddhas*, who have attained perfection, can all be taken as god. They are neither creators nor destroyers. They have conquered their ignorance, passions, and do not require anything. They have attained *kaivalya* or *nirvāna*.

Jainism takes the world as perfectly real, with all its plural beings. The world according to it is a function of six externally existing substances, five material and the one spiritual. Jainism believes man has an eternal conscious substance within him known as *jīva* (soul). In fact, all living beings have souls within them; only the soul of man is most developed, because consciousness in it is the most manifest. Mans' soul is potentially perfect, and is capable of attaining infinite power, infinite knowledge, infinite faith, and infinite bliss (*ananta chatusthaya*), i.e. Godhood. There is a belief in life after death in the form of rebirth, the transmigration of the soul from the old body to the new one. *Moksha* is the final liberation of the soul from the chain of birth and rebirth (Tiwari, 1983).

Jainism believes that the present state of man is the state of bondage, which is due to his own past *karmans*. Actions done with passion are the poison of the soul and it is these, which cause the soul to be reborn. Thus, Jainism believes in all the chief Hindu doctrines of *karma*, rebirth, bondage, and liberation. Man suffers due to his own *karmans'* and there is no other explanation for human suffering. Liberation can be attained not by offering rituals to gods and goddesses, but by following the path of three jewels—right faith, right knowledge, and right conduct. Jainism lays utmost emphasis on the value of moral conduct, under which *ahimsā* is the most emphasized virtue. Of others, purity, chastity, non-attachment, compassion, love, fellow-feeling etc. are much emphasized. Jainism extols the life of a monk or a celibate who has renounced everything and is engaged in spiritual elevation by following a path of rigorous moral and spiritual discipline (Tiwari, 1983).

The followers of Jaina religion are divided into four categories according to gender and the strictness with which the members practice the injunctions set down by the religion. Namely: the *Yatis* or *Sadhus* or *Munis*—the male ascetics; A*rjikās* or *Sādhvis*, female ascetics; *Sravakās*, male laity and *Sravikās*, female laity. All members of the community undertake vows, to assist them in their final goal of reducing *karma* and attaining *nirvanā*. This organization of the community from earliest times is one of the important reasons put forward for the survival of Jainism in India as against Buddhism (Sangave, 1997).

The major points of difference between the two sects are as follows: The *Digambara's* believe that a monk who owns any property, for example, wears clothes, cannot attain salvation. The *Śvetāmbara's* assert that the practice of complete nudity is not essential to attain liberation. The *Digambara's* hold the view that women are not entitled to *moksha* in this life. On the contrary, the *Śvetāmbara's* believe that women can reach *nirvanā* in this life. According to the *Digambara's*, once a saint had attained *Kevala Jñana* (omniscience), he needed no food, but could sustain life without eating. This view is not acceptable to the *Śvetāmbara's* (Sangave, 1997).

Jaina doctrines may be broadly divided into philosophical and practical. Jaina philosophy contains ontology, metaphysics, and psychology. The practical doctrines are concerned with ethics, asceticism, and the life of the laity. Aside from the difficulties in interpretation of the texts from Pāli and Prākrit languages in which they were written, a vast amount of Jaina literature is lost.

Basic Principles of Jaina Philosophy

The most celebrated text, the implication of which forms almost the entire theoretical foundation of the Jaina philosophy of being is: '*The real is characterized by birth or origination, death or destruction, and sameness or continuity*'. Umasvati (1st century AD) was the first to evolve a systematic exposition of the philosophical aspect of the Jaina religion. According to the postulate embodied in his text, everything real must have the triple character of productivity (*utpada*), destructibility (*vyaya*), and at the same time, permanence, or persistence (*dhrauvya*) underlying it. Conversely, whatever lacks the one or the other of this triple nature is a mental abstraction having no title to reality. Productivity and destructibility constitute the two aspects of change and may therefore together be characterized as the dynamic aspect of reality, the static aspect being represented by permanence or *dhruvatva* (Padmarajiah, 1963).

According to Jaina cosmology, there are six fundamental substances constituting reality: soul, which is sentient and formless; matter, which has form; and medium of motion, medium of rest, space, and time, which are formless substances.

The Upanishad maintained that Being is one, permanent, without beginning, change, or end. In opposition to this view, the Jainas declare that Being is not of a persistent and unalterable nature. Being, they say, 'is joined to production, continuation, and destruction'. This theory they call the Theory of Indefiniteness of Being. Any material thing continues forever to exist as matter; this matter, however, may assume any shape and quality. While the brāhmanical speculations are concerned with transcendental Being, the Jaina view deals with Being, as given in common experience (Jacobi, 1975).

The Jainas are opposed to the materialistic conception of the soul as identical with the body. In their opinion, the principle of life is distinct from the body and it is most erroneous to think that life is either the product or the property of the body. It is because of this life principle that the body appears to be living. This principle is the soul. The defining characteristic of soul (*jīva*) is consciousness. Intuition, knowledge etc. are its different forms. Since it is formless, it cannot be perceived by the sense organs. We know it by introspection and inference (Mehta, 1969).

The soul as the bearer of life is called *jīva*, and since it is animate, a living being is called a *jīva*. There are infinite souls in the universe. The number of *jīvas* is infinite as in the *Nyāya-*

Jainism

Vaisesika, Samkhya-Yoga, and Purvamimamasa schools. Like them, Jainism also does not accept the illusory character of the *jiva* as defined in the monastic Vedānta. The total number of souls remains constant forever. It neither increases nor decreases. Within the different individual grades and classes of beings, decrease or increase naturally will occur, with the exception of the delivered souls whose number is not subjected to any decrease. A soul is not all pervasive. By contraction and expansion, it is capable of occupying varying proportions of the countless space-points of the universe. Souls are of two categories, liberated and worldly. The liberated souls are perfect and pure. They possess four infinities: infinite comprehension, infinite apprehension, infinite bliss, and infinite power. Ordinarily, however, all the other *jivas* excepting a few released pure souls (*mukta jiva*) have all their power, purity, and knowledge covered by a thick veil of *karman* matter, which has been accumulating in them from beginningless time. The worldly souls are further divided into mobile souls and immobile souls. The mobile souls are further divided into four classes—the five sensed, four sensed, three sensed, and two sensed. The immobile souls possess only one sense, touch. They are divided into earth bodied, water bodied, fire bodied, air bodied, and plant bodied. The soul is not identical with the body. It is an independent entity, which is essentially conscious. The worldly soul is equal in extent to its own body. It is the possessor of material *karman*. Its existence is proved by direct experience (Schubring, 1962; Roy, 1966; Mehta, 1969).

Concept of Knowledge: The Jainas recognize two modes of knowledge—the external, for the apprehension of external objects, and the internal for the apprehension of self-consciousness. The existence of an objective reality, beyond and beside consciousness, and apprehended in perception, is asserted by the Jainas. The relation between knowledge and object is external with regard to physical objects though it is different in the case of self-consciousness. In knowing any object, the self knows itself simultaneously. Had it not been so, none else could have imparted this knowledge to it. In self-consciousness the subject of knowledge (*jnānin*), the object of knowledge and knowledge itself are different aspects of a single concrete unity. Further, there cannot be *jnāna* without *jnānin* since that would make the former foundationless (Roy, 1966).

Modes of Consciousness : "The Jaina advocates the tripartite classification of the modes of consciousness. All plants experience only feeling, animals experience feeling, and conative impulse. All persons experience feeling, conation, and cognition. In order of development, feeling comes first, then conation and then cognition. The embodied self has knowledge and perception of external objects, desires pleasures, and dreads pain. It acts for the attainment of good or the avoidance of evil, and experiences pleasure or pain. It is a knower, an experiencer, and an agent. Thus, the distinction of cognition, feeling, and conation is clearly recognized. There are five kinds of cognition: sensuous knowledge, testimony, clairvoyant knowledge, telepathic knowledge of other minds, and omniscience. Perception, memory, recognition, reasoning, and intuition are the different kinds of cognition. Pleasure, pain, and indifference are the three kinds of feeling. Attachment, aversion, and delusion are affective conative states. Emotions, passions, instincts, and volitions are also recognized" (Sinha, 1961, p. 50).

Next to the sensual organs, the inward sense, or either, the reason is essential for spiritual imagination. With animals and human beings, *sannā* (emotion) is connected with their coming into existence by procreation, with the gods and the inhabitants of hell with their possessing it in their pre-existence. Those who possess the *sannā* are called *sanni* and so the *kevalin* is *no-sanni-no-asanni*, since he has come to be beyond the *sannā*. The ten *sannās* are the primitive emotions or instincts owned by all beings (with the exception of the *kevalin* and the *siddha*). They are directed towards the nourishment, fear, sex, splendor, anger, pride, deceit, greed, worldliness, and all carnal desires. Of the four, first fear shows up acutely with the inhabitants of hell, nourishment with animals, sex with human beings, and splendor with the gods, the remaining being chronic. Apart from depending on the respective *karman*, these four depend on imagination aroused by information, on thinking of it independently, and furthermore, on the concrete causes as cowardice, empty stomach, too much flesh and blood, and on possession. Imagination, no matter whether it depends on the activity of the five outward senses, or on that of the inner sense, proceeds from the primary perception over the will, to cognition, and ascertainment, to the act of imprinting the perception in the mind (Schubring, 1962).

The Jaina Concept of Reality : The Jaina hypothesizes the reality or the factuality of relation because of direct and objective experience. Thus, reality is not merely inferable, but also as an indubitable perceptual fact. He does so, in opposition to what he considers, as the aprioristic dialectic of Buddhism. By implication, of the Vedānta also, wherein the mind imposes its own forms upon, instead of obeying the dictates of the events of the objective realm. This is the spirit underlying Prabhachandra's contention that the Buddhist seriously errs, not merely by ignoring what is directly perceivable, viz., the relational element, but also in describing it as a conceptual fiction (*kalpanā*), which is anything but perceptible. Hence, the Buddhist cannot deny the reality of this phenomenon in the light of objective experience. However, the Jaina still chooses to escape from this reality by the severe austerity measures as part of the vows that he undertakes (Padmarajiah, 1963).

Law of Karman : The Jaina approach to the problem of evil and suffering is practical. Being a non-theistic system, it does not have any occasion to tackle the problem in the way in which it is raised and answered in the context of Semitic religions. It does not ask and answer the general question as to why there is evil in this world. Rather, it raises and tries to answer the specific questions to why a man suffers. The Jaina answer to this is that man suffers due to his own past *karmans*'.

Besides believing in the law of *karman* in a general sense that the Hindus and Buddhists systems believe in it, Jainism believes in it in a very specific sense, that of particles of fine matter (Tiwari, 1983).

The Jaina meaning of *karman* is not work or deed. According to the Jaina conception, *karman* is an aggregate of particles of very fine matter not perceptible to the senses. The entire cosmos is full of *karmic* matter, which has infected the soul from time immemorial. Through the actions of the body, mind, and speech, *karmic* matter enters the self. It is tied to the self according to the strength of passions, viz., anger, pride, deceit, and greed. First, there is an influx of *karman* particles due to activities. At the same time, bondage (*bandhā*) takes place owing to passions. The particles of *karman* produce various types of effects (Mehta, 1969).

Karman is classified into eight fundamental types: comprehension-obscuring (*jñānavaranā*) *karman*; apprehension-obscuring (*darsanavaranā*) *karman*; the *karman* which produces pleasure and pain, called the feeling-producing (*vedanīya*) *karman*; *karman* that obscures right belief, and right conduct, known as deluding (*mohanīya*) *karman*; *karman* that determines the length of life, called age determining (*āyus*) *karman*; *karman* which forms the body called physique making (*nāma*) *karman*; *karman* that destines a position in society, known as status determining (*gotra*) *karman*; and *karman* that impedes the infinite energy of the self, called the power obscuring (*antarāya*) *karman*. Our worldly existence is dependent on these eight types of *karman*. There are numerous sub-types to these. Of these, the first four are obstructive (*ghātin*), whilst the remaining four is unobtrusive (*aghātin*). They are further classified under the heads of virtuous (*punya*) *karman*, which yield happiness and pleasure in life, and sinful (*pāpa*) *karman*, which produce sorrow and pain (Mehta, 1969).

According to Jaina thought, souls are eternal substances of indefinite size since they contract or expand according to the dimensions of the body in which they are incorporated for the time being. Their characteristic mark is intelligence, which may be obscured by extrinsic causes, but never destroyed. Souls are of two kinds, mundane (*samsārin*) and liberated (*muktā*). Defilement of the soul takes place due to *karman* matter entering it. The *karman* particles stick to the soul due to work of passions. Anger, pride, fraud, and greed are denoted as passions, and they for their part result from *karman*. The freedom from passion, however, and hence the purification of the soul leading to *moksha* can be realized in life only by the Jaina monk (or nun) (Schubring, 1962; Jacobi, 1975).

Hence, whatever suffering one has is due to ones past specific *karmans*'. So, none but an individual is responsible for all his sufferings. Any sort of life whether seemingly happy or miserable, is a symbol of suffering, because life as a whole is essentially full of limitations and imperfections, and imperfection itself is the greatest evil. Hence, what is to be avoided is any future birth. For that, all sorts of actions, done out of passions and desires, whether good or bad, are to be avoided, as they attract *karman* matter. They are the causes for the continuance of the body and taking rebirth. So long as matter is associated with the soul, there can be no end to suffering. So to avoid suffering completely, one has to get rid of the continuous chain of birth and rebirth. That is possible only through the attainment of knowledge and performance of only non-attached actions (Tiwari, 1983).

The *Triratna* or Three Jewels : The Jaina view of life after death is similar to the Hindu view. The ultimate destiny of man is *kaivalya* or moksha. As bondage is the association of the soul with matter, moksha is complete dissociation of the soul from matter. This dissociation is complete only when matter already accumulated with the soul is completely annihilated and any further influx of matter is completely checked. By pursuing the path of *Samyag Darshan* (Right Faith), *Samyag Jnana* (Right Knowledge) and *Samyag Charitra* (Right Conduct) one can attain moksha. These three are known as *Triratna* (Three Jewels) in Jainism (Tiwari, 1983).

The following eight essentials are given in Jainism for Right Faith (*samyag darsana*). Absence of doubt about scriptures; absence of desires for the worldly pleasures; absence of doubt about the attainment of spiritual path; a clear and un-confusing vision about the ideal; augmentation of spiritual qualities; re-establishing deviation from truth; sense of affection towards the followers of right path; and preaching the importance of truth. There seems to be a controversy regarding the exact connotation of right faith. Some define it as a belief in the nine Jaina categories. Some define it as a belief in six substances and nine categories. Some define it as faith in the dharma devoid of violence and in the way of life prescribed by the *Jins* and *Kevalis*, some define it as belief in Jaina scriptures and teachers and so on (Tiwari, 1983).

Right Knowledge is knowledge about the true nature of things and the distinction of the soul from the material substances is necessary.

Right Conduct is conduct based on detachment. Jainism gives a long list of actions constituting the right conduct for a householder and for a monk separately. The five vows mentioned here are necessary for all. The five vows are known as *panchāmahavrata* in Jainism.

Ahimsā (Non-violence): Violence in any form is strictly prohibited in any form and any denomination. *Ahimsā* is to be practiced not only in deed, but also in thought and words.

Satya (Truthfulness): Abstinence from giving false statements or telling a lie. Mere statement of fact is not truth. Truth, if it is harmful to others, should be avoided. It must be spoken with beneficent intentions. Other wise it will offend or harm somebody and that will be *himsā*.

Asteya (Non-stealing): Besides stealing, it includes within it the avoidance of all sorts of dishonesty and conceit.

Brahmacharya (Celibacy): Jainism extols the virtue of celibacy much more than any religion. Acceptance of any form of sexual conduct including the thought of it is a violation of this vow.

Aparigraha (Non-possession or non-attachment): This stands for not only abstinence from excessive material possession but also for the avoidance of desire for such possessions.

The Self in Jaina Thought

Mahāvīra expressed his understanding of human nature and human ways and doings through numerous parables. According to the first type, man has various attributes, and he retaliates in various ways. According to the second type, human beings also differ in descent, strength, and beauty. In the preference these attributes are given, they differ in that some are sociable and others are not in their faculty of either causing or healing wounds. A third type is concerned with mutually exclusive opposites. The heterogeneousness of man results from their *karman* matter (Schubring, 1962).

During the time of its specific bodily existence, the individual possesses more than one body (*sarira*). Their number is five in all, but their distribution among the different beings differs. They all have the *karman* body (*kammaga sarira*), and the fiery body (*teyaga sarira*) life long. All beings with one to five senses permanently own the earthly body (*uraliya sarira*). Both the gods and the inhabitants of hell always live in bodies of transformation (*veuvviya sarira*), but other beings do so only temporarily, while the body of transposition (*aharga sarira*) merely applies to human beings and in special cases only (Schubring, 1962).

The Jaina emphasizes the causal interrelation between self and body, although the relation between them is external. A change in one always involves a physical antecedent and a psychical antecedent, one being the substantial cause and the other the external cause. The self is the substantial or constituent cause of an emotion, while *karman* matter is its external or indirect cause. A change in *dravya karman* or physical *karman* immediately produces a change in *bhāva karman* or consciousness. It produces an emotion. *Dravya karma* is the cause of *bhāva karma*, which is the cause of an emotional state. An emotion is the effect of karmic thought, which is the effect of *karmic* matter. The direct and immediate cause of an emotion is *bhava karman* or karmic thought. However, its indirect or external cause is *dravya karman* or karmic matter.

There is contiguous coexistence of the soul and karmic matter with each other. There is no direct causal action between them. The karmic particles merely by proximity cling to the soul because of their adhesive quality. The soul becomes adulterated with karmic particles. This adulteration is not due to direct causal action of karmic matter upon soul. The soul develops an inclination towards matter because of its emotional states. This inclination is an external condition of karmic matter. Material particles of *karman* so determined somehow bind to the soul and cloud its intrinsic omniscience. Thus, the Jaina steers a middle course between parallelism and interactionism (Sinha, 1961).

The Social Self in Jaina Thought

Mahāvīra's similes deal with man in general. The main principle of Jainism is *ahimsā* and freeing oneself from the bondage of *karman* matter. This total freedom can be achieved only by renouncing the world. For achieving this goal, the Jaina has to undertake numerous vows. Paradoxically enough, it is the laity, in whom the teachings have taken root that the number of restrictions exceeds those accepted by the monk. This is due to the larger diversity of the civil life in which the laity still stands. The duties that a laity is bound to observe must be derived from those observed by the monk (Schubring, 1962).

All rules of conduct are so designed as to secure the aim as early as possible. As there is no outside agency to help the individual in his efforts to secure salvation, it is natural that more importance was given to the individual. Jaina ethics took pains to provide for the welfare of both the society and the individual. It recognized the need for taking care of the society, and aspired to bring the highest conceivable form of good within the individual's reach. The social aspect of an individual's life was never ignored. An individual was never conceived as separated from the society and social life. social life was never considered an impediment to ones' spiritual progress if necessary precautions are taken. These precautions are included in the twelve vows of a layman. These vows play a good part in the life of an individual, as well as the whole community. The individual, who adopts the twelve vows, or some of them, is left ample freedom to fulfill all his worldly duties. They enable him to remain in fullest concordance with worldly propriety and etiquette even if he happens to occupy any responsible post, which requires energetic and violent acting in the interest of the state (Sangani, 1997; Sangave, 1997).

The rules of conduct for laypersons are divided into twelve *vratas* or vows, eleven *pratimās* or stages in householders' life, six daily duties, and thirty-five rules of good conduct. The layperson begins with the avoidance of the five *aticāras*, i.e. shortcomings of faith. Namely, doubt or skepticism (*sankā*) desires of sense pleasures (*kānksa*), disgust for anything (*vicikitsā*), for example, with a sick person, thinking admiringly of wrong believers (*anyadrsti-praśamsā*), and praising wrong believers (*anydristi-samstava*). This will enable a layperson to observe vows, which marks the first stage of right conduct (Sangave, 1997).

The vows are of two kinds, small and great. The small vows (*anuvratas*) are for the laypersons, and those who practice the great vows (*mahāvratas*) are the ascetics. The layperson is enjoined to observe twelve vows: five *anuvratas*, three *gunavratas*, and four *siksavratas*. The *anuvratas* are the fundamental or primary vows that he observes. The *gunavratas* and *siksāvratas* are the supplementary or minor vows to enhance the strength of the *anuvratas*. The five *anuvratas* are related to *ahimsā, satya, asteya, brahmacharya,* and *aparigraha*. Since these are observed partially by the layperson, they are called *anuvratas* in his case. An ascetic observes them completely, and therefore, in his case they are known as *mahāvratas* (Mehta, 1969).

The Twelve Vows : The five main vows are as follows: i) *Ahimsā*—to be free from injury, ii) *Satya*—to be free from falsehood, iii) *Asteya*—to be free from theft, iv) *Brahmacārya*—to be free from unchastity, v) *Aparigraha*—to be free from worldly attachment. Laypersons cannot observe these vows strictly and therefore they are allowed to practice them as far as their conditions permit. For the fixing of these five vows in the mind, there are five kinds of *bhāvanā's* as attendant meditations for each of the vows and every Jaina is expected to think over them repeatedly. Further, he must meditate that the five faults that need to be avoided in the vows are pain personified and are of dangerous and censurable in this as well as the next world. Moreover, he must meditate upon the following virtues that are based upon the observance of these five vows. These are: friendship with all living beings (*maitrī*), delight at the sight of beings better qualified or more advanced than ourselves on the path of liberation (*pramoda*), compassion for the affected (*kārunya*), and tolerance or indifference to those who are uncivil or ill-behaved (*mādhyastha*) (Sangave, 1997).

In order to practice the five main vows, the seven *Sīlavratas* or supplementary vows must be practiced. These are i) *Digvrata*—taking a life long vow to limit his worldly activity to fixed points in all directions; ii) *Deśavrata*—taking a vow to limit the above also for a limited area; iii) *Anarthadanda vrata*—Taking a vow not to commit purposeless sins; iv) *Sāmāyika*—taking a vow to devote particular time everyday to contemplation of the self for spiritual advancement; v) *Prosadhopavāsa,* taking a vow to fast on four days of the month; vi) *Upabhoga-paribhoga-parimāna,* taking a vow everyday limiting ones' enjoyments of consumable and non-consumable things; and vii) *Atithi-samvibhāga,* taking a vow to take ones' food only after feeding

Jainism

the ascetics, or in their absence, the pious householders (Sangave, 1997).

In addition to the above twelve vows, a householder is expected to practice in the last moment of his life the process of *sallekhanā* or peaceful death. *Sallekhanā* is described as the giving up of the body on the arrival of unavoidable calamity, distress, old age, and disease, with a view to increasing spiritual merit (Sangave, 1997).

The householders' life has been divided into eleven stages or *pratimās*. These form a series of duties and performances, the standard and duration, which rises periodically and which finally culminates in an attitude resembling monkhood. The eleven *pratimās* are as follows:

> *Darsana pratima* : Possessing perfect, intelligent, and well-reasoned faith in the doctrines of the faith and their applications in daily life.
>
> *Vrata pratimā* : keeping up the twelve vows and the extra vow of *sallekhanā*.
>
> *Sāmāyika pratimā* : Worshipping daily three times a day. Worship means self-contemplation and purifying ones' ideas and emotions.
>
> *Prosadhopavāsa pratimā* : fasting regularly, as a rule, twice a month.
>
> *Sacitta-tyāga pratimā* : Refraining from eating uncooked vegetables, plucking fruits from a tree etc.
>
> *Rātri-bhukta-tyāga pratimā* : Abstaining from food after sunset.
>
> *Brahmacharya pratimā* : Maintaining sexual purity now assuming the stricter aspect of celibacy and not decorating ones' person.
>
> *Ārambha-tyāga pratimā* : Abandonment of worldly engagements and occupations.
>
> *Parigraha-tyāga pratimā* : Divesting oneself of wealth by dividing the property amongst heirs. In addition, training one to bear hardships, incidental to a life of asceticism.

Anumati-tyāga pratimā : increasing the rigor of living in the direction of asceticism and refraining even from giving advice in family matters.

Uddista-tyāga pratimā : After renunciation of householder's life, retiring into the forest and adopting the rules laid down for the guidance of ascetics.

The thirty-five rules of good conduct are rules that would assist him in following the vows. If he would carefully observe these rules of conduct, he would come into possession of the following twenty-one qualities, which every person should possess. He would be serious in demeanor, clean as regards both his clothes and person, good tempered, popular, merciful, afraid of sinning, straightforward, wise, modest, kind, moderate, gentle, careful in speech, sociable, cautious, studious, reverent both to old age and ancient customs, humble, grateful, benevolent, and attentive to business. These rules are essential for the Jaina, as there are no external agencies to assist him in his road to salvation. The merits or demerits he acquires, or the *karman* matter he attracts, are dependent on his actions. Thus, the importance of individual behavior cannot be understated (Sangave, 1997).

Status of women : From the time of Pārasvantha to the present, women have been admitted to the religious order of nuns. The *Digambaras* hold the view that women cannot become perfect without being reborn as men. As nudity is essential for perfection, women cannot abide by this, thus their incompetence for direct salvation. The *Śvetāmbaras* however, have no such restrictions. However, both the sects maintain that in the monastic life, the nun is inferior to the monk, and is prohibited to study certain texts. A nun of thirty years standing is inferior to a monk of three years, who can be her teacher. This attitude may stem from the monks belief in the superiority of a celibate life—or conversely a fear of sexuality, as they considered a woman as the temptress that perpetuated the misery that was life (Pruthi & Sharma, 1995).

Jainism

The general trend in Jaina literature is that women, by nature, are bad. In the *Tandulaveyaliya*, we are given etymologies of various synonyms of 'woman'. She is called '*Nārī* (*nā-ari*) because there was no worse enemy for man than she is. She is '*Mahilā*' because she charms by her wiles and graces. She is called '*Padmā*', because she accelerates a mans' passions. She is called '*Mahitiya*' because she creates dissension. She is '*Ramā*', because she delights in coquetry. She is called '*Anganā*' because she loves the *anga* or body of men. She is '*Josiya*', because by her tricks she keeps men under her subjection. She is '*Vanitā*' because she caters to the taste of men with her various blandishments. The essentially evil nature of women is also illustrated in various tales" (Pruthi & Sharma, 1995, p. 165).

The generality of Jainas considered women as desirable, though the influence of the tales would have affected their perception of women, and hence their attitude towards them. However, woman, in her role of mother, is held in the greatest of esteem, the Jaina monks were no exception to this. It is difficult to associate motherhood with celibacy, and Jaina theologians do not hold the dogma of immaculate conception.

In present times, for all practical purposes the Jainas are becoming a sect of Hinduism. They are thus influenced by Hindu imagery and stereotypes of both man and woman. As in the *Manu Smriti*, the Jaina texts state that a woman, when a child must be kept under the control of her father, when married under her husband and when a widow, under her son. Thus, a woman is never allowed to live independently. Further, we are informed women may have freedom as much as they may like in the discharge of their duties towards their husbands and children. However, they must not interfere in matters that properly belong to men's sphere, their minds being extremely fickle and superficial, like 'a drop of water on a lotus leaf'. No one who accepts the participation of women in activities other than domestic duties can thrive for long. In addition, it is under a mans' control that a woman achieves her desired end, 'like a sword in the grip of a man' (Handiqui, in Sangave, 1997; Pruthi & Sharma, 1997).

Achārya Amitagati's *Subhasitaratnasandoha*, considered important from the point of view of Jaina ethics, treats the female body as a sum of all impurity. Hence in its opinion the woman is 'the treasury of all sufferings', 'the bolt barring the city of heaven', 'the pathway to the dwelling of hell' etc. (Winternitz, 1933).

In contradiction to these, many stories of devoted and chaste wives are also told. Hereby, taking the description of women to another stereotypical extreme. Achārya Somadeva, as a practical thinker gives his judgment in '*Nitvakyamrtam*', that women are neither good nor bad. They have neither an innate merit nor blemish but become just like their husbands. This view is more balanced and reflects social reality. It is also noted that such harsh remarks about women are not generally accepted in society. They are made with a view to blacken the character of women in order to warn the lustful monks to keep aloof from feminine charms that might overcome their reason. Remarks like "*striyo hi visamam vism*", i.e. women are indeed the worst of poisons, are made while advising the ascetics to abstain from the desire of women (Jain, 1947; Sangave, 1997).

The Emotions in Jaina Thought

The Jaina regards feelings as modifications of the soul substance. They are due to the infra-atomic particles of *karman* matter, which encrust the soul. They are the effects of the environment upon the self in an embodied condition. The Jaina thinkers recognize the affective value of sensations (Sinha, 1961).

Emotions are mirth or laughter, indulgence in sentient pleasure, non-indulgence in it or languor, sorrow, fear, disgust, sex feeling of a woman, sex feeling of a man, and a eunuch's sex feeling. Passions are anger, pride, deceit, and greed in different degrees of intensity. There are four instincts: The instinct for food (including the preying instinct and the like); the instinct of fear based on the instinct of self-preservation; the sexual instinct or the mating instinct; and the instinct of acquisition including the instinct for collection; and the instinct for possession. Instincts are modified, controlled, and even eradicated by severe discipline. Suicide defies the instinct of life; celibacy conquerors the sexual urge; saints eradicate the instinct for acquisition, collection, and possession; omniscient persons overcome even hunger and thirst (Sinha, 1961).

The Jaina divides emotions into two main classes: *Sakasāya* emotions and *Akasāya* emotions. The former are gross which have a tendency to stain the purity of the soul. The latter have no such tendency to corrupt the soul.

The *akasāya* emotions are the following: Mirth or laughter, attraction, repulsion, sorrow, fear, disgust, sex feeling of women, men, and eunuchs.

The *sakasāya* emotions are the following: Anger, which springs from thwarted desire. When a person is thwarted, obstructed, or opposed in the attainment or enjoyment of an object of desire, he is thrown into a stage of anger. Pride or conceit, which consists in self-glorification due to the possession of cherished objects. Deceit by means of which, an object of desire is sought to be attained. Greed or craving for an object, which is not yet attained. These gross emotions are called passions. There are many passions, which are formed out of the four primary passions. They are but modifications of the soul-substance or different forms of its agitation (Sinha, 1961, p. 161).

The *sakasāya* emotions are of four degrees of intensity. They are irresistible, over-powering, strong, and mild. The most intense and durable passions are called *anantānubandhi*. The passions in this state are permanent. The next degree of intensity is called *pratyākhyāna*. The passions in this state are less durable. The next degree of intensity is called *apratyākhyāna*. The passions in this state are less durable. The least degree of their intensity is called *samjvalana*. The passions in this are the least durable. They are momentary and quickly disappear. Anger, pride, deceit, and greed are gross emotions or passions, which stain the purity of the soul. They are but violent forms of desire, which is a craving for possession or enjoyment of an object. They produce a disturbance in the soul, throw it into a state of agitation, and interfere, more or less with calmness of thought. This emotional agitation of thought is called impure thought. Passions are impediments to self-knowledge and self-realization. Only those persons who have extirpated all passions, which have a tendency to taint the soul, can be on the path of righteousness. Those who are agitated by passions can never realize the self. Attachment and aversion are the internal causes of bondage, and determine its duration and intensity (Sinha, 1961).

A detailed effect of the passions is demonstrated in the *Dasavaikalikā*, which according to some scholars contain the original words of *Mahāvīra*. The passions depend on impressions made by all colors, different kinds of smell or taste, and the four sensations warm, cold, soft, and rough, and this they have in common with the central offences and all other sins. They result in an existence in hell. The latter two represent a delusion of a friendly, the former of a hostile nature. All details offered with regard to the passions (except greed) derive from the sphere of the monk. Anger arises with the experienced or anticipated confiscation of pleasant things or with the act of supplying someone with unpleasant ones, and it is aroused by ones' self-satisfaction wounded by the teachers. Pride (*māyā*, a synonym for *mana*) is entertained towards ones' ancestry and family, physical strength and handsomeness, erudition and asceticism, gifts, and prestige, visits by gods and goddesses, and finally, towards ones' standing above the average of the masses by ones' knowledge and faith. Fraud means all that contradicts truth[1] (Schubring, 1962).

The Jaina recognizes three kinds of pleasure—physical, mental, and spiritual. Spiritual pleasure is the feeling of freedom of the soul from the burden of *karman* particles. It is independent of the senses. Affective consciousness or feeling

Jainism

is of three kinds: pleasure, pain, and pure feeling. Pure feeling is the innate bliss of the self, which is infinite, eternal, and independent of the senses. It is the spiritual experience of the pure self. It is the enjoyment of the self by itself. It is supersensible spiritual bliss due to the experience of the innate purity of the self. It is not due to *vedaniyā karman* (Sinha, 1961).

The Jaina regards pain as a modification of the soul substance, which is in the nature of suffering due to bad action or *karman* particles. It is due to the contact of undesired objects with the sense organs, and an object of aversion. The Jaina recognizes physical and mental pain, but denies the existence of spiritual pain (Sinha, 1961).

Through the Prism

The details of Jaina philosophy and ethics are beyond the scope of this study. At the onset, it should suffice to state, that various aspects of Jaina philosophy and ethics have met with considerable refutation from the Buddhist philosophers. Even between the two major sects—the *Digambaras* and the *Śvetāmbaras*, there is considerable refutation of each other's philosophical perspectives (Bhaskar, 1972). A cursory reading of these indicates a degree of confusion even for scholars of Jainism. Added to this is the fact that a vast amount of Jaina literature is either lost or not accessible. In addition, an analysis by scholars has brought forth evidence that perspectives may have been added, deleted, or ignored during the period of the schism of the Jaina sects into *Śvetāmbara* and *Digambara*, each trying to prove his own antiquity and authenticity. Hence, what the followers accept as their philosophy can be stated as being the essence of the main four points and the elaborate rules of conduct that are laid out for the house-holder to follow. The influence of the *Tīrthankara* that a given society follows, and the assimilation of regional and local customs, that are part of the cultural background of the people, would also be evident. What appear to be followed are external rules of conduct. The rules for monks are equally elaborate to assist in their attainment of moksha. In this work, I restrict the discussion to the main issues under concern, the self and emotions, and aspects of the philosophy and ethics that have a direct bearing on the lives of the Jaina. Thus keeping within the premise that self-construal is vastly influenced by the philosophy that guides a society.

According to the Jainas, the self is the subject of knowledge, object of knowledge, and knowledge itself. They are different aspects of a concrete unity. In Roy's (1966) analysis, "the Jainas seek to establish a new mode of knowing object. Consciousness according to them is necessary so that we may demarcate animate objects from inanimate ones—*jīva's* from *ajīva's*. However, consciousness is identical with a sort of life-principle. This is nothing but an attempt to describe subjectivity by making it something external. It is only an objective attitude that can describe the soul in terms of physiological principles—like life as the Jainas do. As they regard the soul as an object, they demarcate it into different levels according to the number of sense organs that the bodies of the individuals possess. No subjective approach can think of such objective gradations. Therefore, the Jainas ultimately reduce subjectivity to the status of an object by interpreting it in the objective attitude" (p. 138).

The soul is potentially the possessor of infinite knowledge, infinite intuition, infinite power, and infinite bliss. However, these qualities remain covered and mutilated because of its beginningless association with matter, which is concrete and real, and not imaginary and unreal as the idealist Buddhist or the monist Vedāntist would like us to believe (Pruthi & Sharma, 1995). The question raised at this point is, does not this combination of the soul and *karman* matter become its basic nature. What prompted the philosopher to seek a goal that liberates him from his basic essence, that has been his condition from "beginningless time"? Is it an infinite regression into nothingness that eliminates pain?

Jainism

According to Zimmer (1975), the Jaina philosophy is of profound pessimism. The round of rebirths in the world is endless, full of suffering, and of no avail. Of and in itself, it can yield no release, no divine redeeming grace; and the very gods are subject to its deluding spell. Therefore, ascent to heaven is no less a mere phase or stage of delusion than descent to the purgatorial hells. Because of meritorious conduct, one is reborn a god among the gods; due to evil conduct, a being among the beings of hell or an animal among the beasts. However, there is no escape, either way, from this perennial circulation. One will continue to resolve forever through the various spheres of inconsequential pleasures and unbearable pains unless one can manage somehow to release oneself. But, this can be accomplished only by heroic effort and a long really dreadful ordeal of austerities and progressive abnegation.

From the Jaina point of view, the special dignity of the human being consists solely in the fact that he is capable of becoming enlightened, free from bondage. This ideal is expressed in the legendary biographies of the Buddha's and *tīrthankara*'s and is taken seriously and literally as an ideal for all. It is regarded as open to man, and steps are needed to realize it. The way of perfectibility taught is that of yogic asceticism and self-abnegation (Zimmer, 1975).

For the Jaina, right faith, right knowledge, and right conduct are essential for the attainment of moksha. Right faith enjoins the absence of doubt about what the scriptures state. In other words, an injunction against thinking afresh. The philosophy accepts reality as a fact and not an illusion. It accepts the objective reality, which can simultaneously be apprehended subjectively. Right knowledge is therefore knowledge of nature, as it exists. However, the rules of conduct and the ultimate aim persuade him to shun nature as it exists—his instincts, needs, and desires as a sentient being. This is a primary dichotomy in Jaina thought.

In its analysis of the psychology and destiny of man, Jaina philosophy regards the life-monad (*jīva*) as different from the "*karmic* matter" (*a-jīva*, non-*jīva*), by which it is bound down and withheld from liberation. This is a view that Jainism shares with Sankhyā philosophy. In the Sankhyā, the life-monads (there called *purusās*) are strictly distinguished from lifeless matter (there called *prākriti*), and the goal of mans' spiritual effort is conceived of as the realization of the separation of the two. This radical dualism of the early Jaina and Sankhyā views is in striking contrast to the well-known "non-dualism" of classic Brāhmanism. As developed in the Upanishads and *Bhagavad-Gītā* and supremely stated in the Vedānta, 'all things, in all their aspects, are but reflexes of that one eternal self—Ātman Brahmā—which is in essence beyond all definition, name and form (Zimmer, 1975).

An opposing doctrine is that of Maskarin Gosala, who was a contemporary of Mahāvīra. He professed the doctrine of *a-jīva*, the prefix 'a' signifying "as long as". According to him, "as long as the life monad" (*a-jīva*) has not completed the normal course of its evolution (running through a fixed number of eighty four thousand births) there can be no realization. The natural biological advance cannot be hurried by means of virtue and asceticism or delayed because of vice, as the process takes place in its own good time. The destiny of man is framed by a rigid law that of the evolution of the life-monad. No divine grace or human zeal can interrupt or interfere with this unalterable principle of bondage, evolution, and release. When the time at last arrives and eighty four thousand existences have been attained, release simply happens, just as everything else has happened—by itself. In response to this determinism of Gosala's principle tenet which allowed no place for voluntary human effort, Buddha is quoted as having declared this imposing antagonists teaching to be the worst of all the contemporary erroneous doctrines. For the *a-jīvika* doctrine, that no amount of moral or ascetic exertion would shorten the series of rebirths offered no hope for a speedy release from the fields of ignorance, through saintly exercises (Zimmer, 1975).

Jainism

Gosala's doctrine does not dismiss mans' moral conduct as insignificant. For every living being, through its characteristic pattern of reactions to the environment, betrays its entire multi-biographical history, together with all that it has yet to learn. Its acts are not the cause of the influx of fresh *karmic* matter, as in the Jaina view. It only reveals its position or classification in the general hierarchy, showing how deeply entangled or close to release, it happens to be. Our words and deeds announce to ourselves just what milestone we have come to. Pious acts, then, are not the causes, but the effects; they do not bring, but they foretell release. Jainism, like Buddhism, disagrees with Gosala's fatalistic interpretation of the graduated roles of the play, asserting that each human individual is free to make his own escape (Zimmer, 1975).

Instead of Gosala's mechanistic biological order, Jainism asserts the power and value of the morale of the individual. The force of thoughts, words, and deeds, which if virtuous, stainless, and unselfish, lead the life-monad to enlightenment. However, if bad, egocentric and unconsidered fling it back into the darker, more primitive conditions, dooming it to an existence in the animal kingdom, or to live among the tortured inmates of the hells (Zimmer, 1975).

Can man's actions truly be unselfish, without egoism? The yearning for freedom is as much an act for the 'self' as we know it. Jainism, Hinduism, and Buddhism, offer very arduous and largely unattainable means of release. Contrarily, Gosala's doctrine holds up the hope of an inevitable rise in the status of the soul, and ultimate release. This is irrespective of the acts of commissions or omissions. This perception may give man the ability to accept himself and his life for what it is, rather than condemn him for attracting bad *karman* matter. It presents us with a view to accept human nature as is. As is stated in the *Quran*, "man is made from the goodliest of fabric to the vilest of vile". Every individual may ultimately be destined to achieve freedom or *moksha*.

This perception may not urge man to develop ethical

and moralistic behavior; for that matter neither has the morals or threat of a hell or rebirth of a belief system. Ethics and morals are relative to the society and situation in which an individual lives. These are largely a product of an individual's life experiences, and what he makes of them. Doctrines advocating human endeavor to attain moksha, over thousands of years, have not succeeded in eradicating behavior that invites 'bad' *karman* matter. We still see the same spectrum of behavior now—from the vilest of vile to the goodliest of good—as had been observed then. As this is the spectrum of human nature, growing out of its interaction with the environment.

While Vedic speculations are concerned with transcendental being, Jainism deals with being, as given in common experience, i.e. 'man as man'. Like Hinduism, it considers the present state of man as the state of bondage that is due to his own *karma* (although the meaning of *karma* in the two are different). In its description of man as man, Jainism recognizes and accepts his emotionality. However, the emotions are considered the cause of attracting karmic matter, and hence viewed negativistically. The ideal being an emotionless state. This goes against the principles of the inherent nature of the species. It recognizes the frustration-conflict-emotion cycle, and offers means to cope with it. This coping is based on the structure of its basic philosophy and ultimate goal of life, that of attaining moksha. The means it prescribes are extreme asceticism. Although social bonds and responsibilities are stressed, Jaina philosophy is primarily individualistic, as the onus of attracting good *karman* matter rests entirely on the individual. In the process, it denies the role of social interaction as causative in the emotionality of an individual. Ideally, the onus of responding affectively to a situation should depend on the individual, the reality of the matter points towards interactionism.

Thus, there is a dichotomy in the demands of an interdependent social culture, and an independent religiophilosophical thought. For the ultimate aim is the region of supreme isolation (*kaivalya*), and to become the isolated one (*kevalin*).

In its recognition of nature, why does it choose to discount the instinctual needs of man that are essential not only for his survival, but for the survival of his species? Right conduct is conduct based on detachment. However, the Jaina too recognizes the difficulty of maintaining the vows of *ahimsā*, *satya*, and *brāhmacharya*, and offers concessions to these. He is permitted *ahimsā* in the course of his duty, if it is so required; permitted a white lie, if the truth were to hurt another; permitted indulgence in sensuality if the need arises. This, in fact, is normal behavior irrespective of the moral or ethical code that an individual follows.

The most important doctrine of the Jainas is *ahimsā*. As all matter is considered '*jīva*' or a life-monad, no *himsā* (violence) should befall it. The Jaina monks avoid as far as possible the squeezing or touching of the elements. For example, he cannot cease breathing, but to avoid giving possible harm he should wear a veil before his mouth, thus softening the impact of the air against the inside of the mouth. Only in the cessation of life, can the soul desist from any harm. Paradoxically, it prescribes violence to the self. Firstly, by its extreme measures, and through the principle of *santhara* or *sallekhana*. As Parihar (2001) reports, this centuries old practice continues to thrive among the Jaina community. It is the termination of living by fasting 'when all purposes of life have been served or the body becomes unable to serve any purpose'. It is not to be adopted in the hope of acquiring either fame, a position in society or to get rid of physical pains. Preventing *santhara* invites social ostracism. While people deify *santhara*, there is a debate on. Aside from the aged choosing this route, instances of young persons opting for it are also reported.

Is this socially sanctioned suicide? Many feel that *santhara*, like *sati*, are not really a voluntary act because the person is only acting in accordance with social and religious conditioning. In contemporary times, as in the past, interpersonal and intrapersonal problems have existed. Are we addressing the individual self at two levels here? Through this practice, the social self is venerated. The private self, in the throes of angst, finding its release in a philosophy that permits self-annihilation. As we have, and will consistently see in all philosophies, the private self is a persona non-grata, the social self is the prime focus at a mortal level, the ultimate being the abstract 'pristine pure state'.

The Jaina recognizes the difference between emotions and instincts. Like Jung, it also holds the view that the will to live, sex instinct and the will to power are the primal urges of human nature. Along with these instincts, in accordance to its karmic theory, the instincts of hunger and thirst, too are impediments towards the attainment of the final goal of life—that of eliminating all karmic matter from the soul. Thus, although the primary level of the organism, i.e. the biological self, the body according to our definition, is accepted, its relevance is discounted. Severe discipline and austerity measures are to be undertaken to eliminate instinctual needs.

Although Jainism aims towards this ideal, it recognizes that it is not a path approachable by all individuals. Therefore, it has a gradation in the level of human life. The socio-philosophical structure, the rites and rituals, are directed towards attaining this distant goal. While celibacy, as a prime means of abstaining from attachment and sensual pleasure was no doubt enjoined on the monks, according to the Jaina text *Vavahāra Bhāsya*, sexual indulgence was permissible to the monks in exceptional cases. A monk who found it impossible to control himself was allowed to have relations with a courtesan on payment of her prescribed fees, for relief. This sanction however was of the type that permitted a monk to eat forbidden food in distress, and was not to be used indiscriminately. There was also a belief that learned monks and Brāhmins were capable of producing geniuses in dull women. Intercourse with a strictly celibate monk was also considered a cure for sterility in women. The Jaina text *Acharanga* mentions, women of the household in which monks lived as guests often approached the holy men for cure of sterility or for obtaining illustrious sons (Pruthi & Sharma, 1995). The vow of chastity has an extremely vast effective range. The prescriptions cohering with it do not refer to normal sexuality only, but they frequently also indicate events of sexual pathology. Among the cases resulting from frustrating desires, we find the apparitions of godly persons of opposite sex to which either monks, or nuns surrender (Schubring, 1962).

Instead of finding our answer in the attainment of moksha, we need raise some questions here. Humankind is a social animal. Humankind does not survive in isolation. What prompted the philosophers to arrive at a principle of behavior that goes against the inherent nature of the species? The vow of celibacy if followed forcefully would have annihilated the species. Why then did this concept, of the original sin and celibacy arise in the mind of man? A desire to escape from the trials of life? A fear of existence, a fear of sexuality? Fear prompting a negativistic perception of woman, the sensual being, in touch with her physicality and emotionality, ironically, through the process of motherhood. Fear creating a misogynist perception of her as the conduit of sensuality. Is it a thought process emanating from a depressive state of mind? Troubled with the trials of life, the individual feeling the need to return to a state of infantile purity and bliss. A period of life without thought and feeling—as recalled by the adult mind. A state when the mind was a 'tabula rasa' or the 'empty cabinet' described by Locke.

Are these philosophies a response to the existential angst of an individual? Life in infancy, as far as the adult mind can reconstruct a memory of, was bliss. As an exercise of thought, the individual, then extending himself into a fantasy of infinite regression, reaching the point of 'pure bliss'. From this fantastical state, he retraces his steps to the real world. Finding the cause of his existence in the 'original sin'. Are these philosophies then, starting from a troubled mind, seeking escape from life? In the process negating the female in her totality. At the individual level, finding a way out only through denial of his biological self, and finally through self-negation? These questions can be directed to all philosophical systems holding similar views.

These questions demand an answer. As Kakar (1996a) analyzes, this cultural psychology is the psychic representation in individuals of their community's history and social institutions. "The cultural injunctions perhaps do not affect the act of coitus or regulate its transports. What they can do, though, is to increase the conflicts around sexuality, sour it for many, and generally contribute towards its impoverishment. This can effectively block many men and most women from a deep full experience of sexual love and the mutual cherishing of bodies, the only containers we have for our souls. Cultural injunctions become significant for the family since a fundamental aspect of the relationship between the parents involves the meaning of each child in terms of the parents' conscious and unconscious fantasy around the act that produced the conception" (p. 22) Ironically, despite such attitudes, we have one of the highest population growth rates in the world. Reality doused by colors of ideals, finding its existence in the nature of the species. Is ours then, a deluded reality?

So much power is assigned to women due to her feminine nature, that men have to be extremely wary of her. Can we infer in this recognition, the completeness of women—in touch with her instincts, emotions, and self? The fear of these compelling society to develop aggressive and passive, physical, social and psychological means of power to curb her personhood. Ironically, the man is also living within the bounds of this gender fear. As this state of affairs has existed since eons, the fear has been converted to power, her strengths perceived as weaknesses. Gender relations progressing on erroneous cultural perceptions, which are accepted as truth. The implications of this are seen in gender stereotypes that individuals endeavor to live by.

Aside from giving concessions to the needs of the body, there is a dualism in the Jaina perception of instinctual needs, which represent the biological self. Ironically, although *ahimsā* is the principle doctrine, *himsā* is permissible on the self. In a philosophy that recognizes the worth of each *jīva* or life-monad, is not curbing the needs of the biological self at a physiological level and the private self at a psychological level, *himsā* against the self? At a social level, the caste system too perpetuates *himsā* on the social self. In addition, social customs discriminating against women, all belie the practice of *ahimsā*.

The individual is thus in a vicious circle of being born with karmic matter, in a body that needs fulfillment; following cultural norms that inflict psychological pain on others, attracting more *karman* matter. The force of *himsā*, at a psychological level, makes him respond emotionally, thereby attracting more *karman* matter. For the ordinary man, with ordinary strength of will, there is no way out.

For the Jainas, negation of the self is the only route to moksha. In accordance with the role self-castigation plays in the system, even the biography of *Mahāvīra* scarcely speaks of intellectual struggles and exertions but all the more of the enormous physical efforts directed to suppressing human nature, and, in the end, yielding both omniscience and omnivision as a reward for them. Ultimately the physical side comes to the front completely. Godhood instead of personhood is the goal of Jainism.

NOTE

1. As in Hinduism, it provides a good analysis of the reasons for the emergence of the emotions at a psychological level. Frustration of needs is recognised, thereby accepting the needs that human beings are governed by. Their observations are not restricted only to instinctual needs, but psychological needs as well. What we can convincingly state is the commonality of these affective states, irrespective of the cultural background. Can we thus infer that these are common through the species? In cross-cultural analysis the difference, when it appears,

can be attributed to language factors, situations that bring about the said emotions, the social permissibility, and acceptability of such emotions. Thus we can conclude that emotions are common through the species, it is the socialisation that gives it the individual culture specific colours. The cultural philosophies need to be scrutinised, not for the theoretical viewpoints that they present, but rather, the observations of human nature that they present – either explicitly or implicitly through the rules of behaviour that they lay down for society. A consistent observation is the fear of human sexuality. It was there, it will always be there, as on it depends the survival of the species. The question to be raised is why the fear, and why the abhorrence for so natural and basic an instinct? Neither has the notion of sin associated with it, or the multitude of misconceptions associated with it, curbed the instinct from a moralistic perspective.

5

Zoroastrianism

About the beginning of the second millennium B.C., according to archaeological record, the so-called Aryans or Indo-Iranian people appeared on the north-eastern frontier of Mesopotamia. Some four centuries later, the rulers of the Mitannia in Asia Minor are found to have Aryan names, while about the same time it would seem that another branch of the Aryan race was making its way into north-western India and overthrowing the high civilization of the Indus valley area. Between these two lines of Aryan movement, laid the lofty plateau of what was to be known as Iran. When Aryan people first settled in this territory is not known, but the available evidence points to their establishment there before the year 1000 B.C. (Brandon, 1962).

Long before Zarathustra gave to his people's faith a definitive form, a dualistic conception of reality characterized the Iranian interpretation of life. There seems to be sufficient evidence endorsing the view that from a very early period there was a disposition in Iran to deify the dual manifestation of power in the universe in such a way that its good and evil aspects were regarded as intimately related in even balance. This was inspired by the recurrent spectacle in the natural world of the struggle between the life giving rain, and the deadly powers of drought, that were a recurrent condition in the region (Brandon, 1962).

The Proto-Indo Iranians included the worship and propitiation of a whole number of gods and goddesses. The Indo-Iranian pantheon included a number of nature divinities deemed to be sometimes good and on other occasions wicked. The Proto-Indo-Iranians worshipped instinctively and often, through fear, and hence excessive sacrifices and offerings were made to the different divinities to appease them. The Proto-Indo-Iranians were nomadic pastoralists, following a patrilineal system within their society, and had no fixed house of worship. Many of their gods were abstract personifications of the elements. Every force of natural element whose manifestation they could see or experience was deified. An unmitigated polytheism was prevalent everywhere (Mistree, 1998).

Disorder, strife, bloodshed etc., was the prevailing conditions in the country. The greater majority lacked noble-mindedness (*ārmaiti*). They consequently had no good form of society (*khshathra*) amongst them. It was a reign not of righteousness (*asha*) but of the evil principle, *druj*. In the opening verses of the *Gāthā* of the *Avesta*, it is stated that confused and distracted humanity approaches God, the supreme creator, with the complaint that evil had encumbered the entire earth and therefore he should send a savior on it. The supreme Lord thereupon names Zarathustra as the savior of humanity and sends him on earth. However mythical this story may seem, it nevertheless shows the perilous state of affairs in ancient Persia in which Prophet Zarathustra first began to live like an ordinary householder with his three wives and children (Navroji, 1928; Tiwari, 1983).

What is Zoroastrianism?

Zoroastrianism is one of the oldest religions of the world, perhaps 2500 to 3000 years old. It is the religion of ancient Persia, and Parsees all over the world even now observe this religion. Prophet Zarathustra, also known as Zoroaster, is regarded as the founder of this religion, and the *Zend-Avesta*, or simply *Avesta*, as its basic sacred text. Reputed scholars today place his birth between 1800 and 1500 B.C. Some scholars postulate that the *Gāthās* (which form a part of the *Avesta*) and the *Rig Veda* are the contemporary works of two groups of people who once shared a common source (Tiwari, 1983; Mistree, 1998).

To the ancient world, Zarathustra's lore was best known by the name of the doctrine of the *Magi*. The Zoroastrian religion exhibits a very close affinity to, or rather identity with, several important doctrines of the mosaic religion and Christianity. The personality and attributes of the devil, and the resurrection of the dead, are both ascribed to the religion of the *Magi*. These are found in the present scriptures of the Parsees. It is not ascertained whether these doctrines were borrowed by the Parsees from the Jews, or by the Jews from the Parsees; very likely neither is the case, and in both these religions they seem to have sprung up independently (Haug, 1878).

Zoroastrianism is predominantly an ethical religion. Its theological premises are based on an essentially moralistic view of life. Zoroastrian morality is expressed in three words, *humat, hūkht,* and *hūvarsht,*—good thoughts, good words, and good deeds, and the greatest of these is good deeds (Zaehner, 1956).

Zarathustra was trained as a priest in an older unknown religion. He refers to himself in his own hymns, the *Gāthās*, as a priest. He also refers to himself as an initiate –'one who knows'. In the later documents of the *Avesta* and in the subsequent Pahlavi literature there is abundant evidence of the existence of established religious beliefs and practices different from those sanctioned or inculcated by Zarathustra and which must consequently represent survivals from an earlier era. Thus, Zarathustra did not create his doctrine ex nihilo, but rather was the reformer of his people's existing faith, expurgating and refashioning the traditional material (Brandon, 1962, Mistree, 1998).

According to tradition, it was at the age of thirty that Zarathustra received a revelatory message from God. By the bank of a river, he had a vision of the angel *Vohu Manah* who appeared nine times the size of a man. He was believed to have held conversations with God himself, questioning the supreme Being about all matters of importance, and receiving always the right answers to his questions. Accordingly, after having been instructed, Zarathustra communicated these accounts of his conversations with God to his disciples and the public at large. The scanty texts which can be traced to the founder himself was very likely not written down by him, but, as was the case with the numerous Vedic hymns, were for centuries handed down orally (Haug, 1878, Tiwari, 1983).

'The angel told Zarathustra that there was only one God, *Ahura Mazdā a*nd that he (Zoroaster) was to serve as his prophet. During the next ten years *Zarathustra* had other visions too, in which each of the angels of *Ahura Mazdā* appeared and revealed further truths to him. *Zarathustra* began to preach religious truths in accordance with his revelations at once, but at first with no success. He was rather condemned by people as spreader of evil spirits. However, ultimately he succeeded in converting at least his own cousin Maidyōimangha. Then he and his cousin traveled to the court of a monarch in Bactria named Bishtaspa. The two cousins tried to convert the monarch, but they could not succeed until Zarathustra healed a favorite ailing horse of the monarch. The monarch and his entire court and Kingdom became the followers of Zarathustra. From here, a turning point comes in the history of the spread of Zoroastrianism. In the years following, Zoroastrianism spread very rapidly by the help of the king, sometimes also through holy wars. Zarathustra was murdered at the age of seventy-seven at the hands of an enemy soldier (Tiwari, 1983).

By nature and vocation, Zarathustra was a prophet, not a philosopher. Like the prophets of Israel, he was not concerned to explain, but to proclaim the new universal truth of which he believed himself to be possessed. According to Brandon (1962), upon a more pragmatic estimate it would seem that Zarathustra's universalism was indeed apparent only and that his world was but the small province in which he lived, mankind, for him being constituted by his neighbours, who seem to have been men of his own race. The racial origin of his nomadic enemies is uncertain; his attitude towards them was one of bitter hostility. Confronted with the spectacle of sin and suffering, the Iranian Prophet was not moved by compassion for the blindness of men; instead his reaction was one of hot indignation and he was eager to strike hard and without pity against the wrong-doer.

In Haug's (1878) analysis, the leading ideology of Zarathustra's theology was monotheism; and the principle of his speculative philosophy was dualism, i.e. the supposition of two primeval causes of the real world and of the intellectual; while his moral philosophy was moving in the triad of thought, word, and deed. The few philosophical ideas, which are discovered in his sayings, show that he was a great and deep thinker, who stood far above his contemporaries, and even above the most enlightened men of many subsequent centuries. His predecessors, the Saoshyant, seem to have worshipped a plurality of good spirits, whom they called *Ahuras*, "the living ones", who were opposed to the *dēvas*. Zarathustra, not satisfied with this indistinct expression of the Divine Being, reduced this plurality to unity. The new name, by which he called the supreme Being, was *Ahura Mazdā*, which means "the *Ahura* who is called *Mazdā*". In translating, the *Ahura* may best be rendered by "living" or "lord", and *Mazdā* by "wise" or "creator of the universe".

Against various deities that people worshipped, Zarathustra taught that *Ahura Mazdā* was the only one God to be worshiped. Zarathustra may have been cognizant of the Aryan tradition, which saw only one reality behind all the various deities that people worshipped in the Vedic age. However, Zarathustra characterized *Ahura Mazdā* in essentially ethical terms. He called him the Lord of supreme good and taught people a life of righteousness and good whereby they could strengthen God's power of goodness (Tiwari, 1983).

The Parsees in India are ethnically of Iranian origin with an ancestry that can be traced back to the province of Khorasan known in ancient times as Parthia. Due to religious persecution a group of Parsees set sail and arrived on mainland India in about 936 A.D. They sought refuge from the Hindu King of Gujarat Jadav Rana, and settled in the land given them, naming it Sanjan, in memory of the place they originally came from in Northwest Khorasan. 'The people of Gujarat addressed the new arrivals as *'Parsees"* from the Persian word *Parsi* a term used in those days by the Gujaratis for any person who came from Iran. The term Parsi denotes race and is applicable today to a group of people who profess and follow the Zoroastrian religion and whose ancestors chose to settle in India. Today, there are only 1,40,000 Zoroastrians in the world (Mistree, 1998).

Basic Principles of Zoroastrian Philosophy

From ancient classical writers, as well as from the tradition of the Parsees, we learn that the religious literature of the ancient Persians was of considerable extent, though the *Zend-Avesta*, in its present state, is a comparatively small book. The Parsees ascribe the loss of most of these writings, known to the ancient Greeks, mainly to the ravage attendant upon the conquest of the Persian empire by Alexander the Great (Haug, 1878, Zaehner, 1956).

According to Zaehner (1956), the surviving *Avesta*, which is indispensable for the performance of the liturgy, is only a fragment of the whole. It falls into three distinct parts. The disparity of these parts enables us to form some idea of the vicissitudes through which Zoroastrianism went, before it became crystallized into a dogmatic religion.

Considering the wide range of subjects embraced by these texts, it would be rash for the reader to assume that they afford him sufficient information for forming a decided opinion as to the character of the Parsi religion. The translated texts contain barely one-eleventh part of the religious literature extant in the Pahlavi versions of existing *Avesta* texts. The latter are even more important than the former, from a religious point of view, as the Parsees themselves consider them authoritative. However, no translator with long experience of the maddening ambiguity of the Pahlavi script would claim finality for his translation. No amount of careful reading can make him certain that he does not misunderstand some essential part of it (Zaehner, 1956; West & Muller, 1995a).

The fountainhead of Zarathustra's religion lies in the hymns—the *Gāthās*, which are reputed to be his own utterances. Divinely inspired and revealed, the *Gāthās* are in the form of exalted poetry, within which lies a myriad of esoteric truths. His passionate utterances seem to have formed the basis of a religious experience leading into a dialogue between himself and his Creator—*Ahura Mazdā*, the Lord of Wisdom. Zarathustra thus, was the recipient of a revelation which when accepted by the ancient Iranians, became a religion, making him the first prophet-priest of the oldest revealed religion (Mistree, 1998).

Zarathustra did not see his God as an omnipotent Being, for he declared in his hymns that God must grow, through the cumulative power of mans' good thoughts, words, and deeds. This in turn he promised would strengthen the power of God who at the end of time, he proclaimed, would become truly omnipotent when evil would be utterly vanquished by the possessors of the truth, the *ashavan* (Mistree, 1998).

Having arrived at the grand idea of the unity and indivisibility of the supreme Being, he undertook to solve the great problem, of the existence of evil and good, and justice of God. Zarathustra solved this difficult question by the supposition of two primeval causes, which, though different, were united, and produced the world of material things, as well as that of the spirit. The one who produced the "reality" (*gaya*) is called "*vohu manah*", the "good mind", the other, through whom the "non-reality" (*ajyaiti*) originated, bears the name "*akem manah*", the "evil mind"; while all that is bad and delusive belongs to the sphere of "non-reality", and is traced to the "evil mind". They are the two moving causes in the universe, united from the beginning, and therefore, called twins. They are present everywhere—in *Ahura Mazdā*, as well as in men. These two primal principles if supposed to be united in *Ahura Mazdā* himself, are not called *vohu-Manah* and *akem manah*, but *Spenta-Mainyu*, "the beneficent spirit", and *Angra Mainyu* or *Ahriman*, "the hurtful spirit". The evil against which *Ahura Mazdā* and all good men are fighting is called *druj*, "destruction or lie", which is nothing but a personification of the *dēvas*. God, *Ahura Mazdā*, is only one, having no adversary whatsoever. *Spenta-Mainyu* was regarded as the author of all that is bright and shining, of all that is good and useful in nature; while *Angro-Mainyu* called into existence all that is dark and apparently noxious. Both are inseparable as day and night, and though opposed to each other, are indispensable for the preservation of creation (Haug, 1878).

Ahura Mazdā presided over a council of seven councilors, who are called "the seven *Amesha Spentas*", i.e., 'immortal benefactors'. They are *Vohu-Manah*, who is regarded as the vital faculty in all living beings of the good creation. *Asha Vahishta*, who represents the blazing flame of fire, the light in luminaries, and brightness and splendor of any kind whatever, wherever it may exist. Light being of the nature of *Ahura Mazdā*, and being believed to pervade the whole good creation, it represents the omnipresence of the Divine Being. *Kshathra-Vairya* (*Shasrivar*) presides over metals and is the giver of wealth. His name means simply "possession, wealth". *Spenta-Ārmaiti*, 'the bountiful *ārmaiti*' representing the earth. She represents the pious and obedient heart of the true worshipper of *Ahura Mazdā*, who serves God alone with body and soul. *Haurvatāt* and *Ameretāt* (*Khordād* and *Amurdād*) preside over vegetation, and produce all kinds of fruits. As the names indicate, they represent the preservation of the original uncorrupted state of the good creation, and its' remaining in the same condition as that in which God created it. They express a single compound idea (Haug, 1878).

Quite separate from the celestial council stands *Sraosha* (*Srōsh*), who is regarded as an archangel vested with very high powers. *Sraosha* seems to have been considered by Zarathustra as a personality. He is the angel who stands between God and man, the great teacher of the good religion who instructed the prophet in it. He shows the way to heaven and pronounces judgment on human actions after death. He is the personification of the whole divine service, including the prayers as well as the sacrificial rites. As he is said to be the guardian of the whole creation, without his protection the world would fall prey to demons. Thus, it is meant that, men must offer up prayers to God and worship him. Should they fail to do so, the good mind (*Vohu Manah*) within them becomes powerless, and the bad mind (*Akem Manah*) takes entire possession of them, instigating them to commit sins and crimes, in consequence of which they will become utterly cast away, both in this life and in that to come (Haug, 1878).

Like *Ahura Mazdā*, his adversary *Ahriman* or *Angra mainyu* or 'arch demon', was, in later times, supposed to be also surrounded by a council. This idea is foreign to the older texts. As head of the infernal kingdom, he represented the "evil mind". This was Zarathustra's philosophical term of the second principle, the 'non-reality'. He produces all bad thoughts in men, and makes them utter bad words and commit sins. His influence is checked by *Vohu-Manah*, the good mind.

Such was the original notion of the two creative spirits, who form only two parts of the Divine Being. However, in the course of time, this doctrine was changed and corrupted, in consequence of misunderstandings and false interpretations. *Spenta Mainyu* was taken as a name of *Ahura Mazdā* himself, and, *Angra Mainyu*, as *Ahriman*, was regarded as the constant adversary of *Ahura Mazdā*. Thus, the dualism of God and the Devil arose. Each of the two spirits were considered as independent rulers endeavoring to destroy the creation of the other, and thus both waged constant war (Haug, 1878).

According to the Zoroastrian viewpoint, the inequalities within our world are not regarded as God ordained, but are held to be the direct result of the constant open conflict between the forces of good and evil. It is the innate nature of evil to be corrupt and destructive, thereby causing continuous affliction upon the whole of creation in the relative world (Mistree, 1998).

Closely connected with this idea is the belief in heaven and hell, which Zarathustra himself clearly pronounced in the *Gāthās*. The name for heaven is *Garodemana*, 'house of hymns'. It is the residence of *Ahura Mazdā* and the most blessed of men. Another general name for heaven is *ahu vahishta*, 'the best life'. hell is called *Drujo demana*, 'house of destruction', in the *Gāthās*. Between heaven and hell is *Chinvat Pěrětu*, 'the bridge of the gatherer', or 'the bridge of the judge', which the soul of the pious alone can pass, while the wicked fall from it down into hell. The belief in the resurrection of the body at the time of the last judgment also forms one of the Zoroastrian dogmas (Haug, 1878).

'The Doctrine of *Chinvat Pěrětu* (The Bridge or Path of Longing) can be said to be one of the most ancient doctrines of the Iranian religion. Here we find Zarathustra giving a promise to those persons who will assist him in obtaining a perfect religio-political authority over the people. This promise is to the effect that he would lead all of them to that ideal existence, which is longed for by them, by imparting to them his beneficial teaching. The bridge of longed-for reward can be attained to only by those men who practice the good doctrines of life and guided by *Ahura Mazdā*. Those who are the enemies of such doctrines shall forever remain "in the house of Lie" instead of realizing "the path of Longing" (Navroji, 1928).

The *Gāthās* speak of 'two intellects' (*khratu*) and 'two lives' (*ahu*). In *Avesta* writings the intellects are called *āsna khratu*, 'the original intellect or wisdom' or 'spiritual or heavenly wisdom', the other is styled *gaoshō srūta khratu*, 'the wisdom heard by the ear. The wisdom gained in this way is, of course, inferior to the heavenly wisdom. Only the latter can instruct man in the higher matters of life (Haug, 1878).

The Self in Zoroastrian Thought

According to Zarathustra, man is by origin, a spiritual being, and his soul, in the shape of what the Zoroastrians call his *fravashi* or *fravahr,* pre-exists his body. Both body and soul, however, are creatures of *Ahura Mazdā*, and the soul is not eternally pre-existent as in many eastern religions. Man, then, belongs to God and to God is his return. Over against God stands the Devil *Ahriman*. He, like God is a pure spirit. They are eternal antagonists and eventually a struggle between them become inevitable. God is all goodness and light, *Ahriman*, is all wickedness and death, darkness and deceit. Creation for God is a necessity in his fight with the devil, and man is in the forefront of the fray. On earth, each is free to choose good or evil. Thus, for Zoroastrians neither evil nor creation is a mystery. There is no problem of evil because it is a separate principle and substance standing over against the good God and threatening to destroy Him. There is, then, nothing mysterious about creation, for God needs mans' help in this battle with the 'Lie' as the principle of evil is frequently called. Being God's creation man belongs to him, but God none-the-less depends on mans' help in order to defeat his eternal adversary (Zaehner, 1956).

The Five Constituents of Man : According to the Greater Bundahishn, man was fashioned in five parts by *Ahura Mazdā*: Body (Av. *tanū*), Breath of Life (Av. *ushtana*), soul (Av. *urvan*), Prototype Image (Av. *kehrpa*), and Guardian spirit (Av. *fravashi*). The *Avestan* writings indicate five powers associated with a mans' self. These are termed *fravashi, daēnā, urvan, baodhangh,* and *ahu.* The significance of these terms, especially of *fravashi* and *daēnā*, are sufficiently important to require a detailed exposition.

The Body: *Ahu* means the life of a human being in which is implied the idea of the earthly existence of man. It is said in the Greater Bundahishn (14.9), that the soul was created first and then the body, for the soul directs the functions within the body. The body of man is likened to the creation of the material world. Clearly then, it is the duty of man to nurture and nourish the physical body in order that the "abode of the soul" may be in harmony with the other physical creations of *Ahura Mazda* (Mistree, 1998; Navroji, 1928).

The Breath of Life : The Guardian Spirit—the *fravashi*, gives the breath of life to man. Its' meaning would be that something, which is associated with a man's self, which, by the high destiny associated with its activity, produces advancement in the condition of good fortune for the world at large. It is the *fravashis*, or, the grand spiritual destinies that first set the entire inanimate nature into activity. The actions in the course of nature are of course the unconscious activity of nature, as different from the free-willed actions of human beings. With every one virtuous action, the spiritual force of beneficent progress gathers strength. The *fravashi* does not interfere with the decision-making process of man and hence unlike the soul, the *fravashi* is not judged at the Bridge of the Separator. The *fravashis* are seen to represent the God-essence within man. They are also believed to be the spiritual protectors of man, who, when in difficulty, can invoke them. The *fravashis* are also said to maintain the natural functions of the body, which upon death cease to exist and hence it is said that the *fravashis* become weakened. Clearly then, **man in the physical world is stronger and more complete than his counterpart in the spiritual world** and it would appear thus, that it is for this reason that the *fravashis* of the dead need sustained prayers and ritual offerings from the living. Upon death, which is deemed a temporary affliction of evil, the *fravashis* once again return to their earlier spiritual abode to wait for the final resurrection of the body, when it is believed that the body will be reunited with its counterparts, the spirit and the soul. Because of this firm doctrinal belief, it is untenable to accept the Hindu or Buddhist concept of reincarnation (Mistree, 1998; Navroji, 1928).

The Soul : The second thing that forms one of the five parts of a man's self is what is called *urvan*. *Urvan* is that which consists of his wishes. These wishes may be either good or bad according to the goodness or badness of the objects wished for. Hence, the *urvan* of a person can be evil as well as good. Hence, when *urvan* and *daēnā* are mentioned together as a good or bad reward the idea is that of the good or bad consequences befalling a person according to his inner desires and outwardly expressed speech and activity. It is essential therefore, that the soul should be in perfect harmony and control over the body in order that it may direct man towards making the right choice. The soul is the instrument that directs the body, the breath of life, the prototype image, and the guardian spirit (Mistree, 1998; Navroji, 1928).

The term *daēnā* figures prominently in the *Gāthās*. The distinction between *daēnā* and *urvan*, lie in the fact that while *urvan* is the willing self of the person, *daēnā* is that part of a man's self, which is made up of his speeches and actions. The *daēnā* of a person is good or bad like his *urvan*. The *urvan*, the willing self, bears the responsibility of good or bad actions while *daēnā*, the character, is only a means by which the consequences befall the *urvan*, the willing-self of that person, since *daēnā* itself is a production of *urvan*. *Baodha* means consciousness, sometimes the understanding power (Mistree, 1998; Navroji, 1928).

The soul fulfils its role through the agency of a number of discernible qualities that an individual is latently deemed to possess. The soul receives its inputs primarily from wisdom, innate reason, and intellect that stimulate the faculty of knowing and the will to act in the soul.

The enemies of the soul are the creatures of the Lie—heresy, anger, vengefulness, excessive desire, disrepute, envy, and any attribute, which is in excess or deficient in man. The Lie, when it attacks man, pollutes his essence and defiles his body by attempting to annihilate the soul; it is likened to "driving a wedge" between them in order that their union may be destroyed. Evil tries to tempt the soul into generating wicked thoughts, uttering wicked words and performing wicked deeds. The greatest triumph of evil is when man succumbs and makes the wrong choice. If the soul is vanquished, it will find itself in hell upon death where it will remain until the end of time (Mistree, 1998; Navroji, 1928).

The soul of man can never be destroyed or eternally damned. The reward or retribution is meted out to the soul at the Bridge of the Separator. The soul, which is judged righteous, returns to its Creator in heaven; while a soul deemed to be wicked is cast down into the abyss of darkness, hell. Thus, man must learn to recognize the nature of wisdom from which arise innate reason, intellect, will and consciousness—qualities that, are discerned by the soul and reflected through mans' conscience (Mistree, 1998; Navroji, 1928).

The Prototype Image: The constituent of man, known as the image or form (Av. *kehrpa*), is believed to be the link that man has to his original abode, which is in Endless Light. Therefore, the *kehrpa* within man keeps watch over, wisdom, intellect, reason, understanding, and memory, so that every person may engage himself in his work (Mistree, 1998; Navroji, 1928).

In keeping with its larger ethical philosophy, Zoroastrianism presents the concept of *khwarr*. Although the soul is the motivating force and the prime mover within man, the *khwarr*, which is the God-given talent within man, must be cultivated to its full capacity because growth, fulfillment, and prosperity are integral parts of Zoroastrianism. The *khwarr* is said to have pre-existed mans' physical birth and Zoroastrianism stresses that man must endeavor to nurture and cultivate his potential talents (Mistree, 1998).

Alongside innate talent, Zoroastrianism emphasizes innate reason in man. Zoroastrian spirituality is not gained through blind faith and belief, but by using the mind, allows man to reason and thereby understand the purpose of life. Innate reason gives man the power to think, infer, and comprehend in an orderly or rational way. It is the faculty of clear vision through which man gains insight into the workings and nature of the physical, psychological, and spiritual worlds. Reason, on a spiritual level, may be recognized as the supra rational which is often allied to the intellectual intuition, a domain in which man begins to understand the eternal and immutable principles of life. Innate reason is one of the components of the mind that has to be trained in order that man may generate fewer wrong thoughts, words, and deeds. Reason on a psychological level, is the power to arrive at the right decision and conclusion, whilst the source of orderly conduct is the manifestation of reason in the physical world. Reason is said to sustain Will and impel it to perform certain actions. Thus, in Zoroastrianism man is encouraged to develop the faculty of reason in order that through controlled will, an individual may choose to generate the right thought, word, and deed (Mistree, 1998).

The lower self in the *Gāthā* is figuratively called the beastly self, and conquest over it is called 'dominion over the beasts'. A merely abstinent man can hardly eradicate the relish of sense-pleasure. It is only when he is engaged in a higher pursuit that the lower pleasures die out. The advice of the *Gāthā* therefore is to follow the inward call of the Higher self. That way we shall get perfection, which way the self inclines (Chatterjee, 1934).

The Emotions in Zoroastrian Thought

Zoroastrianism emphasized the experience of the joys and pleasures of life. In the *Dina-I Mainogi-I Khirad* (opinions of the spirit of wisdom) translated in the Pahlavi Texts (West & Muller, 1995b. Chp. XIX), the sage asked the spirit of wisdom thus: 'Is living in fear and falsehood worse than death?' The spirit of wisdom answered thus: "To live in fear and falsehood is worse than death. Because every ones' life is necessary for the enjoyment and pleasure of the worldly existence, and when the enjoyment and pleasure of the worldly existence are not his and fear and even falsehood are with him, it is called worse than death." In chapter XXX, the sage asked the spirit of wisdom thus: 'Which of any living existence is the worse? And in wisdom who is more unforeseeing?' The spirit of wisdom answered thus: 'a life of him is the worse, who lives in fear and falsehood. And, in wisdom he is the more unforeseeing, who does not provide for the spiritual existence and attends to the worldly one. (Chp. XXXIII) The spirit of wisdom said, the wife is the worse with whom it is not possible to live with pleasure. The child is the worse who does not bring renown. And that country is the worse in which it is not possible to live in happiness, fearlessness and permanence' (West & Muller, 1995a).

According to Brandon (1962), the Evil or the Lie, expressed in the term *'Druj'* connotes not only basic deceit, but also all that evil which must result when the true order of things, *Arta,* is damaged or overthrown. Zarathustra was not concerned primarily to set forth a new doctrine of God and his providence, but to make clear the involvement of man in the conflict between *arta* and *druj.* This had the consequence of forcing upon the individual the choice of identifying himself with one or other of the contending parties by virtue of the quality of his own conduct. Thus Zarathustra, in justification of this novel concept demanded that men should choose their part in this fateful struggle, declares that *Ahura Mazdā* had endowed them with the mental ability to apprehend the moral issue involved. Accordingly, it would seem, that Zarathustra repudiated the ancient tradition in Iranian religion, which held that Good and Evil were equal aspects of divine power. He rejected the moral indifference, which was the inevitable consequence of that view, propounding instead a doctrine of man, which represented him as a responsible moral being, who owed natural allegiance to *Ahura Mazdā* as his creator.

According to Mistree (1998), in Zoroastrian thought, the process of "creative evolution" is an on going one. It is within the cumulative power of man to rid the world of disorder, poverty, misery, or pain, suffering, and eventually death. Grief should be kept to a minimum, as tears for the dead are a hindrance to the progress and well being of the soul. The task of man, therefore, is to bring about the "making wonderful" when God will be made truly omnipotent'.

Through the Prism

The concept of duality in Zoroastrianism is not one based on mere physical power, nor one that alludes to the worship of two antagonistic spirits, but one that is founded upon the intrinsic contrasting natures of the two opposing forces in the relative world. Thus, the role of man in this cosmic struggle, is to assist God in bringing about the final annihilation of evil and the eventual triumph of the forces of good, through the ethical power of cumulative good thoughts, words, and deeds (Mistree, 1998).

Mans' role in this world is to co-operate with nature on the natural plane and to lead a virtuous life of 'good thoughts, good words, and good deeds' on the moral plane. Thus, no religion has been as strongly opposed to all forms of asceticism and monasticism, as Zoroastrianism. It is mans' duty to take to himself a wife and to rear up for himself sons and daughters for the very simple reason that human life on earth is a sheer necessity if *Ahriman*, the evil principle, is to be finally defeated. Similarly, no other religion makes a positive virtue of agriculture, making the earth fruitful, strong, and abundant in order to resist the onslaught of the enemy who is the author of disease and death. On the natural plane, then, virtue is synonymous with fruitfulness, vice with sterility: celibacy, therefore, is both unnatural and wicked. On the moral plane all the emphasis is on righteousness or truth, for evil is personified as the 'Lie', and on the doing of good works in which *Ahura Mazdā* himself 'has his dwelling', for deeds are the criterion by which alone a man can be judged (Zaehner, 1956).

In Zoroastrianism, man is the focal point through whom the theory and practice of the religion are tested and put into action. He is not just a puppet or a pawn in the unfolding of this cosmic drama, but is the most productive, purposeful creation of God. His task is to vanquish the Lie in order to bring about the creative evolution of this world. Unhampered by the shackles of predestination, the role of man is to become the master of his future as well as to mould the relationship that develops between himself and his Creator. It is the task of man to bring about the final renovation and healing of the world, a concept which in Zoroastrianism came to be known as the *Frasho kereti*, the "making wonderful" (Mistree, 1998).

In marked contrast to the positivistic nature of the philosophy, is the depiction of women in it. The Iranian society seems to have followed a patrilineal system. This seems to have influenced the projection of women in the world structure. As per the myth, *Ahrimans'* attack on the world has failed, and he has been thrown back into darkness, by the recitation of the sacred formula by the first man whom he dare not attack. There now follows a very strange episode, which begins the text of the fourth chapter of the *Bundahishn*. 'Nothing the demons say or do can revive their stricken captain until a character described as 'the Whore' makes her appearance on the scene and boasts that she will 'take away the dignity of the blessed man'. At this *Ahriman* instantly revives, and the attack on the material world begins. This is the last we hear of the 'demon Whore' whose attention seems to have been so very decisive. Another text tells us how she succeeded in corrupting the unfortunate *Gayōmart*, the Blessed man. The *Zādspram*, a major Pahlavi text, tell us this:— 'When *Ahriman* rushed into creation, he had the brood of the demon Whore of evil religion as his companion even as a man has a whore woman as his bedfellow; for verily the whore is a demon: and he appointed the demon Whore queen of her brood, that is the chief of all the whore demons, the most grievous adversary of the Blessed man. And the demon Whore of evil religion joined herself to the Blessed man; for the defilement of females she joined herself to him, that she may defile females; and the females, because they were defiled, might defile the males, and the males would turn aside from their proper work. All this seems very un-Zoroastrian, as the reproduction of the species is one of the first duties of man (Zaehner, 1956).

It is clear, however, from this and other passages that woman was held in slight esteem by the Zoroastrians, or at least by a sect of them, for there are passages which exalt the virtues of the housewife, and that the reproduction of males, not of females, was the essential element in the defeat of the Evil One. It would seem that the 'Whore' is the first woman just as *Gayōmart* is the first man. It seems that she was created by *Ahura Mazdā* and fled to *Ahriman* whose consort she then became. The Devil's kiss causes menstruation, a condition abhorred by the Zoroastrians as being in the highest possible degree impure. Thus, man is defiled by woman and ever will be so till the final resurrection when both sexes are called to share in the universal bliss. Through woman who, though created by *Ahura Mazdā*, chose to play the harlot with *Ahriman*, man and all his descendants are defiled. But *Ahrimans'* victory in this respect is only partial, for not only does the union of man and woman make the reproduction of the race of men possible, but woman remains forever subject to man. As always, the stratagems of *Ahriman* ultimately turn to his own undoing (Zaehner, 1956).

Thus, as in the other philosophies, the classical Freudian mother-whore dichotomy is evident here too. 'The female principle, then, appears both as the terrible 'Whore' who lets loose 'so much affliction on the blessed man and the toiling bull, that they will not be fit to live, and as the good mother, the gentle *Spandārmat* whose very name means 'bounteous harmony or devotion'. The Whore, then, is simply the terrible aspect of the female principle just as the Good Mother, *Spandārmat*, the earth, is its kindly and beneficent aspect. They are aspects of the same principle, the eternal female, just as *Ahura Mazdā* and *Ahriman* are the two aspects of the eternal male, eternally divided and in no ways to be reconciled (Zaehner, 1956).

Despite Zaehner's conciliatory interpretation of the 'female principle', a reading of the rules laid down for women present a picture, more in tune with the suppression of women, as an adversary of *Ahriman*. For example, in Chapter LIX of the *Sad Dar*, of the Pahlavi texts (West & Muller, 1995b), "The fifty-ninth subject is this, that in the good and pure religion of the *Mazdā* worshippers, they have not commanded the women to perform the *nyayises* (periodical salutations to the sun and the moon, fire and water). And their *nyayises* are these that three times every day, at dawn, mid-day prayer, and evening prayers, they stand back in the presence of their own husbands and fold their arms and speak thus: 'What speak it; and what is necessary for thee so that I may do it'. For any command, and whatever the husband orders, it is requisite to go about that day. And, certainly, without the leave of the husband she is to do no work, so that the Lord may be pleased with that wife. For the satisfaction of the sacred being is the reverence for the satisfaction of the husband; so that every time that they perform work by command of the husband they call them righteous in the religion. Regarding sin of adultery, chapter LXVII states, it is necessary for women to practice great abstinence from committing adultery—it is necessary to kill her sooner, for the child born of her becomes of another religion, sin increasing in connection with her soul. Despite their emphasis on the 'naturalness of being', menstrous women are viewed as unclean' (Chapter LXVIII, *Sad Dar,* West & Muller, 1995b).

Zoroastrianism also lays emphasis on the education of the child. Parents are directed to teach their children the principles of their religion. They must teach their children the principles concerning good works before they reach their fifteenth year. If they have taught them concerning good works, the parents may claim credit for any good deed the child does; but if the child has not been properly instructed, then the parents are responsible for any sin it may commit on attaining majority. Thus, the child too is inculcated into the practical wisdom of the faith.

Man, for the first time in history was introduced to the concepts of choice and free will based upon an objective and ethical structure. Zarathustra taught that man should exercise this right judiciously within an intellectual framework. Man is thus equipped to discern through volitional consciousness, between the forces of truth and falsehood. Thus, the right of education and knowledge is a cultural given for the Parsees.

In Sethna's (1984) analysis of the Parsi psyche, the average Parsi, belonging to a tiny minority, definitely has many factors in his personality, which arise from interactions with other bigger, religious groups. They have, since coming to India, forbidden any conversions to Zarathustra's religion probably for fear that, idol-worship would creep into a monotheistic creed. Regarding relationships with larger religious groups, Parsees have maintained an aloof stand and have been non-partisan. They have appeared to play it safe by dissociating themselves from inter-religious conflicts. To remain in safety obviously they could not afford to antagonize anybody. Their needs for safety stemmed from insecurity, which in turn stemmed from the fact that they were in a minority. This basic sense of insecurity as related to other large religious groups, led to many attitudes in the Parsees psyche. One was an attitude leading to a conscious feeling of superiority to the large masses of other Indians. This attitude of insecurity has also led to the Parsees always having tried to co-operate as much as possible with any ruling government. The behavior of the Parsees can also be explained due to a sense of panic at being swallowed up by the general Indian culture. The peculiarity of the Parsis' when compared to other Indian minorities is that the Parsis' are an ethnic religious minority, whereas others are only religious minorities. By preventing conversions to Zoroastrianism, the Parsees seek to maintain their ethnic differences. They also seek to maintain some kind of a different identity by behaving more westernized, than their compatriots do. This may have more to do with their emphasis on education and openness to imbibing other cultures with no restriction of going abroad as was the case for the Hindu. This has exposed them to a varied life-style, to which the Hindu is now being exposed. Another attitude is that education must be achieved at any cost.

Sethna (1984) further analyzes that boys are more pampered than girls. This is often very marked so that when grown up, males appear to have less strength of character than females who often have had to fight for privileges at home compared to boys. There are many young men who are unmarried because of extreme attachment to their mothers; or their marriages have failed because they cannot wean themselves from the mother to form a more mature relationship with the wife. Likewise, it seems that many females do not marry because they are looking for 'mature', 'self-sufficient', 'protective' males like their father. Parsees appear to be very orally oriented. They love food, drink, and all the good things of life. They have no feelings of in-bred guilt fostered by religious training. There is no concept (or any resembling it) of original sin. Pleasure is not considered sinful. Hence, Parsees are usually easy going and not guilt ridden.

According to Mistree (1998), 'God in Zoroastrianism is deemed to be totally good and perfect. Hence, that which is imperfect (evil) cannot emerge from God, for if it did, than God would no longer remain totally good and perfect. In Zoroastrianism therefore, God cannot be held to be the harbinger of imperfections such as misery, pain, suffering poverty, disease, or death. Here lies the intellectual strength of Zarathustra's teachings. Whilst others get confused about the tragedies and misfortunes of the world, a Zoroastrian is given a rational and theologically sound conceptual framework through which he may tackle these problems. A Zoroastrian does not need to resort to the theory of reincarnation or believe in a fatalistic divine plan in which man is relegated to being a mere puppet or a pawn in the drama of cosmic evolution.

The Zoroastrian doctrine recognizes and accepts all the dimensions of man. It accepts his physicality and needs arising from it. This is expressed in its concept of the *fravashi*, which comes closest to our concept of the biological self. The concept of *urvan* (the willing self) expresses the private self. Whilst *daēnā* (action), can be interpreted in our concept of the social self. The social self has no bindings, except that of following

Zoroastrianism

the three basic principles of the faith—good thought, good words, and good deeds. As the individual is also urged to use his innate talent and innate reason, the bindings on him may be relatively few. Nevertheless, the reality of social behavior and rules of conduct may be quite different. However, when placed within this open philosophy, the binds may be relatively few.

As a philosophy, Zoroastrianism recognizes the value of the positive emotions of joy and love for oneself and fellow beings. This seems to be its singular emotional strength. Man has the power and the will to fight the enemies of his soul—his thoughts. He is not a victim of past unknown acts. Above all, he has the freedom of choice to accept or deny thoughts, words and deeds that are detrimental to his welfare. Emotions of anger, fear, hate, envy, grief, arise from the influence of *Ahriman* on the individual. Thus, man has the choice of a conscience to guide him. Considering the nature of man the animal, and the physiological basis of emotions, man is inherently composed of the Lie (evil), and thus can never be free from its influence.

Zoroastrianism recognizes the duality of human nature. Although it emphasizes the development of the 'good nature' of man, it does not discount the 'bad nature'. The onus rests on the individual to develop either of these qualities within him. The philosophy has been developed around this duality, taking the good and bad within it. In this sense, it presents a holistic and pragmatic image of man in nature, devoid of any ideal concepts to encumber his growth. Rather, it concentrates on developing ethical and moralistic standards in man. Standards that he can easily achieve, and which are within his abilities to develop.

6

ISLAM

Islam is a world religion and a way of life for millions of its followers. From its inception in the Arabian Peninsula, it has spread over much of Africa, Europe, and parts of China, Afghanistan, Pakistan, India, and Bangladesh, right up to Indonesia. The propagation of Islam has been tumultuous, being spread not only by successive waves of Arab conquerors, but also by the force of the teachings of the *Quran*, and the character of its Prophet. As the eminent historian Professor Philip K. Hitti (1956), has put it, in his *History of the Arabs*, he is the "only one of the world's prophets to be born within the full light of history".

Within the context of our study, it is imperative for us to understand the historical background of Islam and its Prophet. Without this awareness, much of its philosophy and its reason for existence stand to be misconstrued. Alongside, it also brings to our awareness, human nature as it existed in times past, and the basis on which the self-construal of millions of our people is built. Although brief, this sketch should suffice in our understanding of the environment in which developed the Islamic philosophy and way of life.

According to Muller & Palmer (1880/1996), before the birth of Islam, the Arabs were a nomadic race of the desert regions of the Arabian Peninsula. In its valleys lie the holy cities of the Mecca and Medina, and here was the birthplace of Islam. They were a brave, chivalrous, generous, and hospitable people. Pride of birth was their passion and poetry their greatest delight. Alongside, drunkenness, gambling, and plundering were amongst their major vices. They spent all their energies in endless tribal warfare. The position of women amongst them was not an elevated one. Amongst their cruelest customs was that of burying alive female infants. They had virtually no government the best born and the bravest being recognized as the head of the tribe. The religion of the Arabs was *Sabaeanism* or the worship of the hosts of heaven. Living in the midst of vast desert lands, nature in its benevolent fury formed the gods of the people. There were all together 365 idols there in Mohammed's time. *Allah ta'alah*, the God most high; *Hubbal*, the chief of the minor deities; and *Wadd*, a representative of heaven, worshipped in the form of man. *Suwah*, an idol in the form of a woman, *Yaghuth*, an idol in the shape of a lion, were some of the principle deities of the Arab pantheon. Besides the idols of these deities, the *Kabbah*, or chief shrine of the faith contained images representing Abraham and Ishmael. Another object of worship then and of the greatest veneration now, is the celebrated black stone, inserted in the wall of the *Kabbah*. The worship of stones is a very old form of Semitic cult, and the *Kabbah* has been known from time immemorial as *Bait Allah*, 'the house of God'. Belief in 'ginns', witches, and wizards were also believed to have existed. The belief in *Allah* himself was little more than a memory, and as he had no priesthood, and was not the patron of any particular tribe, his supremacy was merely nominal. Christianity had already established itself in Arabia, but its doctrines had not quite taken hold. Judaism was more in accordance with their habits and traditions. Their creed, however, being based on the idea that they alone are the chosen people, was too exclusive for the majority of Arabs, while the numerous and vexatious restrictions of its ritual and regulations for everyday life were ill suited to the free and restless spirit of these nomads. At the time of Mohammed's appearance the national religion of the Arabs had so far degenerated as to have scarcely any believers. The primeval Sabaeanism was all but lost, and even the worship of the powers of nature had become little more than a gross fetishism.

The existence amongst them of Christians and Jews with their monotheistic ideas attracted some of the inquiring minds.

According to Montgomery Watt (1990), the religion by which the Arabs really lived may be called tribal humanism. According to this, the meaning of life consists in the manifestation of human excellences, that is, all the qualities that go to make up the Arab ideal of manliness or fortitude. The bearer of these excellences is the tribe rather than the individual. If they are seen in the life of an individual, it is because he is a member of a tribe, which is characterized by them. The thought that is uppermost in the mind of the individual is that of the honor of the tribe. Life is meaningful for him when it is honorable, and anything involving dishonor and disgrace is to be avoided at all costs.

Against this background was born the Prophet Mohammed. The date generally given of his birth is 571, AD. At the age of six, Mohammed lost his mother Aaminah, and was taken care of by his grandfather 'Abd al Muttalib who took care of him with great affection, and at his death, which was two years later, left him to the guardianship of his son Abu Talib. He spent his following years tending sheep and goats of the Meccans, an occupation that was considered by the Bedouin as derogatory to the position of a male. At the age of twenty-four, he was employed by a rich widow, named *Khadijah*. Later he married her, although she was forty years and he barely twenty-five (Muller & Palmer, 1880/1996).

The first occasion on which Mohammed confided to his wife *Khadijah* that he was the recipient of visions was, as tradition declares, in 610 AD, when he was forty years old. The earliest divine manifestations commanded him to 'recite' what he heard. It was followed by others, which bade him denounce the idolatrous beliefs and practices of his fellow-townsmen, to whom he was to reveal a higher faith and a purer system of life (Levy, 1965).

According to Muller & Palmer (1880/1996, p. xvi), "the revelations were the almost natural outcome of his mode of life and habit of thought, and especially of his physical constitution. From youth upwards he had suffered from epilepsy, which, tradition says, were accompanied by hallucinations. He was also in the habit of passing long periods in solitude and deep thought; and he was profoundly distressed with the falsehood and immorality of the religion of his compatriots and viewed with horror their vicious and inhuman practices. He had for his best friends men, such as his cousin Waraqah and Zaid ibn amr, who had professedly been long seeking the truth, and had publicly renounced the popular religion".

The central point of the new faith was that there is no God but *Allah*. From Mohammed's earliest utterances, it is clear that he claimed to be himself regarded as *Allah's* mouthpiece and the last of his prophets. The *Quran* addresses him directly, to assure him that he is not insane, and to encourage him against men's doubts, it solemnly confirms as true, visions he has seen. Finally, it is suggested that the truth of his message may be seen from the faith of the Muslims (Williams, 1961, Levy, 1965).

This divine communication is seen as the final stage in a series of divine communications conducted through prophets. It is believed that the chain of seers went back through Jesus, Moses, Abraham, and some others to Adam, the first man, who was also the first prophet, because he was the first to whom God revealed himself. In each case, however, the message was changed and deformed by man. Finally, in his mercy, God sent down His final revelation through the seal of His prophets, Mohammed, in a definitive form, which would not be lost. The *Quran*, then, is the Word of God, for Muslims. Muslims therefore regard the *Quran* as immutable and unchangeable, not metaphorically or symbolically but literally. This is a matter of faith for them, and reason can never deflect them from it (Williams, 1961; Zakaria, 1991).

Monotheism, equality, and brotherhood of all mankind forms the basis of Islam. However, different sects have developed based on their belief or non-belief on certain aspects of Islam, and the lineage to which the followers trace themselves, although the basic belief remains the same. In addition to the Shīá and the Sunni's (orthodox group), the numerous sects found within the Indian sub-continent are the Ismaili Bohras, Ismaili Khojas, dau'di Bohras, Aga Khani Khoja, to name just a few. The Sufi sects form the spiritual group within the Islamic tradition.

What is Islam?

According to Haneef (1994), Islam is not a mere belief-system, an ideology or a religion. It is a total way of life, a complete system governing all aspects of mans' existence, both individual and collective. The meaning of the word Islam is "submission" and "peace". In the course of making an individual Muslim— that is, 'one who is in a state of Islam or submission to the One True God'—Islam profoundly affects his thinking and behavior. Indeed, there is no aspect of a persons life, nor of the life of the society which is made of such people, which it does not touch and transform in keeping with its basic concept, that of the Lordship and Sovereignty of God and mans' responsibility to Him. Islam's first requirement is belief and its second action. Out of its concepts and beliefs, a certain attitude toward life, toward ones' self, toward other human beings, towards the universe emerges. A certain kind of personality; a distinctive type of human interaction; a particular mode of worship, of family life, manners, living habits and so on in relation to all aspects of life, takes its development.

The *Quran* literally means 'Reading'. It is a collection of the revelations that descended from God to Mohammed through Archangel Gabriel, over a period of some twenty-three years. It is a mingling of the spiritual and the material, the divine and the mundane. The total reverence of Muslims for their Holy Book baffles non-Muslims. However, this has to be seen in the context of unflinching faith in God that is the basis of Islam (Zakaria, 1991).

Broadly speaking, the Quranic verses, which are intertwined and are not in any specific order, have to be separated so as to classify them under two broad categories: The first part is the nucleus or foundation of the book, and it contains principles and morals, injunctions and directions, warnings and blessings. They embody universal truths, though they were given local color to be comprehensible to whom they were addressed. The second part is the more difficult part to follow. Some theologians describe it as mysterious, and it needs the exercise of ingenuity by the reader to understand its inner meaning. It has parables, allegories, and anecdotes that need to be explained and interpreted, and from which moral guidance again emerges (Zakaria, 1991).

The *Quran* is essentially a moral code of conduct, (Q 2:1) and as such, its method of appeal is necessarily direct. According to the *Quran*, the basic concept of life is that the entire world of creation and everything contained therein is sustained by certain definite laws inherent in each object and in harmony with each other. These laws of nature, the *Sunnat Allah,* are necessarily unalterable and that mans' joy in life should lie in co-operating with these laws and imitating them in his own activity, assisted by the "balance set in his nature" (Q 91:7). These laws constitute the "Will of God", and man is but to try to the best of his ability to conform to them for a life of peace and order. This is "to surrender to His Will"(Q. 2:130). To bring this fundamental point home, the *Quran* repeatedly draws attention to the indifference of man to see clearly the vast panorama of nature and reflect these familiar objects which suggest to him that some "benevolent law" or purpose—*Khalq* or *Rahman*—holds together all that he sees or feels through his senses. It emphasizes that the "heavens and the earth and whatsoever is between them are not created in sport," (Q. 21:16, 44:38–39), rather, for a serious end, that each object of creation is made subject to the laws intrinsic to its nature in order that it may fulfill its function. Man "fitted by nature with a sense of balance and discrimination" (Q. 91:7) is to conduct himself in accordance with the laws of his own being, and in harmony with the laws governing the rest of creation. "That is the right religion" or path of devotion to the ways of *Allah,* says the *Quran*, and for which "man has been fitted by his nature". However, its regret is that man has proved "unjust, indifferent and has corrupted the world" (Q. 33: 72, 30:40) (Latif 1960).

So, whenever the *Quran* asserts that nothing happens against the Will of God, it only means that the laws inherent in the object concerned are at work and have their inevitable course and duration. Mans' role on earth is to understand these laws and conform to them; and whenever he neglects to understand and conform to them, the consequence will naturally prove harmful to him. The Quranic way of expressing this is: "We have willed it so."[1] In other words: a law must have its course: a cause must produce its effect. That is the scheme of life divinely devised or determined and man is not free to alter that scheme, the "Ways of God". This is the main domain of life where man has but to conform or surrender to the Will of God or the laws of life, which sustain it, if he chooses to profit by them of his own free will. The point to note here is that the initiative for movement and reform should lie with man. That is the law—His Will (Latif, 1960).

Next to the *Quran* itself, the most important Islamic textual material is the *Hadīth*, comprising the sayings of the Prophet. There are a vast number of *Hadīths*, which are admitted by Muslim scholars to be spurious. Even among those accepted by the medieval scholars, there are many, which the modernists would reject. No absolute canon of *Hadīth* has ever been established. Certain compilers are recognized as more trustworthy, than others are, and some sects and schools accept *Hadīths* not accepted by others. A man accepted as trustworthy by one school, might not be accepted by another (Williams, 1961).

According to Maqsood (1998), the two most authentic collections of *Hadīth* are those by Bukhair and Muslim. Other respected collections include those of Abu Dawud, Tirmidhi, Ibn Majah and Bayhaqi. The problem of taking guidance from the *Hadīth* is that there is no cast–iron guarantee that all of the sayings are genuine. It has to be admitted that each collection is subject to the selection of human authors, with their own motives and interests. It has been pointed out, for example, that the Prophet's beloved wife Aishah recorded over two thousand *Hadīths*, but less than two hundred of them appear in Bukhari's collection.

"The *Hadīth* literature covers a wide range of individual and collective life, and many of the reported sayings of the Prophet have a very specific and detailed content. This sharply contrasts with the *Quran*, which (barring a few specific injunctions) contains mostly broad principles of conduct rather than specific rules and regulations. Herein lies the utility, as well as the potential danger of *Hadīth*. On the one hand *Hadīth* gives concrete meaning and content to the non-specific and general regulations of the *Quran*, while on the other it is precisely this concreteness of the *Hadīth* that injects rigidity into the institutional system of Islam" (Khwaja, 1977, p. 169).

As Khwaja (1977) analyzes, the prescriptive specificity helps the individual by providing him with concrete and detailed guidance, when the mere affirmation of a general principle may not have helped him to the same degree. On the other hand, such specificity tends to check the growth of the individual through the exercise of his own reason, since it presents him with a complete and readymade concrete rule. Again, while a high degree of specificity may prevent the individual from aberrations, it may prevent him from attaining higher levels of achievement. Now, while the prescription of the *Quran*, are mostly general and non-specific, the prescriptions found in the reported sayings of the Prophet are frequently highly specific. Consequently, while unquestioning submission to the *Quran* does not entail the loss of ones' autonomy but only a measure of restriction within a very wide range of freedom, unquestioning submission to the *Hadīth* entails very drastic restrictions upon ones freedom of thought and action. An excessive concern with *Hadīth* tends to promote a 'rule centric' morality that stresses observance of rules, as distinguished from a 'value centric' morality that stresses devotion to values.

Basic Principles of Islamic Philosophy

The Unity of God : One has to believe in the unity of God by recognizing that the entire universe, both visible and invisible, owes its existence and sustenance to one supreme Being. This, in essence, is Islam's conception of monotheism, which is absolute, unqualified, and uncompromising. "*La ilaha illa Allah*", 'There is none worthy of worship except God', is the concept on which such strong stress is laid that the entire *Quran* seems to be nothing else than an exposition of its implications and a commentary of it. This idea swept off all distinctions of color and race, and every hierarchical conception of life, social and political. It was a revolutionary slogan aiming at the emancipation of man. It restored dignity to human nature by placing man next to God and making righteous living the sole test of superiority of one over another (Latif, 1960, Khwaja, 1977).

The Revelation : The Muslim bases all decisions on the revealed words of the *Holy Quran*. Not one word in the *Quran* is believed by Muslims to be thought or created by Mohammed himself, although he is revered above all humanity as one of the most perfect of God's messengers. Mohammed is important to Muslims because he was the last prophet, the seal of all that was revealed to the prophets before him (Maqsood, 1998).

Life after Death : Life according to the *Quran* is not a cycle. It is a linear line and is to be "carried forward from state to state" (Q. 84:19), from one lower to one higher state or plane. Islam asserts that the present life is but a minute part of the totality of existence. The *Quran* informs man of the reality of another life of a very different nature from the life of this world, of infinite duration. Islam lays the greatest stress on the individuals' accountability to *Allah*. The human beings' life in this world constitutes a trial, during which he prepares himself, either for good or for ill, for the next life of infinite duration. For although mans' body dies, his soul, his personality, has an existence extending beyond the present life; it is a continuous entity whose inner state will accompany it into the Hereafter. It is this state together with ones' deeds, which will determine ones' ultimate destiny (Latif, 1960; Haneef, 1994).

"The True Ambition of a Muslim is to accept or submit (the meaning of the word 'Muslim'); to live out of the will of God so far as is humanly possible, in what ever circumstances he passes along his way of life. *Sharī'a*, which means 'the straight path', is the code of behavior for the Islamic way of life, the law that determines the rightness (*halāl*) or wrongness (*harām*) of any particular action. Thus, *halāl* is that which is allowed and wholesome for humanity; *harām* is that which is forbidden, and harmful. One must search for it, and follow it, through all life's tests and temptations, difficulties and tragedies, consciously considering in every situation what the will of God would be for any individual at any given moment" (Maqsood, 1998, p. 15).

"Every Islamic prayer is a resolve to conform with divine aid to the ways of god or *Sunnat Allah*, in order that one might discharge ones' obligations to ones' self and ones' obligations to others—the *Haq Allah and Haq an-Nas*. Death should thus have no terror for man. What one should fear is wickedness or evil life; and it is against this that one has to seek Divine protection. In whatever man may ask for, he is never to forget his primary need for purity of life. The thought of this life hereafter, which, according to the *Quran*, is "Life Indeed", is to be kept so constantly in view that the present is to be regarded as but a preparation for it. For this reason it is raised to the position of a cardinal belief in Islam, as important to the life of man as every other cardinal belief, to be expressed in righteous work or *Amal-I-Saleh*" (Latif, 1960, p. 166).

According to the *Quran*, every one will have to pass through hell (Q. 19–72–73). The commentators of the *Quran* contend that the text refers to a bridge over hell, which as stated in the *Hadīth*, one has to cross on the Day of Judgment—an idea that runs parallel to what prevails in Zoroastrianism. The *Quran*, however, makes no specific reference to the provision of such a bridge. Whatever the nature of hell or heaven, it is to be admitted that life in either sphere must eventually subserve some ultimate divine purpose common to all humanity who according to the *Quran* mark a distinct stage in creative evolution. The process has necessarily to continue. Heaven and hell, whether they are mere states of the soul or otherwise cannot therefore remain so for all times. That will be stagnation and the stultifying of the purpose of evolution. Hence, it is that the *Quran* takes particular care to disclose the destiny of man. "From state to state" or from one plane to another", shall ye assuredly be carried onward" (Q. 84:19) (Latif, 1960).

The *Quran* makes it repeatedly clear that every one, whether righteous or unrighteous, will have to carry with him to the next stage in life the reactions of his deeds indelibly impressed on his soul. His action, his thought, his speech, his feeling, his imagination, even his fancy, will cling to his neck tenaciously and mark the character of the life he has lived. "And every man—we have fastened to him his bird of omen upon his neck; and we shall bring forth for him, on the day of resurrection, a book he shall find spread wide open. Read thy book, thou art accountant enough against thyself today" (Q. 17:14–15) (Latif, 1960).

These two states, heaven and hell, will be experienced in physical form by the new bodies with which *Allah* will raise men up; they are not merely spiritual or psychic states. Moreover, while we do not know the exact nature, the *Quran* tells us that the inhabitants of heaven will experience some things, which will remind them of their life on earth. The happiness and beauty of it will far exceed anything one can imagine, and that the ultimate triumph and bliss for those who have attained Paradise will be nearness to their Lord (Haneef, 1994).

As for those who have deserved hell, theirs will be a temporary or permanent state of torture depending on their inner condition and the nature and extent of their sins. The *Quran* describes hell as a state of intense, fearful burning and agony without respite, among the most horrifyingly loathsome surroundings and companions. Atheists and polytheists will be placed in hell, though they will be suitably rewarded for their good deeds in this world. But the most awful as part of the suffering of its inhabitants will be the terrible, inescapable awareness that this is the destiny, which they deserved and brought upon themselves by rejecting *Allah* and ignoring the guidance which He had conveyed to them through His messengers. Hell and heaven begin for man in this very life; for, whatever good or evil he does, at once becomes a part of him, and begins to give him a foretaste of heaven or hell to follow. The good deed will promote spiritual elevation; the evil deed, its own downward feeling. If man could but realize the ugliness of his deed before his death and feel sincerely repentant, and retrace his steps, there is always the grace of God to bring him peace of mind (Latif, 1960; Khwaja, 1977; Haneef, 1994).

Angels : The Holy *Quran* mentions the two guardian angels for each human, who take note of everything. "When the two angels meet together, sitting one on the right, and one on the left (appointed to learn his doings), not a word he utters, but by him is an observer ready (to note it)" (Q. 50:17–18). However, thanks to God's grace and mercy, the record of a persons' sins and failings only lasts until that person repents. The moment a person is truly sorry, the record is wiped clean again. On the other hand, if a person does good, or even if they only intend to do good without actually doing it, it always counts to their credit. This is expressed many times in the *Hadīth* (Maqsood, 1998).

Neither the *Quran* nor the Prophet has made any claim that the *Quran* and the *Sunnah* was the end of human knowledge. Of all the divine attributes with which man has to endure himself for his task, knowledge commands precedence. "To acquire knowledge is binding on all believers, both men and women" (Ibn Maja). Knowledge enables the possessor to distinguish right from wrong, it lights the way to heaven; it is our companion when friendless: it guides us to happiness, it sustains us in adversity; it is a weapon against enemies and an ornament among friends. By virtue of it, *Allah* exalts nations, and makes them guides in good pursuits, and gives them leadership; so much so, that their footsteps are followed, their deeds are imitated, and their opinions are accepted and held in respect" (Ibn Abd al-Bar: Fadl al-'Ilm) (Latif, 1960; Hassnain, 1968).

However, one thing the *Quran* makes perfectly clear. Knowledge does not consist in the mere assemblage in ones' memory of ideas or material on this or that subject. The Book insists on reflection as an indispensable aid to the proper acquisition of knowledge. Knowledge in the Quranic conception covers every field of life—the life of the vast universe working around man in immediate contact as well as remote, and the life of man himself moving onward with a knowledge of his past. An acquisition of knowledge therefore imposes on him the exercise of not merely his intellectual and physical faculties, but his spiritual: and nothing is prohibited to him in Islam except, probably, probing that beyond which his reason or intuition has been incapable of advance (Latif, 1960).

Maqsood (1998) has summarized the Principles of *Sharī'a*: As the first principle, humans should consider all the things that *Allah* has created and bestowed, for the benefit of humanity. Humanity was given control over the earth and was expected to utilize the vastness of all its resources wisely and well. Only a very few things are prohibited, and the prohibitions are always for specific reasons.

The second principle of *Sharī'a* is that anything that has not specifically been forbidden falls under the general principle of the permissibility of things, and is allowed by *Allah*. If no evidence is found (for making a thing *harām*), then the writer or teacher who forbade it has wrongly usurped the prerogative of *Allah*, and has committed the sin of making *harām* what *Allah* had allowed. It can and does happen, and the Prophet specifically warned against it. As far as living habits are concerned, the principle is of freedom and conscience— nothing is prohibited except what *Allah* Himself has prohibited.

The third principle of *Sharī'a* follows from this—if a thing is prohibited, then anything that leads to it is also prohibited. For example, as sex outside marriage is *harām*, so also are seductive clothing, private meetings between people who might be tempted, and so on. In other words, that which leads to *harām* is also *harām*.

The final principle of the *Sharī'a* is that necessity removes the restrictions, and the person who does the *harām* thing out of necessity is not held to blame for it.

He further interprets, "The ideals to be aimed at, that will form the perfect Muslim character, are kindness, modesty, gentleness, courage, steadfastness, consideration for others, and the general desire for the promotion of the happiness and welfare of society. Pride and arrogance are neither attractive qualities nor acceptable ones for the Muslim, for Islam teaches that no individual is superior to another except in the amount of faith and performance of good deeds" (Maqsood, 1998, p. 23).

The Self in Islamic Thought

Man, Islam asserts, is a unique creation of *Allah*, possessing an obvious, outward aspect—the physical body—and a hidden, inner aspect—the mind, emotions and soul. The uniqueness of mans nature lies in the fact that he has been endowed with freedom of choice and judgment between right and wrong. The capacity to think, transmit knowledge, feel and act, and an immortal soul which lives on after death of the physical body have not been given to other creatures. Although mans body dies, his soul, his personality, has an existence extending beyond the present life; it is a continuous entity whose inner state will accompany it into the Hereafter. Thus, man is a composite of many aspects, levels and functions, the totality of which represents the reality of human nature (Haneef, 1994).

The *Quran* divides the movement of human life into two broad periods. Firstly, there is the period of mans' making until he receives consciousness by the 'spirit of God' being 'breathed into him', and he becomes an embodied soul. The period beginning with this moment and continuing thereafter crossing the line of what is termed 'death' is the period that matters. It is this, which the *Quran* has in view, when it asserts: "From state to state shall ye assuredly be carried onward". The earlier movement has indeed a biological setting. The subsequent is clearly indicated by the *Quran* to be spiritual in form and character. The former refers to a physiological development as in the mother's womb. The biological mould, form, or '*taur*' is completed in the emerging child, which thereafter merely expands its physical dimensions until death overtakes them. The 'spirit of God', as the *Quran* points out, is breathed into him when he emerges as a child, gathers increasing consciousness, and develops individuality. It is this spirit or ego, as it is styled by philosophy, which is addressed by the *Quran*. It is that which does not disappear with the disappearance of the body. It retains its individuality and assumes an independent existence the moment it discards its physiological covering or association (Latif, 1960).

During the early period or before the 'spirit of God' is breathed into him, no responsibility is attached to man in the making, since he is not conscious of the movement. The question of responsibility arises the moment consciousness begins to be at play. The first stage in this period, which closes with what is called 'death', is the basic stage of preparation for all subsequent stages. It is the stage of freedom of will and action or of willing co-operation with the laws of life helped by the balance set in the nature of man. What follows is but a continuation of it. 'Your creation and resurrection are but like a single soul' (Q. 31:27) (Latif, 1960).

Human life, according to the *Quran*, is to express itself in a system of activity promoting peace and harmony in life, and that subject to that end in view and in conformity with the principles underlying it, man has every freedom to will and act. Moreover, there is an assurance to every individual:

"On no soul do we lay a responsibility greater than it can bear" (Q. 2:286) (Latif, 1960).

The culture of Islam is but an expression of this process. Whatever ones' role either in ones' family circle, or in society at large, or even in his private closet, one has to be mindful of his dual responsibility. To be so mindful is '*khair*' or good, and not to be so is '*sharr*' or evil. The distinction is to be upheld in every sphere of life's activity—physical, intellectual, spiritual, social, economic, and political. It is this distinction, which also underlies the principle distinguishing the '*halāl*', the permissible or the lawful, from the '*harām*' or unlawful. Life thus viewed, every action of man assumes a spiritual significance (Latif, 1960).

Islam accepts suffering as a natural part of life. Everybody faces suffering, fears, and disappointments. *Allah* grants the conditions of your birth whether you are born wealthy or poor, intelligent or stupid, beautiful or ugly, and so on. It has nothing to do with the will of the parent (Maqsood, 1998).

According to the *Quran*, folly brings its own suffering. That is fate, the law of life, and the decree of God. Fate or *taqdir* is used in the *Quran* in three broad senses. Firstly, there is the field of what we may term the divine initiative or of the operation of the laws of nature—*Fitrat Allah* or *Khalq Allah* or *Sunnat Allah*. They are signs of a plan of existence, necessarily conceived in advance or pre-determined even as every human plan is pre-determined before it is put into action. Mans' responsibility lies only in the nature of the use he makes of these laws. Every reaction to them is *taqdir*. Secondly, there is the field of human initiative. That too is *taqdir*. Lastly, there is the reaction on our life of the deeds of others. Sometimes they bring us joy that may seem unexpected. But the very ability to feel the joy proceeding from the good deeds of others is the result of a process of righteousness in us. Even that is *taqdir*. Sometimes, the deeds of others bring us pain and suffering. *Taqdir* in this context expresses itself in one of two ways. It may be that those who have thus suffered had not in proper time anticipated the rise of evil tendencies in others and exercised proper check on them by every reasonable means open to them or it may be that they knowingly abstained from interference. They have to pay the penalty for the failure to do so. Here comes in the injunction of the *Quran*, the injunction designated as *Jihad* (Latif, 1960).

According to Latif (1960), *Jihad* literally means exertion or striving against all that is evil, whether in thought, feeling, or action. That is an essential condition of a peaceful life; so much so, that the most trying form of it is the *Jihad* against ones' own evil ways. Fighting with arms those who are out to disturb the peace of the world or bent on the destruction of the good in life is *Jihad*, as commonly understood; but *Jihad* with ones' self is indeed a hard task. Hence, it is called '*Jihad-e-Akbar*', the greatest of *Jihads*. To abstain from this *Jihad* in ones' own personal case is to let the 'self' disintegrate. Like wise to abstain from remonstrating with the evil around by thought or deed as the case may demand, is to be a party to the disintegration of corporate happiness for man. The ill deeds of other men involve us in the result of their ill deeds whenever we abstain from putting a check on them. It is the penalty one has to pay for letting others freely indulge in evil deeds. Such is the view, which the Prophet of Islam takes of this issue.

The Emotions in Islamic Thought

According to Khwaja (1977, p. 94), "Islam does not preach asceticism. It has a very balanced approach to the various dimensions of human personality or the needs of man. It is the only religion, which is fully practicable for all men. It does not degrade the physical needs of man like food or sex. The pursuit of the means of livelihood, marriage, and the procreation of children, are not only permitted as concessions to the flesh, but are regarded as the duties of a good Muslim, equally important as other religious duties. In fact, there is no distinction between the spiritual and the profane in Islam.

Everything depends on the motive (*nīyat*) of the individual. All actions from prayer to entertainment can be performed in the spirit of devotion and service of God. In such a case every moment of ones' life is said to be spent in the worship of God (*ibādat*)".

Islam teaches that although you should fear the Day of Judgment if your life has been full of sins for which you never repented, death should not be feared. It is only human nature to shrink from pain and suffering, but Muslims are to do their best to bear all such trials with patience and fortitude. Death is the natural end of human life—it cannot be avoided, and no one escapes it. On the other hand, many people long to die, because they are unhappy or in pain, but *Allah* requires them to go on living. In addition, when death claims someone near to him, he does not indulge in excess of grief. For not only does Islam forbid this but also it is inappropriate in one who believes. Rather, he prays for *Allah*'s mercy and peace on the departed, and takes his living and dying as a lesson and example (Haneef, 1994; Maqsood, 1998).

Qutub (1964) states, in its treatment of man, Islam recognizes in principle, all the natural emotions and does not repress them, but permits the practical performance of instinctive acts to an extent such as may give a reasonable degree of pleasure without causing any harm to the individual or community". Love for God being held as supreme; fear of God being a prime deterrent for man. Anger is an emotion that clouds reason; grief is an affront to God for discounting that which he has willed. There are Quranic injunctions, and sayings of the Prophet to guide the individual to deal with the panorama of human affect.

Through the Prism

The soul, according to Islamic view, exists on a linear continuum. From one state to another, it passes, never stagnating at a point. In its sojourn on earth, Islam views man as man. Life and consciousness is breathed into him by *Allah*, so that he lives his life in accordance to the nature that *Allah* has provided him.

Islam accepts the material aspect of life. Materialism, in this sense, is living in the world of nature, in accordance with the principles of nature. However, this has to be lived out according to the laws laid out by *Allah* in the *Quran* and the principles of right behavior as explained by the Prophet in the *Hadīths*. To do this, the Muslim is urged and encouraged to work toward acquiring and achieving the necessities required for this life on earth. Materialism in this sense does not overshadow the spiritual aspect of the Muslim. He is profoundly aware and accepting of *Allah*, the source of all life. Unflinching faith in this abstraction is the basis of his life. As a natural corollary to this, emotions are viewed as an innate part of the individual.

The innate nature of man is expressed by the *Quran* in a paradox, each side of which is meant to be equally true. "Surely, we created man of the goodliest fabric; then we rendered him the vilest of vile" (Q. 95: 4–5). Every thinker in every age has had to recognize this paradox in human nature. Says the *Quran* in continuation of the paradox for the sake of clearing the issue raised therein: "Then we rendered him the vilest of the vile, save those who believe and work righteously" (Q. 95: 5–6).

Islam accepts man as a biological entity, with natural needs that have to be fulfilled. It permits him full enjoyment of the pleasures of life. From the perspective of our definition of the components of "self", Islam recognizes the biological self as an important element in the totality of the individual. Islam prohibits the renunciation of life, as this would mean discounting an important aspect of ones' self, and an affront to *Allah*, by denying that which He has given.

These prohibitions are a very comprehensive and eloquent listing of the basics of human nature. A cursory glance at the behaviors that are to be curtailed by these injunctions, and the social situations that they arose from, indicate their presence in the innate nature of man. One may well state that these arise from the "animal" nature of man. Man is an animal. These behaviors have been noted right from the time of the *Vedas*, to the *Bible*, to the *Quran* and right up to present times. Affects of hate, anger, giving rise to violence, greed, the insatiable need for power, are all perceived in man from the times past. The Prophet recognized mans' instinctual needs, and thus formulated rules that man could abide by, being true to his nature, keeping within the social context of the times. Making the object of love a distant Superior Being, serves to curtail mans' need for power, thereby sustaining his allegiance to him. This figure, which has essentially given him birth, is the benevolent parent of every child, who rewards him when he behaves, and punishes him when he doesn't, fear, being the key element of control. Ironically, love for a fellow human being is not really encouraged, as there are enough rules which permit expression of anger even violently towards loved ones, due to some transgression. Perhaps this too is in keeping with the essential nature of man. Evidence of violence towards our own species, whatever justification we may put forth, is evident at any moment in time, of humankinds existence.

According to Khwaja (1977), a critical concept of man is the prerequisite of a mature and adequate conception of God. The concepts of suggestion, resistance, defense mechanisms, neurosis, neurotic fear or anxiety, need for violence and power in man, effects of unfulfilled needs, pain and suffering, are highly significant for understanding the dynamics of human behavior and for a genuine and authentic commitment, as against from inauthentic faith. But almost no notice has been given to the above concepts by Muslim thinkers, apart from literary critics and poets.

In Brandons' (1962) analysis, there is one important aspect of Mohammed's doctrine of human destiny, which must not be overlooked, namely, the position of women. Mohammed's teaching was addressed primarily to men, and, his picture of delights awaiting the faithful in paradise is conceived in terms of masculine tastes. According to his view, women were definitely inferior to men. Thus, in *Surah* iv.38 he declares: 'The men are overseers over the women by reason of what *Allah* hath bestowed in bounty upon one more than another, and of the property which they have contributed (a reference to the marriage price which was so important in Arabian society). It is in keeping with this estimate that in the same *Surah Mohammed* allows men to have as many as four wives, and of concubines as many as they could afford. This neglect of women in his teaching about human destiny vis-à-vis God must surely be judged as evidence of Mohammed's unconscious acceptance of the traditional evaluation of women in ancient Semitic society (Brandon, 1962).

As the *Quran* is primarily a book of moral teachings, dealing with man the social animal, the social self, is of prime importance. Islam preaches a holistic philosophy of brotherhood of mankind, equality amongst all, freedom to acquire knowledge and reason, acceptance of the individual and his needs, a democratic outlook in polity. Why, then, is there an observed discrepancy between Islamic society as it exists, and its philosophy? More so, when they are strict adherents to the *Sharī'a*? What are the implications for the individual? Is there a dissonance within him?

To address these issues, we review further aspects of Islamic philosophy that have a bearing on the social self, and consequently, the private self.

As Khwaja (1977) elucidates, once a Muslim commits himself to the *Quran*, as the infallible Word of God, he cannot at the same time claim to follow his own independent reason or go wherever the argument leads him. In this sense, there is a conflict between commitment to revelation and commitment to reason, or between faith and autonomy. If one commits oneself to the *Quran*, he will have to subordinate his own judgment to the Divine judgment in case of conflict between them. A conflict only shows that human reason is in error and is unable, for some reason or other, to comprehend the truth of the Quranic judgment. In all such cases, the individual is very likely to realize his error provided he sincerely and

Islam

patiently tries to grasp the truth of the Divine judgment in question.

He further analyzes (p. 136), "The traditional view of revelation does not create any difficulties so long as the letter and the spirit of the *Quran* accord with the ideals and aspirations of the believer, even though he may be unable to live up to them in actual practice. However, the moment his authentic evaluations differ from some Quranic command or prescription, the logical implication of the traditional conception of revelation is that he should surrender his personal and private judgment to the Divine command. This is the only straightforward and intellectually honest opinion, provided he accepts the traditional conception of revelation. However, if he is unable to surrender his authentic judgment even after the most careful, honest, and prayerful search for authentic existence, then the surrender of his individual judgment would not heal the tragic split in the depths of his being. Even if he were to surrender his spiritual autonomy on the ground that the finite human mind can never fully grasp the infinite wisdom of God, he will still suffer from the pangs of a deep existential conflict. The faith of such a person would be haunted by ghosts of the reasons, which he has buried for the sake of an unqualified commitment to revelation. Such a person can never feel satisfied either by the surrender of his spiritual autonomy or by the traditional Islamic hermeneutic. For such a person the *Élan* conception of God (this *Élan* is the Divine discontent, or the aspiration or quest for the perfect) and of revelation does not generate any existential conflict or tension in the depths of their beings."

For Latif (1960, p. 65), "Three questions pose themselves in the beliefs of the *Quran*. Is man under Islam, free to will and act? What equipment does it suggest for him as an aid to righteous action? Moreover, what exactly makes an action righteous? Expressions confront us at every turn in the *Quran* proclaiming that nothing happens except as God wills. Yet, responsibility is attached to mans' action, and hopes of reward and fears of punishment are held out. And then, as against this, stand out a host of verses calling upon man to exert his mind and choose between right and wrong; and he is told: "God does not change the condition of a people unless they first change that which is in their hearts" (Q. 13:12) "man shall have nothing but what he strives for" (Q. 53:40), "whatever suffering you suffer, it is what your hands have wrought" (Q. 42:29). What is one to make of these apparent contrarieties crossing and re-crossing each other? Is man after all free to will and act or not free at all? Is there a way out? Such were the questionings, which in the early centuries of Islam divided the Islamic society broadly into two warring camps one called *Qadriyah*, or those who believed in the freedom of will. The other *Fabriyah*, or those who believed in pre-determination or absolute divine control and direction of human action. The determinist outlook not merely triumphed in the conflict, but has ever since clung to the Muslim mind and robbed the *Quran* of the corrective it had offered".

Observes Sir William Muir (quoted in Wadia, 1923, p. 44) "In Islam the relation of *Allah* to the world is such that not only all free will but all freedom in the exercise of the intellect is preposterous. God is so great and the character of His greatness is so pantheistically absolute that there is no room for the human. All good and all evil come directly from *Allah*. Hope perishes under the weight of His iron bondage and pessimism becomes the popular philosophy". Says Clarke (quoted in Wadia, 1923), Islam saw God but not man; saw the claims of Deity, but not the rights of humanity, saw authority but failed to see freedom, therefore hardened into despotism, stiffened into formalism, sank into death. According to Latif (1960, p. 65), "criticism of the *Quran* of the type disclosed here may be unpalatable to a Muslim but he has only himself to thank for it. The initial responsibility for it belongs to the doctors of Muslim theology in the Middle Ages and to their successors as well, who through an inept approach to the Quranic concept of the "Will of God"—the abiding basis for right human activity—have kept the meaning and purpose of the *Quran* concealed from the mind of man, giving thereby a handle to willful critics to read rank fatalism in Islam".

Although Islam seems to follow the humanist tradition, Engineer (1985) states, it is clear in Islam the concept of freedom implies the freedom to act, not the freedom to choose. The moral ideas pronounced by God can be realized only by adopting them in practice. There is no question of choice. Those who act contrary to them perpetrate 'evil', although they are free to act as they like.

However, Muslims believe that their destiny is predetermined, and nothing happens without the will of God. This belief goes contrary to the other teachings of the *Quran*, which state that man is the master of his life. It is within his own hands to direct the course of his life. He determines his future place in heaven or hell, through his right or wrong actions. Muslims who argue for predestination as well as those who seek to preserve mans' free will have each been able to find support in the *Quran* for their views (Williams, 1961).

At one level, it provides good reasoning, but at another, it absolves caretakers from taking adequate measures to nurture the future of their child. This is also linked to the issue of whether man has free will or not. How the individual deals with this "if God willing" attitude will depend on other factors such as his personality, (in the conventional sense), upbringing, social environment, and opportunities, including the dogmatism of his adherence to his scriptural injunctions. If he does not think, he may just flow with the tide, and if he chooses to take hold of his life, he may be able to carve out his destiny. It is akin to following the straight and narrow path and meeting up with just what is laid out in front, or walking roads with forks, and making choices at each crossing. The issue here is freedom of will—the choice of recognizing ones' true self.

From the individuals' perspective, he is still bound by confines of tradition, which do not permit him to exercise his adult faculties of reason. The child is not permitted to become a mature adult. The individual is functioning from predefined roles—his social self—the masks he wears to present himself in the way he is expected to. Although Islam does recognize the biological self, the belief system, with its emphasis on sin, lays the foundation for guilt for transgressions. The individual finds himself in a bind, as at one level, he is expected to encourage his reason—the unique faculty presented by God to man alone. At the other end of the spectrum this reason is not sufficient for him to exercise his restraints, hence he needs the power of an omnipotent conscience governing his behavior. Thus, for those lacking in power, this would be sufficient to set up the frustration-guilt cycle, leading to forms of aberrant behavior and stark pathology, or diminution of personal needs, leading to a shared normative social neurosis.

The way a person chooses to believe may ultimately depend on other personality and intellectual factors of the individual. These being governed by the environment in which he has been raised. Hence, social learning, subjective experiences, and the individual mode of thought, supports or urges the individual to think of new answers to the questions that he faces. Aside from faith and belief, education has a role to play in the formation of his personality.

Neither the *Quran* nor the Prophet has made any claim that the *Quran* and the *Sunnah* is the end of human knowledge. The dichotomy between experience and the teachings in the *Quran* in relation to education may be quite lost on the laity. Firstly, his lack of education prevents him from developing his cognitive abilities. The injunctions within the *Quran* prevent him from asking questions. In addition, his dependency on the mullahs' for the interpretation of the *Quran*, make him vulnerable to their perspectives, which may be guided by larger socio-political factors, making him vulnerable to their interpretations.

At this point, we digress to the issue of the language of the *Quran*, which is Arabic. A language that is not part of our daily usage, thus making us dependent on a second hand perspective. The laity being taught just what he needs to know to develop and keep his faith. The language itself is given to multiple interpretations, based on the orientation of the interpreter. To give an example, the concept of "*taqwa*" has

Islam

elicited two different interpretations. Khwaja (1977) interprets it as "leading a balanced life'; whereas, Haneef (1994) interprets it as "an attitude comprised of love and fear of *Allah*". One interpretation implying a conscious rational choice, the other based entirely on fear. Such contrariness is replete in the various interpretations of the *Quran*, and the *Hadiths*, particularly with regard to rules of social behavior. Thus, in the childs' formative years, the way in which these concepts are explained would influence his personality formation—one based on independence and confidence, the other on fear.

Due to socio-political factors, the education of a large number of Muslims is in madarsas. Gurumurthy (2000) states, "A *madarsa* is a nursery run by Muslim theologians for children. Together with verses from the *Quran*, these children are taught that the only truth is the divine truth taught in the *Quran*, and the *Hadith*. Virtue lay in unthinking obedience". The effect of this is apparent, as one sees the glaring difference between what the *Quran* says, and the functioning of Islamic society today. Their unwavering stance of referring back to an era when Islam was the purest—i.e. during the period of the Prophet and the four caliphs, harks back to a time when the rules were laid down to meet the exigencies of the social situation during *that* period. To demand that contemporary society too lives according to those rules is a retrograde step. The contemporary Indian Muslim may be living in a no mans land where he is taught to have total faith and belief in one thing, and on the other, he observes situations in a rapidly changing society that are contrary to the interpretations of his faith, as are presented to him. He may thus opt to become a true believer of his faith—leading to a strict adherence to his group identity, or he may choose to distance himself from the communal life, but still adhere to his faith and belief in *Allah*.

Titus (1959, p. 200) states, "The faithful were warned (by the *Maulvis*) that the end of "western" education was sure and certain infidelity, and that those who attended such schools, or permitted their sons to do so, would be accounted apostates. Even life itself was threatened in order to prevent the introduction of such a serious innovation, with all its implications for the religion of Islam, as viewed by the conservatives. The result of this attitude on the part of the learned leaders of the community was that for many decades, Muslims in India fell farther and farther behind their Hindu compatriots in the matter of education. For, the latter were not at all slow to avail themselves of new educational facilities, and to adapt themselves to changing circumstances".

This absence of a broad based, liberal, scientific education prevents the Muslim youth from having a holistic picture of life in present times. His worldview, and hence himself, would be like the proverbial frog in the well, considering just the sky above his head as the entire universe. This, in fact, holds true for any group with a narrow perception of the world in present times.

Although the Islamic way of thought presents answers to righteous living, the reality and experience of the Islamic way of life is far from the injunctions and beliefs of the *Quran*. This dichotomy between learning and experience is observed in the lives of individual Muslims and Islamic societies. Larger socio-political factors have obliterated the democratic way of life that the *Quran* prescribes. As expressed by Engineer, (2001), "The *ulama*, who interpreted the *Quran* and the *Hadith*, did so under the influence of feudal values. Many of them went against the spirit of Islam and justified the feudal hierarchy. The few who resisted were isolated and lost out. The *ulama* support (and control) ruling establishments and use Islam to legitimize authoritarian rule. Any movement for human rights is condemned as a western conspiracy against Islam, although human dignity and freedom of conscience are central to the teachings of the *Quran*". He rightly pleads that "Muslim intellectuals must reflect on why Muslim countries have not been able to usher in true democracy, despite the claim that Islam is democratic in spirit".

Equality and brotherhood of all mankind forms the basis of Islam, although gender equality does not form a part of this. Over the years the shape of this equality has taken a different form. In the social sphere, the influence of Hinduism on Islam has nowhere left a more definite mark than in the creation of caste distinctions, which indicate social status as clearly as they do in Hindu society. This, together with the religious divisions, which are undoubtedly more numerous here than in any other country of the Muslim world. The implications for the individual are just as many, as the atrocities meted out in the name of caste and class distinctions.

According to Engineer (1992), the *Quran* was the first scripture to have conceded so many rights to women and that too in a period when women were much oppressed in the major civilizations. Yet, later Islamic jurists drew much from the Arabic traditions and resorted to formulations, which curtailed, if not trampled upon, women's rights. The *Quran* never intended to place undue restrictions on the movements of women, nor did it require them to completely hide their faces while moving out of the house. Yet, the leading jurists required women not to move out of their houses except in an emergency and even to have their faces covered. The rights given by the *Quran* were taken away by the jurists in view of their situation and yet these *shari'ah* rules are enforced even today when the context has changed.

To give an idea of how women came to lose the social status given them by Islam in latter-day Islamic society, Shaykh, (1964), illustrates what an ideal woman was thought to be. 'An ideal woman speaks and laughs rarely and never without a reason. She never leaves the house, even to see her neighbours or her acquaintance. She has no women friends, confides in nobody, and relies only on her husband. She accepts nothing from anyone, excepting her husband and her parents. If she sees relatives, she does not meddle in their affairs. She is not treacherous, and has no faults to hide, nor wrong reasons to proffer. She does not try to entice people. If her husband shows the intention of performing conjugal rites, she is agreeable to satisfy his desires and occasionally rouses them. She always assists him in his affairs. She does not complain much and sheds few tears. She does not laugh or rejoice when she sees her husband moody or sorrowful, but shares his troubles, and cheers him until he is quite content again. She does not surrender herself to anybody but her husband, even if abstinence would kill her. Everyone cherishes such a woman'.

Engineer (1992), comments "The woman does not have an existence of her own. The *Quran* does not approve of this. It gave her an independent existence of her own and an active role in life in her own right. It is unfortunate that in Islamic society, women are seen only in their medieval image, not in the revolutionary Islamic image portrayed in the *Quran*". Thus, in Islamic society too, the women live in a schizoid world of personal needs and social ideals.

The *Quran* itself states that man has been given both aspects of good and vile within him. The implication being that there is no "pristine pure" state of man. Aiming for pristine purity is aiming to become God. Man has to live within the bounds of his nature. He has the choice to decide what aspect of his nature plays the greater role in his life—the good or the bad. Whatever he chooses, according to Islam, he will bear the consequences in hell or heaven, before moving on to the next state of life.

NOTE

1. Although at an abstract level, one can well understand this as functioning according to the laws of nature. But this form of abstraction would surely come from a more sophisticated intellect. For the man with a normal level of intellectual thought processing, this may well take on as an injunction from a more "anthropomorphic" form of God. This would be further substantiated by the beliefs in ginns and angels, and the other more directive injunctions given by God, and further supplemented by the spectre of God waiting on the Day of Judgement, reviewing his records and sending him to heaven or hell. As the description of both these places are quite vivid, belief in nature is bound to be overtaken by a belief in an unseen anthropomorphic being.

7

Sikhism

Sikhism began with the teachings of Guru Nānak Dev (1469—1539 A. D.). This new religion was nurtured by nine other Gurus who succeeded him: Guru Angad (1539—1552 A.D.), Guru Amar Das (1552—1574 A.D.), Guru Ram Das (1574—1581 A.D.), Guru Arjan Dev (1581—1606 A. D.), Guru Hargobind (1606—1644 A. D.), Guru Har Rai (1644—1661 A. D.), Guru Har Krishan (1661—1664 A. D.), Guru Tegh Bahadur (1664—1675 A. D.). After the establishment of the *Khalsa* (1699), Guru Gobind Singh (1675—1708 A.D.) the tenth Guru ended the line of living Gurus and conferred Guruship on the *Guru Granth Sahib* or the *shabad* or the 'Word' of the Lord.

A superficial survey of the literature might well suggest that the pattern of Sikh history, like its contemporary expression, is simple and straightforward. This impression should be dispelled, for they misrepresent both the pattern of Sikh history and the nature of modern Sikh society. Historical antecedents and contemporary realities are both much more complex than the stereotype would suggest (McLeod, 1996).

During the time of Guru Nanak, the conventional patterns of religion did not command universal acceptance. Customary religion had numerous challenges and of the dissenting movements, three were of particular importance. There was, first, the tradition of *Vaishnav bhakti* which had spread to Northern India from the south, and which in the north was associated, above all other names with Ramanand. For *bhakti* (devotion) the essential religious response was love, and in *Vaishnav bhakti* this love was directed to one of the *avatars* of Vishnu. Secondly, there was the ancient tradition of *tantric* yoga, expressed in northern India during this period by the numerous adherents of the Nath sect of yogis. Thirdly there were the members of the Sufi orders, numerically far fewer than the adherents of orthodox Islam, but exercising a perceptible influence on the religious thought and practice of Hindus and Muslims. Emerging from this confluence of influences was the *Sant* tradition of Northern India. According to McLeod (1976), it was this *Sant* tradition that provided the basis of Guru Nanak's thought, an inheritance that he interpreted in the light of his own personality and experience. In addition to these is the dominant influence of Islam, as this was the period when Punjab was under Islamic rule. However, there is wide spread disagreement regarding the question of the relative impact of Hinduism and Islam, and the notion of "syncretism" of these two traditions (Singh, 1976). While some authors confidently portray Sikhism as being more of a redeemed Hindu religion (Wing-tsit, C. et al, 1969, Bradley, 1963) other authors assert a greater influence of Islam than of Hinduism (Hutchinson, 1969; Smart, 1976).

Many Sikhs look at their religion not as a philosophy of synthesis but as a new, revealed religion with little debt to the existing traditions. According to this tradition, Guru Nanak's revelation came directly from God. He had a direct vision of the truth and the very first words he uttered after the revelation were: "I am neither a Hindu nor a Muslim." His statements show his belief that God had commanded him to preach an entirely new religion, the central idea of which was the brotherhood of man and the fatherhood of God, shorn of ritualism and priest craft. He conveyed his message to the world in the common language of the land. This was in contrast to the scriptural languages like Sanskrit and Pali, which were not known to the masses. He introduced the *Gurmukhi* script to provide a simple medium for the communication of ideas. Sikhism is, therefore a distinct religion, which has its own scripture, its own sacred city, its founder, and the line of Gurus (Mansukhani, 1968; McLeod, 1976; Singh, 1997b).

Singh (1997) states, "Clearly, religions or any philosophic systems for that matter do not arise in a vacuum. A novel fresh way of living must reflect on the old even if only to reject it but in that process becomes influenced by what it has rejected. Therefore in most beliefs and practices, a pattern of continuity between the old and the new is never very difficult to discern" (p. 24).

Alongside this rich matrix of religious thought were the political upheavals and constant strife with Muslim invaders and the Mughal Empire, and subsequently its strife with the British invaders. Thus, in its brief five hundred years history, the Sikhs fought with zeal against foreign invaders to maintain the sovereignty of the nation. In addition, in its most recent history, the battle with the Indian government culminating with the attack on the Golden Temple by the Indian army in 1984.

Guru Nanak was a Khatri of the Bedi sub-caste and that accordingly he belonged to a respected family. He was brought up in a Punjab village and his growth to manhood took place during a relatively settled period. In McLeod's (1976) analysis, it meant "a life dictated by the agricultural nature of the village economy and consequently by the seasonal round characteristic of rural Punjab. It would have been a round of contrasting cold and heat, of labor in the fields and enforced rest during the months of summer barrenness, of the striking resurrection of the land of the men's spirits with the breaking of the monsoon rains, and of the regular festivals marking the high points in this annual cycle. All of this would inevitably have constituted the stuff of his childhood experiences" (p. 228)

The sources for the life of Guru Nanak are generally unreliable. Much of the information is gleaned from the *janam sakhis* or the traditional biographies. He was born in 1469 and grew up in his father's village of Talvandī, a village in Sheikhupure district, 65 kms., West of Lahore. His father was a village official in the local revenue administration. As a boy he learned, besides the regional languages, Persian and Arabic.

He was married in 1487 and was blessed with two sons. In 1485 he moved to the town of Sultānpur where he secured employment in the service of the Muslim ruler Daulat Khan Lodhi, as an official in charge of stores. From Sultanpur he began a period of travels within and perhaps beyond India (McLeod, 1976; Singh, 1997b).

By all accounts, 1496 was the year of his enlightenment when he started on his mission. He traveled extensively, visiting numerous places of Hindu and Muslim worship. He spent twenty-five years of his life preaching from place to place. Many of his hymns were composed during this period. They represent answers to the major religious and social problems of the day and cogent responses to the situations and incidents that he came across. Numerous miracles are attributed to him during his travels. During these tours, he studied other religious systems like Hinduism, Jainism, Buddhism, and Islam. At the same time, he preached the doctrines of his new religion and mission at the places and centers he visited. Since his mystic system almost completely reversed the trends, principles, and practices of the then prevailing religions, he criticized and rejected virtually all the old beliefs, rituals, and harmful practices existing in the country. This explains the necessity of his long and arduous tours and the variety and profusion of his hymns on all the religious, social, political, and theological issues, practice and institutions of his period. Finally, on the completion of his tours, he settled as a peasant farmer in the village of Kartarpur on the bank of the Ravi River, and it was there that he died, probably in the year 1539 (McLeod, 1976; Singh, 1997b).

The adherents of the Sikh faith were drawn mainly from the Khatri and Jat society. The Khatris are an urban-based mercantile community, some of whose members are to be found living in villages. Trade has been their distinctive occupation, although many are to be found in administration, clerical employment, and industry. In contrast, the Jat are a rural and agrarian community consisting largely of peasants and landlords. Although the two communities belong largely to Punjab, representatives of both have migrated elsewhere in India and overseas, mainly to U.K., Canada and U.S.A. Thus, within the *Panth* leadership drawn from a mercantile community (Khatri) secured a substantial and increasing following drawn from an agrarian (Jat) community. This Jat incursion was of considerable importance in the evolution of the *panth*, particularly for the development, which took place during the seventeenth and eighteenth centuries. Thus, conventional values of Jats, Khatris, and others will be evident in the Sikh community.

A theology of Guru Nanak as opposed to Sikh theology must omit the contributions of Guru Amar Das, Guru Ram Das, Guru Arjan, and Guru Gobind Singh, and of concepts, which evolved during the eighteenth century. In the case of the third, fourth, and fifth Gurus the omission concerns amplifications that are certainly valuable, particularly Guru Arjan, which involve no significant modification of the pattern, set out by the first Guru. With Guru Gobind Singh, however, comes the institution of the *Khalsa panth*, and finally with his death in 1708, and the consequent termination of the line of the personal Gurus, the function of the Guru had been vested in the scripture (the *Adi Granth* or *Guru Granth Sahib*) and in the corporate community (the *Khalsa panth*). For modern Sikhism the scripture exists as a channel of communication between God and man, but obviously, this could be no part of Guru Nanak's theology. It must be understood, however, that this doctrine, its significance notwithstanding, is no more than a supplement to the teaching imparted by Guru Nanak. The theology of Guru Nanak remains the substance of Sikh belief (McLeod, 1976).

What is Sikhism?

The word "Sikh" is derived from the Sanskrit *"shishya"*, which means 'disciple'. Sikhism is an evolutionary theory about the spirituo-empirical development of man. It is not an institutional religion as greatest emphasis has been laid on the evolution of Moral Conscience (Guru) of man, i.e. on the Individual Morality as against Collectivism. The Society of Man of Moral Conscience has been praised. The Gurus laid down the path on which to tread. The tenth Guru defined Khalsa as the "Man of Moral Conscience" or the "Pure One". It does not refer to any religious community. It is truly said that a society has no conscience, but a 'Society of Conscientious Men' is a 'Society with Conscience', which is the only holy association, worthy of all praise (Singh, 1979; Singh, 1997d).

The *Adi Granth* or *Sri Guru Granth Sahib* is the religious scripture of the Sikhs as well as Guru eternal for them. The basic words in the expressions listed is *'granth'* meaning a book, *'sahib'* and *'sri'* being honorifics, *'gurū'* indicating its status as a successor in the gurū-ship after Guru Gobind Singh, and *'Adi'*, literally original, first or primary. The *Guru Granth Sahib* is an anthology of the sacred compositions of the gurūs and some of the medieval Indian saints. The latter came from a variety of class and creedal background—Hindu as well as Muslim, high caste as well as low caste. One criterion for choosing their verses for the *Guru Granth Sahib* apparently was its tone of harmony with the teachings of the gurūs. Guru Arjun, the fifth Guru, prepared the anthology in 1603–4. To it were added by Guru Gobind Singh, the tenth gurū, the compositions of Guru Tegh Bahadur, the ninth gurū. Even before the time of Guru Arjun, *'pothis'* or books in *Gurmukhi* characters existed containing the holy utterances of the gurūs. The Sikhs held the *'bani'* or word revealed in great veneration even before the *Guru Granth* was compiled. It was equated with the guru himself. Guru Arjun (A.D. 1563–1606) prepared the sacred volume, and the first copy was calligraphed by Bhai Gurdas (1551–1636) (Singh, H., 1997).

The authors of the *bani*, poet-philosophers as they were, were themselves non-conformists and unconventional in their outlook. This applies more particularly to Guru Nanak and Sant Kabir—whose poetry constitutes the core of the *Guru Granth's* thought—content. The ethical principles, values, and obligations that have found exposition in the *Gurbani*, presented as they are through the medium of poetry, are not to be found in any definitive logical pattern or order, but are free expression of the poetic minds. One has to glean ethical elements from *Gurbani* and place them in a system, classification, or framework, according to one's light (Singh, 1981).

Since they were conveying their message to the mass of the people both Hindus and Muslims, with a view to evoking a response in the very depths of their hearts, they have for obvious reasons, used in their hymns the then current words and symbols from Indian, Persian and Arabic languages. And yet, one thing is patent even from a cursory study of the *Guru Granth Sahib* that the Gurus have, as was essential for the proper understanding of a new gospel, made the meaning of each concept, symbol and term employed by them, unambiguously clear (Singh, 1997c).

The making of the *Granth* was no easy task. It involved sustained labor and a rigorous intellectual discipline. Selections had to be made from a vast amount of material. Besides the compositions of the four preceding Gurus and of Guru Arjun who himself was a poet with a rare spiritual insight, there were songs and hymns by saints, both Hindu and Muslim. The genuine had to be sifted from the counterfeit. Then the selected material had to be assigned to appropriate musical measures and transcribed in a minutely laid out order. A precise method was followed in setting down the compositions. First came the *shabads* by the Gurus in the order of their succession. Then came *chhands*, *vars*, and other poetic forms in a set order. The compositions of the Gurus in each *rāgā* were followed by those of the *bhaktas* (devotees) in the same format. *Gurmukhi* was the script used for the transcription (Singh, H., 1997).

In the Sikh system, the word Guru is used only for the ten prophet-preceptors—Guru Nanak to Guru Gobind Singh, and for none other. Now the *Guru Granth Sahib* fulfills this office, which was so apotheosized by the last Guru, Guru Gobind Singh, before he passed away in 1708. No living person, however holy or revered, can have the title or status of Guru. For Sikhs, Guru is the holy teacher, the prophet under direct commission from God—the ten who have been and *Guru Granth Sahib*, which is their continuing visible manifestation (Singh, H., 1997).

The development of Sikhism was marked by an event, which took place on a particular day in the year 1699. The tenth Guru, Gobind Singh, having observed the growing hostility of both the hill rulers of the neighboring areas and the Mughal authorities, and having reflected upon the weakness of his followers, reached a momentous decision. This decision he put into effect during the *Baisakhi* festival of 1699, and the result was the founding of the *Khalsa Panth*. The *Khalsa* is best described as an order, as a society possessing a religious foundation and a military discipline. The religious base was already in existence and a military tradition had been developed, but something much stronger was required. The military aspect had to be fused with the religious, and this Guru Gobind Singh achieved by promulgating the 'Order of the *Khalsa*' (McLeod, 1996).

The Guru gave the *Khalsa* the social ideal of equality and close brotherhood. There was to be no distinction of birth, caste, class, or color. All were equal in social status, and had the same rights and privileges. He, thus, enunciated the principles of liberty, equality, and fraternity. He gave them names with the suffix *'Singh'*, meaning lion. The giving of the name 'Singh', which was current among Hindu martial classes, to all men was a step to eliminate the caste identification as a person's caste could be identified by his surname. With the standard surname, the 'Singhs' became one family. Sikh women were similarly given the common suffix *'Kaur'* (princess). He made them take on an oath to observe the five "k's": The *'kesh'* or long hair—the most reasonable explanation for this symbol is that Guru Gobind Singh desired to provide his *Khalsa* a natural military uniform, the least expensive and most impressive permanent costume. Besides, he deemed it necessary that their heads should be properly guarded from sword cuts and *"lathī"* (rod) blows by means of long hair and turbans. *"Kanghā"* or comb, indicated cleanliness. *"Kirpān"* or dagger, depicted power and prestige. The *kirpān* emphasizes two important principles, which the Guru wants the Sikhs to remember, namely, his duty to confront injustice and oppression, and second to stop him from escape into withdrawal and monasticism. *"Karā"* or steel bangle developed an iron will and destroyed evil effects of misfortune. It was a permanent substitute of *"rākhi"*, a thread tied by a sister on the wrists of brothers, reminding them of their duty to help and protect them, and a reminder of the promise made to the Guru and the *panth*. And *"kachha"* or a pair of knickerbockers aimed at agility, as it was more convenient than the long *dhoti* of Hindus and the loose trousers of Muslims. These symbols gave the *Khālsā* a semblance of unity, brotherhood, and equality. They developed group consciousness (Singh, 1976; Singh, 1997d; Gupta, 1997).

The *Khālsā* was required not to do five things: to shave or cut hair, to smoke, to eat halal meat of the animal killed in the Muslim style, to wear a cap, and to worship tombs, graves, relics of cremation and cherish superstitions (Singh, 1997d; Gupta, 1997).

Guru Gobind Singh declared the following five deliverances for his disciples: *Dharam Nāsh* or freedom from previous religious practices and customs; *Karam Nāsh* or the obliteration of the past bad deeds; *Janam Nāsh* or giving up the family influences and caste effects; *Sharam Nāsh* or the disappearance of hereditary professional distinctions as all the callings were given equal respect and status, *Bharam Nāsh* or discarding the rituals prescribed by previous practices. The five rules of conduct for the general observance of the Sikhs: before beginning every work or enterprise, prayer should be offered, they should help one another and serve the *panth*; they should practice riding and using arms, a Sikh coveting another's property would go to hell; Regarding sexual matters the Guru advocated faithfulness to one's wife (Gupta, 1997).

Different sects in Sikhism have developed, based on the traditions that the followers adhere to, their characteristic attitudes towards the *panth* and their role within it. The *sahaj-dhāri* (or *Nanak panthi*) are those who do not emphasize the Sikh identity as a means of enhancing social or ritual state. They follow the Guru, but are not *amrit-dhāri*, (*Khālsā panthi*), i.e. baptized into the *Khālsā*. The *amrit-dhāri* Sikhs are baptized into the *Khālsā* and are adherents to the rules of the *Khālsā* (Singh, 1976).

Sikhism is a whole life, a *"miri-piri"* or *"sant—sipāhi"* (saint—soldier) religion. The terms are synonymous and convey a single concept, and not a combination of two concepts. For, the Guru's concept of God or spirituality is incomplete or partial without an essential and inalienable combination of the spiritual life with the empirical life. Spirituality and its attributes have to be expressed in and to enrich the latter. Empirical life without drawing moral sap from the former remains egoistic, chaotic, and barren. In Guru Nanak's system, God himself is engaged in the socio-spiritual development of man. He does not want the spiritual man to withdraw to Him, but wants him to be the agent of his altruistic will. Man has not been left alone by God to fight lone battles with evil. He is a benevolent helper, enabling man to remove and shed his imperfections resulting from egoism at the present level. The spiritual man, as stated by Guru Nanak has to ferry others across the turbulent sea of life. The concept of personal salvation, as in some other religions, by withdrawing from the empirical life is distinctly denied (Singh, 1997d).

Basic Principles of Sikh Philosophy

Sikhism is a monotheistic faith. It recognizes God as the only One. God is the creator and the universe is his creation. The universe is in time and space. It is changing and is governed by fixed laws. The Creator is different from the creation, which is limited and conditioned. As Creator, God is free. Any laws known to man do not determine Him. He is not the material cause of the universe. But, no independent *prakriti* is assumed. "God created the world of life, planted *"Naam"* (Immanent God) therein, and made it the seat of righteousness" (Mansukhani, 1977; Singh, 1997a).

In the Sikh scriptures, emphasis has solely been laid on the functional qualities of God and nowhere has God been described in a particular form. Guru Nanak in the prologue to *Japji* (the words of the *Guru Granth Sahib*) has defined God as "One God, Who is unchanging and immutable, Whose Name is Reality, the Creative Personality, without fear and without enmity. He is Immortal, Unborn, self Existent, one can find union with Him through evolution of Moral Conscience (Guru)." He is defined as *karta purkh*—the Creative Personality. Personality exists where there is intelligence, mind, will, reason, individuality, self-consciousness, and self-determination (McLeod, 1976; Singh, 1979).

God is both Transcendent and Immanent. He is both in the Universe and outside it. While time, space, and change are features of the becoming universe, God is eternal, self-existent. He cannot be conceived or explained in empirical terms. He is beyond time and beyond space. The Immanent aspect of God has been variously described as His Will that directs the universe, His Word that informs the universe, and his *Naam* that not only creates the entire universe but also sustains and governs it. God creates the universe and becomes Immanent in it, being at the same time Transcendent. This Immanence of God is only a symbolic way of expressing God's connection with the world (McLeod, 1976; Singh, 1979).

The Gurus call God the "Ocean of Attributes, Values, and Virtues." This aspect of God is of importance in indicating the spiritual and moral trends and the character of Sikhism. A God of attributes lays down the ideals for which man has to work (McLeod, 1976; Singh, 1979).

Everything is governed by His Will. Just like the Attributes of God, Gods Will, too, can be exercised only in a changing world and towards a goal. The very idea of a Will implies a direction and an aim. Natural laws are indeed acknowledged and regarded as a significant part of God's communication with mankind. They are not, however, the ultimate basis for behind them lays a will that is expressed in terms of decision of giving and withholding. Without this divine grace, a man is helpless. If, however, God chooses to impart it the way of salvation lies open (McLeod, 1976; Singh, 1979).

God has been described as one who never takes birth, nor takes form. All pantheistic ideas as flowing from the idea of reincarnation are repudiated. There are three other corollaries to this concept. The first is that man can never become god and that god and man are not identical. Secondly, it indicates that the aim of spiritual effort is not merger in God, as in other systems, but to be in tune with Him. This has a crucial significance in determining the human goal, and in showing that the entity of man is distinct from that of God. The two can never be one, though man can be his instrument. Thirdly, it shows that spiritual activity does not stop after the final achievement, as he has a role to perform in carrying out the Will of God (Singh, 1997a).

God has been called Gracious and Enlightener. A God of Will and a God of Grace have a meaning only in a becoming world, wherein alone, His Grace and Will can operate (Singh, 1997a).

The Sikh Gurus have given the word *"Naam"* a distinct and significant meaning, which is far different from that of the mere *"naam"* or psychic factors as understood in the traditional literature. Since *Naam*, Gods' Immanence, has not only created the world, but is also supporting, controlling and directing it, the same cannot be unreal or illusory. In fact, *Naam's* immanence in this world guarantees its being a place of righteous activity and not being a fruitless, unwanted or capricious creation. According to the *Guru Granth Sahib*, it is not *naam* and *samsara* (world) that are opposed, but *naam* and *haumain* (egoism); it is not worldly activity as such that has to be given up, but it is only egoistic, and selfish activities that have to be shed (Singh, 1997c; Singh, 1997a).

Naam is the only real basis of Morality without any religion. God is infinite and the Gurus do not impose any limitations in realizing him. *Naam* is the total participation of the self and is Spontaneous (Singh, 1979).

Naam makes us free from all types of bondage. We begin to act freely and express our opinion in favor of truth, justice, and fair play. We reject all types of compulsions and accept no coercion. To be free means to do what one loves to do. A godly man will always love Truth and act truthfully. *Naam* therefore is the highest form of experience of Truth and Freedom, while compulsion and coercion are its opposites. Where there is *naam* there is no coercion and domination or undue submission. The greater the experience of *naam* in anyone, the greater is the moral courage and freedom in him. A man who loves all humanity is the truly free man in this Universe. Such a man at the same time is not afraid of anything. He cannot be intimidated, bribed, or beaten into submission. This is the only true way of established relationships with fellow human beings, i.e. based on love, equality, and freedom (Singh, 1979).

The Sikh doctrine of *"māyā"* points out the impossibility of grasping the actual world in the verbal net of man's mind and the fluid character of those very constructions he creates.

Guru Nanak bāni presents *"māyā"* from the objectivist as well as the subjectivist points of view. Firstly, as in common parlance, the term *māyā* denotes wealth or riches. An individual engrossed in the worldly possessions is *māyādhari*, who remains oblivious of the spiritual aspect of life. Secondly, attractions of the worldly life in general are characterized as *māyā*. Thirdly the phenomenal world or the universe itself is *māyā*, which is identical with nature at all levels—physical, biological, mental,—created and established by the Divine ordinance. This view depicts *māyā* at the height of objectivity, as a living, operating, seemingly endless, and colorful world of names and forms. Human consciousness, which is a part of the phenomenal world of *māyā*, not only mirrors this world, but engages itself in the un-covering of its depths and the discovering of its truths. In the Nanak-*bāni*, one prominent subjective aspect of *māyā* is the passionate self of man, his sensuous, possessive, egoistic nature. Another aspect is represented by human attachment with the world—the *moha-māyā* or infatuations that prevent man from rising above his individuality and relativity (Singh, 1981).

Thus, *māyā* and nature (*qudrat*) seem identical in the Nānak-*bāni*. The world of nature may be taken as *māyā* incarnate, denying any special or extraordinary existence to *māyā*. This amounts to asserting that the world exists in its own right as established by Divine Will, and not as a product of some supposed intermediary, namely *māyā*. It also means that the order of nature is not to be considered as illusion, pure and simple. We must not associate any real value with the phenomenal world, because as the teaching goes, it is neither ever lasting nor eternal. However, it may be 'illusory' in the sense that it appears to us permanent, whereas its real status is that of creation. Accordingly, the world is not rejected as illusion in the Nanak-*bāni*. It is the *qudrat* (creation) of the *Qādir* (creator) whose creativity is not in doubt anywhere in the *bāni* (Singh, 1981).

This interpretation of the concept of *māyā* in Sikh terminology has far-reaching consequences. It pulls the Hindu mind out of the slough of indolent introspective pre-occupation, and subjectivism, generated by the belief that the whole world of the appearances in which man is born to pursue his socio-political life, is no more real than a phantasmagoria in the minds of the gods above. By giving a foundation of solid reality to the world of appearance, this re-interpretation of the concept of *māyā* conforms to a sense of reality, feeling of urgency, and objectivity to the whole frame of mind of man. This is necessary for the all-out effort to speed up the evolutionary process through the human will, and this is the core of the percepts of Sikhism, as a way of life. This concept of *māyā* does not impel a man to renounce the world and is not inimical to economic pursuits (Kaur, 1990; Singh, K., 1997).

The *Vārāsā* hymn, (*Guru Granth Sahib*, p. 464) refers to the acts of eating, drinking, and dressing; to all worldly affections; to the colorful phenomena of life and its species; to virtue and vice, to ego and pride, to air and water, fire and earth. This description by itself and in itself is a poetic transcript of the philosophic conception of nature as the sole category of reality, postulated in modern naturalism. The point of departure is the attribution in the hymn, to the powers of nature to the supernatural master, whose ordinance prevails in the order of nature (Singh, 1981).

Sikhism upholds belief in the doctrine of *karma*. Man is held morally responsible for his deeds and accordingly rewarded or punished. Simultaneously, the Sikh doctrine also holds that man's actions are causally chained to his character that in turn is carved out of his heredity, experience, and his social environment. Man acts according to his nature. If it is so, he cannot be held responsible for his actions since he acts within the 'determined' limits. Alongside, God also endows him with the autonomous power of free will or choice. He is capable of exercising this choice independently of his nature. Thus, he is constantly reminded in the *Gurbāni* to exercise this choice rightly and make his own destiny. To the extent that man chooses and acts independently of his nature, i.e. his desires, habits, and perspectives of life, he is responsible for his actions. The autonomous power of free choice is the divinity in man or the inner voice of conscience that guides him through life. Man comes to know the Will of God through it (Kaur, 1990).

The use of human rationality and a sense of discrimination have a distinct place in moral life. Sikh theology being non deterministic, man has a distinct moral freedom and responsibility in the choice of his actions. It is this exercise of right choice that determines his spiritual progress. For the moral life of man two virtues, namely humility and love find the highest priority in the Guru's ethical system and the discipline prescribed for the seeker (Singh, 1997a).

Sikhism thus proclaims the dynamic reality and authenticity of the world and life. The world being real, creative work and virtuous deeds are of fundamental importance. This emphatic assertion of the reality of the world is a clear departure from the Indian religious tradition. The Gurus were extremely conscious of this radical and fundamental change they were making. That is why, both in their lives and in their hymns, they have been laying stress on this aspect of their spiritual thesis, lest they should be misunderstood on this basic issue. Living in this world is not bondage for them but a rare opportunity. In India, generally the householder's duties were not believed to be conducive to higher spiritual attainments. That is why one had to renounce worldly activities and take to the life of a hermit or *Sanyāsi*. For the Gurus, the world is a place of beauty. Man's struggle therein provides an opportunity for his progress. Hence the arena of man's and the mystic's work has to be in life and life alone. A householder's life is an essential moral responsibility of man. The seekers' training has to take place during the course of a moral life and not in a monastery. The psyche can be properly conditioned only when it is subject to the stresses and strains of the social environment of man. It is his deeds in the world that alone form the basis of his spiritual assessment. The Guru therefore emphasizes that 'one gets not to God by despising the world' (Singh, 1997a).

The prejudices against women and castes, idleness of yogis and ascetics, hypocrisy of priests and Brahmins, and inequalities in the economic field and the amassing of wealth have been condemned. Similarly in the political field, the oppression of the rulers, the tyranny of the invaders, and the corruption of the officials have been deprecated (Singh, 1997a).

Action and activity, howsoever good, involve the use of force, because action and force are synonymous. Action not involving force is a contradiction in terms. Therefore, except by some miracle, it is impossible to bring about a change in the social or institutional environment without the use of requisite force. Immorality does not lie in the use of force, which is inevitable for all living, whether moral or immoral, but it lies in the direction or purpose for which force is used. As a prophet of a new religion he made it once and for all plain that, so long as one worked in the midst of social life, all arbitrary prejudices against meat-eating or the use of force as such were wrong and meaningless. Both reason and force are neutral tools that can be used for good and evil, for construction and destruction. The Gurus unambiguously accept the use of both of them as the means of religious functioning and progress. In doing so, they made the major departure from the earlier *bhakti* and religious traditions (Singh, 1997a).

As far as human values are concerned, at least five intrinsic values are mentioned in *the Gurbāni*, which may be treated as the highest values of the Sikh faith.

1. *The secret of alphabet :* This is the value of the light of learning, of enlightenment, the promotion of which brings the glow of wisdom in one's life. *Gurbāni* accords an exalted place to learning and enlightenment. Without an awareness of the essence of existence and life, altogether deprived of intellectual endowment, without acquisition of a sense of language, and unable to decipher even 'letters of the alphabet' one cannot hope to follow the teachings of scriptures and cleanse the mind of sinful disposition (Singh, 1981).
2. *Humanism :* The humanism of *Gurbāni* is indicative of love for the divine, on one hand, and love for humanity and welfare of all the other. It offers a synthesis of humanism and theism. It is through reverence of humanity, through service and benevolence, through compassion and justice, that love of human beings becomes possible. It may take the form as the mutual love of wife and husband, which is made a symbol of the music of life for the Lord in

Gurbāni. The social and humanistic spirit of *Gurbāni* becomes amply clear from the advocacy of the virtues of forgiveness and compassion. *Gurbāni* commends the virtue of non-attachment, *not* renunciation. Another commandment repeated so often in *Gurbāni* is to renounce lust, wrath, covetousness, infatuation, and pride. These five evils flourish in the affliction that is egoism. Their cure lies in banishing the direction given by the passions and bringing the mind in tune with the Enlightener's teaching (Singh, 1981).

3. *Ecstasy :* The aesthetic value in *Gurbāni* is the value of the balanced state of the human mind, for which symbols like *sehaj* (equipoise), *ānand* (bliss), *vismad* (wonderment) have been employed. This state may result from the ecstasy of meditation on *Naam*, from treading the path of spiritual awareness, realizing the 'Absolute Truth' inside and outside and absorbing oneself in it. When the individual examines his body and being, when he has an insight into the inmost of his mind and finds the light of that very spirit present, when he recognizes his own 'essence' he obtains a uniform view of the light within and of nature's objects and forms without. It is in such a state of equipoise that all anguish and suffering vanish, the stage of *nirvana* is acquired, and the mystical awareness brings forth an experience of absolute blissfulness (Singh, 1981).

4. *Absolute consciousness :* Mystery of the Spirit, of which the individual's aesthetic sense produces a beatific state of ecstasy, the intuitional vision of the same mystery furnishes one with the highest knowledge, which the *Gurbāni* names *Brahman-Gyāni* (Absolute Consciousness). To the knowing individual endowed with intuitive insight, the secret of "drop in the ocean and ocean in the drop" opens up (Singh, 1981).

5. *Emancipation in life :* In terms of the *Gurbāni*

ideology, the state of emancipation in life may be regarded as the highest value and ideal of human life. Blissful ecstasy and absolute consciousness cannot be separated from this state. The individual who is liberated in life seeks nothing for his personal benefit, not even *mukti* or salvation—he longs only to be worthy of Lord's love. He has discovered a way of life that makes it possible to attain salvation even while one is engaged in playing and enjoying oneself, in eating and drinking, and dressing oneself—and this very course is the ideal way of life, according to the *Gurbāni*. This is not the ideal of spiritual peace attainable after death; this is the consummate style of life tempered with truthfulness (Singh, 1981).

The Self in Sikh Thought

The doctrine of *haumain* is basic to Sikh theology. *Haumain* is the "I" of the normal individual psyche. According to the Gurus the world came into being by individuation. Evidently, for the growth of life, this creation of an individual self, of *haumain* in every being was essential. There could be no animal life without there being in each organism a center of consciousness. *Haumain* has thus, enabled the evolution of life. Every man is equipped with many kinds of organs and faculties. These faculties, including his thoughts, are subservient to his individuality, self or ego. Throughout the evolution of life, this ego-center, or *haumain* has been the instrument and guardian of his security, welfare, and progress. Without a deep commitment to the interests, preservation and progress of the self, to the exclusion of every other being or self, life could never survive the battle against challenges from the environment. This ego, or *haumain*, has been the best means of securing the survival and the progress of life from amoeba to man. It is impossible for one's thought system, intellect, or reason to be anything but self-centered, the same being subservient to the individual self or ego-consciousness.

It is this organic condition of man that the Gurus call *haumain* or ego. Mans' consciousness being self-centered, he is constitutionally incapable of looking to the interests of others (Singh, 1997a).

The Moral Self in Man : It is "I" in a person that is conscious of both the behavior of the self and the behavior of others. The whole approach of Sikh teachings is the evolvement of a strong 'Moral self'. The Gurus make it clear how from the smallest speck of life, man has evolved after millions of years and myriads of births. Although man is mainly an animal, he is distinctly superior to other animals. His superiority lies in his two attributes that the other animals do not possess. First, in his sense of discrimination, i.e. his awareness of his own thinking process and his capacity to deliberate over his thinking. This clearly emphasizes that man has the sense of making judgment and choice, i.e. a moral sense to distinguish right from wrong. The Gurus state unambiguously that a social or civilized life is not possible unless man develops his internal discipline or moral life, which alone can make for progress of man in social life. The second superior attribute of man is that, although he is at present at the egoistic state of development, he has also the capacity to develop a link with the Universal Consciousness, the Basic Reality of Gods (Singh, 1979; Singh, 1997d).

Evolution of the Real Self in Man : Man is required to face the realities of life in a disciplined manner. He is to maintain the internal harmony by his objective and moral approach in his day-to-day dealings. Unbridled desire for acquisitiveness, uncontrolled and undisciplined indulgence in sensual pleasures and egocentric behavior result in impulsive living and destruction of an integrated personality. It is the voice of God within us, which guides us to lead a balanced and moral life. In this way the Real self in man is evolved. The basic requirement of the Real self is the self should be an object of examination to the self; it looks at itself as it looks at objects. It judges its own actions dispassionately and objectively and makes suitable amends. The Gurus in the *Guru*

Granth Sāhib repeatedly use the words *"aap apai nun khāyā"*—the self eats away the pseudo self. Good character cannot be found without effort. One needs to exercise constant self-watchfulness, self-discipline, and self-control under the guidance of the 'Moral Conscience'. This leads to the path of peace of mind, tranquility, harmony, pleasure, and inner strength (Singh, 1979).

The Voice of God is the "Will of God" : It is the Divine teacher or the "Sat Guru". The "Will of God" is not external will imposed on us, an arbitrary law framed by a heavenly tyrant, who is a stranger to us and does not know our nature and problems. "The Will of God" or the "Voice of the Moral Conscience" is precisely our "real being", the best in us, which is just, good, and approved by God. It is not a strange law that demands our obedience but the silent voice of our very selves. There is the dynamic effect of the environment on us in the sense it conditions us. However, this cannot create personality. In us is the dynamic self and the dynamic Moral Conscience. The self in union with the Moral Conscience will form the Dynamic Moral self, which can resist or even change the traditions and the social environment. This is one of the most vital differences between man and the lower animals. The lower animal can only modify itself and cannot influence others. Man with his rationality can bring about change in himself as well as the environment (Singh, 1979).

The Moral Conscience is developed not by implanting prohibitions against doing wrong but to develop love for good, honesty, and sincerity. There should be an internal urge to act righteously and truthfully, this is what is the positive conscience. If such a conscience is developed, the evil is avoided automatically and without repression. It makes possible deliberations and is a mature positive conscience. It coordinates and regulates our behavior and what is right and best comes out spontaneously. It has no regrets for not accruing the immediate material gains by adopting unfair means. The urge (morality) and the will (self) unite to form the moral self as one whole. What we ought to do and what we want to do coincide. There is no internal conflict between the self and Conscience. Conscience should therefore be an ally of the moral life and not its policeman. We should not be forced to conform to the moral code by the fear of punishment to do wrong, but should imbibe love for righteousness. This is the positive thinking. Freedom lies only in the spontaneous functioning of the total integrated personality. This *sehaj* or *achint* is the spontaneous activity as opposed to the compulsive activity due to the fear of freedom from the instinctual slavery. All other activities other than spontaneous activity are false, superficial, and mechanical (Singh, 1979).

Presently, man is at the *'manmukh'* (egoistic) state of consciousness, but he has the capacity to be linked with the Universal Consciousness, or to be a *'Gurmukh'* who works in line with the Fundamental Reality by being its instrument. The Gurus repeatedly state that at the *manmukh* stage, mans greatest malady that blocks his progress is his egoism or *haumain* consciousness. The struggle against the elements and environment having largely been won, man finds himself incapable of dealing with his own species. All his rational capacities and talents are still the equipment of the egoistic man, and for that matter, are governed by his ego-consciousness. His intellectual capacities being subservient to his ego, consciousness cannot be used for the benefit of another person. Just as a mans lungs cannot breathe for another person, his rational capacities cannot help being selfish, since they are directed by his ego-consciousness. The altruistic tendencies developed in man as the result of cultural conditioning over the years are only superficial or conditioned. Spontaneous altruism is constitutionally and psychologically impossible in the egocentric or *haumain* governed man. The moment the struggle for existence becomes keen, the basic self-centeredness of man comes into play. Thus, start all the conflicts of man, social as well as national and international. Hence, the fundamental importance of moral life in Sikhism, as it is the only spiritual means leading towards God Consciousness (Singh, 1997a; Singh, 1997d).

A truly moral person will never identify himself with supernatural powers or powerful persons to incorporate their magical powers within the self to become powerful. He will utilize the good part of his instinctual energy to develop the psychological processes of perceiving, learning, remembering, judging, discriminating, reasoning, and imagining. He tries to follow the instructions of the preceptor and tries to live up to the ideal. He is a man of moral convictions but never imitates or flatters others (Singh, 1979).

The progress from self-centeredness to God consciousness is progress from a virtually determined or a mechanistic state to a free and creative state. A moral act involves voluntary decision on the part of one's consciousness. It is the result of his free will or decision or choice. It is, thus, a clear step on the path from being determined to being free; it is an effort to rise from the state of *haumain* to the state of God Consciousness or creative freedom. It is, indeed, a spiritual act (Singh, 1997a).

The Gurus have explained their views about the spiritual goal of man by enunciating five principles. All of them point to the same conclusion about the ideal life. (a) The assessment of man, Guru Nanak says, will be made on the basis and character of his deeds. (b) Higher than truth is truthful living. It is just a symbolic way of emphasizing that the ideal is to live the active life of truth and not only to know 'Truth' as an end in itself. The goal is to live an active and creative life. According to *Gurbāni*, a practical life of truthfulness, fidelity, self-control and purity, is higher than the metaphysical truth. This is a virtue of truthful discipline and principled conduct. *Gurbāni* does not advocate a form of effort or activity that leads man to take pride in his own power and to disregard the potentialities of the Divine power. As an ethical virtue, effort provides the inspiration to "accomplish one's task through one's labor." This is a homily to the individual to "lead a life of effort and activity, and to enjoy oneself in earning one's livelihood." He, who exercises the virtue of effort, need not lead a life of dependence. Fortitude, valiance, or fearlessness is a cardinal virtue. (c) Guru Nanak specifically raises the question as to how one can be a true human being, or an ideal man. Then he himself provides the answer: "By carrying out the Will of God". The Gurus conceive of God as a God of Will, Dynamic, Attributive, and Creative. God is always nurturing the world with a benevolent eye. For man, the ideal life is to carry out His Will. The goal is not only to establish union with God, not only to know His Will, but after having done that to carry it out. The ideal is not blissful union as an end in itself, but union in order to be God's instrument or agent in the world. Therefore, in Sikhism it involves continuous moral activity. (d) All exhortations to man are to achieve ideal of God consciousness by the practice of virtues. (e) *Naam* is creative and attributive. *Naam* is working in the world with benevolence and love. This is the goal of Sikhism (Singh, 1981; Singh, 1997a).

The Sikh teachings are based upon the principle of creativity—to rely upon one's own powers. Man should not regress to the animal life of inertia and rest but should go forward and treat the whole life as a process of birth and strive for further progress and should not at any stage consider himself to have attained the finality. Creativity is the positive view of human behavior, while the negative is conflicting and restrictive behavior. In negative behavior, one does not respect the right of others for freedom and progress and jealousy stands in their way. This leads to unending conflicts in human relations. It is generally said that conflicts are harmful and hence they should be avoided. This is the escapist approach and is not a correct attitude as only confronting the evil boldly and not running away from it develop character. The situations that arise make us wise and give necessary immunity to resist the evil. If one avoids conflicts, he becomes a smoothly running machine. If all desires are met without any effort, then the feelings become flattened out. There is always the instinctual conflict going on within us. We transcend from the animal within us by self-awareness, imagination, and creativeness (Singh, 1979).

The Social Self

The implications of the *Gurbāni* follow logically in the percepts of social behavior. Guru Nanak emphasizes the social responsibilities of a Sikh. The primary responsibility is the acceptance of equality between man and woman in the religious and social field. Guru Nanak clearly states, "Why downgrade woman, when without woman there would be none." The Sikh Gurus were the first to raise their voices against sati, and they instituted widow remarriage. There is no activity within the Sikh religion reserved exclusively for men, nor is there any, which is closed to them. This is important to note because in many religions a woman may not read the scriptures, lead the prayers, or perform many of the other priestly functions, particularly if she is menstruating. There is no ritual purification ceremony required of her once a month. If in a Sikh service men and women sit on separate sides, it is based on custom, culture and tradition, and not canon (Singh, I. J., 1997).

The second responsibility is of maintaining equality between man and man. This was a direct blow to the social ideology of *varnāshram dharma*, which gave scriptural sanction to the hierarchical caste system. All are expected to share of the *karah prasād* and the *langar* (food served from the community kitchen of a Gurudwārā) regardless of the their own caste or of the food sources of the offering. This ensures that high castes consume food received, in effect, from the hands of lower castes or even outcastes and that they do so from a common dish.

The third social responsibility that Guru Nanak emphasizes is the importance of work to sustain life. A total participation in life and social responsibility in all fields are desired. The rejection of asceticism, monasticism, *sanyāsa* and celibacy, and instead the acceptance of a householder's life, and the necessary creation of a society concerned with the socio-political problems of man.

The fourth social responsibility Guru Nanak stresses is about the sharing of wealth. Thus, Guru Nanak stresses the twin ideas about the brotherhood of man, the sharing of wealth to eliminate poverty and maintain equality in society.

The fifth social responsibility, where Guru Nanak radically departed from all the contemporary religious systems, including Sufism, Santism, and Christianity, was his approach towards injustice and oppression of all kinds in society. He pointed out the greed and hypocrisy of Brahmin priests and Mullahs, the blood thirsty corruption and injustice by lower and higher rung officials in the administrations, the misrule, oppression and irresponsibility of the local rulers, their inability to give security, fairplay and peace to the people, and brutal and barbaric butchery of the people. This was an assessment of the prevailing turmoil and conditions in society, which the Guru felt needed to be changed. In Guru Nanak's ideology there was nothing like private personal salvation. Just as God of Love is benevolently looking after the entire world, in the same way, the godman's sphere of activity and responsibility is equally wide, and is unhedged by any self-created barriers. This is the fundamental difference between a salvation in religions catering for individuals and a universal religion catering for the spiritual well-being of society as a whole (McLeod, 1996; Singh, 1997e).

The Emotions in Sikh Thought

There are two main types of instincts, which all living beings are endowed with—the Life instinct and the Death instinct. Guru Nanak called the Life Instinct as *sanjog* (union) and death instinct as *vinjog* (separation). Guru Nanak in *japji* states, "God has implanted in man the Life Instinct and the Death Instinct, and thus exercises His Will on him." Life Instinct drives the individual to all the positive manifestations of life, of reciprocal attraction, union, and constructiveness. This finds expression in sympathy, spiritual love, friendship, admiration, affection, enthusiasm, tenderness, devotion, and sexual activity.

It works for creativity, growth, development, and union. Death Instinct is aggressive and destructive in nature. It accounts for such feelings as antipathy, aversion, malice, hate, anger, and rebellion. Violence and aggression to cause destruction are deeply implanted in the human nature and are its essential components (Singh, 1979).

Forces that are considered as evil are *kaam* (lust), *krodh* (anger), *lobh* (covetousness), *moha* (attachment), and *ahankāra* (pride). These forces are not evil by themselves. They are natural instincts produced in man, through the organs given to him by God. For instance, *kaam* (lust) as a natural instinct is not evil so long it is confined within limits of any accepted law of morality. Without this instinct, the progeny of human race would have ended. Similarly, other natural instincts of man are intended to serve essential and useful purposes. They are not evil so long as their use is confined to such purposes within the law of morality. But these natural instincts become evil when they are acted upon by '*haumain*' of man. *Haumain* in its bad sense stimulates his natural instincts to desire more of everything and by means, which may not be consistent with the law of morality (Singh, 1969).

Sikhism does not encourage fear. It does not believe in a system of punishment or the inducement of rewards. In place of fear, it advocates personal courage. It believes optimistically in the ultimate victory of the moral order. Sikhism preaches that we should neither cause fright to anyone nor be afraid of anyone. This healthy spirit has been responsible for the Sikh's willingness to offer his life for his faith. True heroism, requires a lack of fear and a lack of hatred (Mansukhani, 1977).

Inhibition is the result of the suppressed passions, and its consequences are most serious. Human nature is deformed and the value of man's latent positive spiritual forces is distrusted. Sin becomes man's only pre-occupation, he detects sin everywhere in himself, and in others, he becomes a negative hostile to life. The severe restrictions that the ascetics impose on themselves for normal pleasures of life lead to impairment of qualities of good humor, generosity, frankness, sympathy, and compassion. Their hostile drives against themselves make them cruel. Love, which gives gentleness to a man and makes him pleasant, kind, and generous are totally wanting. The Gurus teach us that the only effective way to overcome sin is the positive way of life, knowledge, creation, through an aspiration towards beatitude, noble, and sublime. The Gurus do not disregard the human world in all its miseries. Instead of renouncing the sinful world, they encourage man to meet and mingle with it. The Gurus say, "one is emancipated while laughing and playing in life and living a full life" (Singh, 1979).

Generally, emotions and reason do not exist together. The emotions are the outburst of the state of tension and excitement caused by certain events and the feelings. When a person is emotionally aroused, any amount of deliberate suppression and care in thinking causes disturbance in the nervous system. Reasoning on the other hand requires a calm mind. At the same time, without emotions, a person feels emptiness and loneliness. The emotions to a desirable level are necessary, which should always be balanced by reason, thus helping evolve a state of *emotional reason*. This is possible only when man develops the sense of objectivity and transcends his self. When there is a selfish motive, the mind becomes prejudiced having no regard for rationality. The reason is twisted to suit one's own purpose. The sense of objectivity is to be developed and the self should be an object to itself. The higher self in man should be able to examine the actions of the self as the self would examine the actions in others the self must remain self-conscious and should not be swayed by the emotions (Singh, 1979).

Through the Prism

The most fundamental implication of the Gurus spiritual system is an inalienable combination between the spiritual life and the empirical life of man. They have stressed that there can be no spiritual progress of man, unless spirituality is expressed in life and deeds. Spiritual and empirical progress are inter-linked and inter-dependent (Singh, 1997d).

The Sikh doctrine recognizes and accepts all the dimensions of man: his biological, social, and private self. Numerous hymns portray the human body as a treasure of most valuable elements, including the spiritual truths of life (Singh, 1981). It lays utmost stress on developing the inner voice or the self of the individual. The route to achieving this is well laid out in the development of the Moral self, thereby reaching the Real self. It does not negate any aspect of mans' reality. On the contrary, it considers this as the *only* reality.

Sikhism emphasizes the discovery of the private self. The more one is aware of himself in his relation to others, the less he is subjected to their influence. A self conscious and self-reflective individual would never become a slave of others and barter his freedom. Individualism in an interdependent society is the social ideal. A highly individualistic person frequently acts because of his own considered wishes and goals and is not so completely motivated by common perceptions and understandings as most people are. Individualism and self consciousness prevent the persons to be swayed by emotions; they engender resistance and social distance and thereby separate people and prevent them from acting together as a single collectivity of persons, as in crowds, or as a collectivity of ideas and sentiments, as public opinion and propaganda. Sikh teachings lay stress on this way of life (Singh, 1979).

There is no inherent dichotomy in the belief system between the individual and his social expectations. The concept of original sin is not found in Sikhism, nor the idea that woman is conceived any differently or is any less. In the Sikh view human birth is special for in the human condition man can aspire to be divine. Sikhism is a religion of joy, not of sin. Human birth is not a fall from grace, but not to fulfill its potential and its destiny would be. Knowledge is not sin; its abuse and misuse would be sinful. The sin is not in being human but in *not* becoming all we can be as humans (Singh, I. J., 1997).

An important implication of the Sikh theory of evolution is that the Gurus attribute faults and evil in society to the imperfections of man. They repudiate the concept of a fall, Satan, or Devil. There is no obsession with sin or any system of sacrifices to atone for one's moral lapses. All such myths or concepts are rejected. It has been stated that man at present is at the stage of imperfection; and hence, like the infant, he has to be helped to move and run, and not to be obsessively punished for not being able immediately to gain speed. In fact, they declare that God is benevolently helping with His Will and Grace the process of human evolution. Grace implies freedom, choice, and creativity. As such, it is the source of morality. It gives the seeker optimism and hope, for God is interested in his destiny, future, and progress. Thus, the ideal of individual salvation as an end in itself is not there (Singh, 1997d).

In most other religions, worldly life is opposed to spiritual life. In Sikhism, it is a self-centered life that is opposed to spiritual life and not worldly life as such. The Gurus consider the world to be real and accept life and its responsibilities in its totality. Their spiritual system, therefore, involved the use of all the available tools, including reason and force, for the purposeful progress of man. Their acceptance of the many facets of human nature, their acknowledgement of the emotions of love and joy, give the Sikhs a distinctive characteristic in their ability to enjoy life the way it is. As a rule Indians are sensitive about fun being made of them. The Sikhs are an exception to this rule. Aside from the philosophy that rejoices life, this attitude is born out of a sense of confidence in their proficiency in any sphere of activity, physical or mental, in any profession.

Although religious belief can provide a powerful bond, it would nevertheless be naïve to assume that the conventional values of Jats, Khatris, and others would involve no tensions within a religious grouping, which included such distinctively different groups with their own traditional customs and norms. The cultural traditions of the Sikhs have their base in the larger Hindu traditions.

Although Sikhism promised an equal place to women, predominant society then and now does not; therefore the practice falls far short of the preaching. In many matters however, Sikhism delivered in its voice against sati and instituting widow remarriage. The position of Sikh women within society is not very different from the rest. The Sikh society strongly sanctifies the patriarchal social structure in which marriage, motherhood (especially of a son) and service to husband become the most valuable attributes of women. The freedom of conscience, thought, and will that are prescribed by the belief system are in contradiction to the social norms. Thus, the dichotomy that arises within the Sikh emerge not from within the belief system but rather, between the belief system and the culture, custom, and tradition. These have a far greater role to play in the daily lives of the individual man and woman. All of these have raised acute problems of identity and cohesion.

The dividing line between the Hindus and the Sikhs is so thin that those who wish to maintain the separate identity of the community strenuously advocate features that emphasize the difference between them. The long unshorn hair strictly symbolic with no pragmatic use or value remains the centerpiece of Sikh identity. For women, wearing of their turban over their long hair appears to have less to do with their understanding of Sikhism and more to do with the cultural constraints or with the particular school of thought or teacher who have influenced them. A Sikh's long hair and unshorn beard are in effect the only things that mark him out as different from the Hindu. His name, family associations, deportment, religious practices—in fact nothing else, serve the same purpose. Therein lies the secret of the concern of the orthodox elements over the increasing practice amongst certain sections to discard these external symbols of their faith. The orthodox are willing to overlook defections of the spirit but not of form (Singh, 1976; Singh, I. J., 1997).

As I. J. Singh (1997, p. 33) states, "The reverence shown by most people for tradition is misplaced and only serves to spare the living the inconvenience of having to do their own thinking. By hiding behind tradition, we shift responsibility on the dead who cannot answer. By wrapping tradition in an aura of holiness, we create guilt in the living for even daring to question it". Many in the new generation have successfully grafted the western-oriented, outer-directed exploratory attitude towards life on to their own Sikh heritage, because the two have always been quite compatible. However, in their attempt to maintain their distinctive identity, one of the major implications of the Sikh thesis, universalism, is disregarded. The Gurus did not assert exclusivism. Considering the exclusiveness of other religions, Guru Nanak's system is unique in its universalism (Singh, D. 1997d).

As in other belief systems, the failure in the deliverance of the precepts of the Gurus does not lie in the beliefs. It rests in the interpretations and the increased dogmatism of the followers. So much so, that it seems as though man is incapable of dealing with the freedom of conscience, will, and action that is presented to him. It seems that man is unwilling to choose this path of freedom in his goal to attaining, not only a sense of well-being, but also peace and fulfillment.

8

Contemporary Psychology on Self and Emotions

The perceptions of the "self" have varied from metaphysical, to static, to dynamic perspectives; to mind devoid of body, as pure consciousness, with the body as a mere appendage, to debates on whether the self is the knower or the known. Baumgardner & Rappoport (1996) in their analysis of recent debates about psychology's concept of self suggest the emergence of a decentralized, flexible, and pluralistic self in contemporary culture. With a paradigm shift of perceiving emotions as disorders to emotions as natural processes, emotions have occupied a central place in mans' quest for understanding himself. Following is an overview of the range of concepts and perceptions on the self and emotions in contemporary western thought.

Western intellectual tradition traces questions about the self back to the Greeks. Socrates maintained that, the universal man and not the particular man must be the object of our study. His teachings were about the soul, and were more ethical and metaphysical[1]. According to Plato, all men are essentially the same because they share the same essence or nature of man, which makes them all 'human', despite individual differences. Aristotle emphasized the individuality of man. He further made the distinction between the physical and nonphysical aspects of human functioning. This led other philosophers to speculate about the nature of consciousness, thought, and knowledge. From the ancient Greeks, also comes the idea of the "persona", where ones' self is not his "true self" but rather a role that he plays before others. A more positive usage of the word "person" dates back to Latin theology. This usage derives from a Roman official, Boethius (480–525), who states, a person is "an individual substance of rational nature" (Roy, 1966; Byrne & Maziarz, 1969; Strauss & Goethals, 1991).

The Self in Contemporary Western Psychology

After a long hiatus, due to the dominance of the behaviorist school, the study of "self" has again gained momentum, because of the acceptance of the relevancy of subjective processes. Further, an interdisciplinary approach to the question of "self" has added dimensions that hitherto were not considered. In the following sections, I look at some of the contemporary perspectives on self, which have their moorings in the past. Traditionally the study of the self has been divided in terms of the study of the "concept of self", that is, 'what is the self?' and the "self-concept", that is, 'how do I perceive my self?' However, the two are intrinsically linked. Hence, it is imperative that they are viewed together, eliminating the subtle distinction between the two. I review these theories based on the biological self, the social self, and the private self. Although each approach presents its unique perspective, an integration of these gives us a complete picture of contemporary western psychological perspective on "self".

Critical Issues in Self-Theory

The critical issues in the theorizing of the self have been: the self as fact or fiction; self as knower versus the self as known; self as structure (static) versus self as a process (dynamic); self as one or many.

According to Dennet (1991), the human self that ultimately emerges from the complex process of the development of the zygote is not anything real. For him, the individual is a fictional character in a story told by the brain.

He thus urges that the self is a fiction, an abstract object like the physicist's 'center of gravity'. The selves are useful organizing concepts, the characteristics of which are being constantly written and re-written by the brain. Harré (1991), like Dennet, thinks that the selves are not real. However, in adopting a social constructionist view, he proposes that the self emerges not from the individual human organism, but from the social relations within which it exists. Accepting this position, Gergen (1991) claims that the self is a fabrication. The very properties we attribute to ourselves (our internal states) are themselves fabrications. What we call 'self-knowledge' is merely socially conditioned interpretation that has little to do with the intrinsic properties being interpreted. So-called break throughs in self-knowledge are merely realizations that alternative, more satisfying ways of interpreting ourselves are available. He states that we have so much data, which we scan selectively, that we can justify almost any label we choose. Even the way we decide whether someone's actions (including our own) were caused by the persons volition or by external causes—how free someone is –is also in large part socially determined.

The theories of divine providence involve a static all-inclusive causality on the part of God with respect to man. Kohut's (1984) self-psychology contains primarily a static structural concept of self. The primary threats to the self consist in the failure of the environment to provide the ingredients necessary for the optimal development of an intact self, with the result that the self that does develop is structurally weak. Structural weakness of the self is the critical element in pathology, and maladaptive coping with inner conflict is simply one of the many manifestations of this primary structural weakness. There is an implicit dynamic aspect to Kohut's self-psychology in its conception of the individual's struggle to maintain self-cohesiveness and to resume developmental growth (Eagle, 1991).

Byrne & Maziraz (1969) express that man develops, progresses, and indeed evolves. He is not only static but also dynamic. Thus, he cannot be adequately represented in a three-dimensional perspective; he must be seen, as it were, moving through the fourth dimension of time. Amongst the prominent 20th century thinkers, Heidegger and Sartre agree in their emphasis on man as being dynamic rather than static. This realm of constancy in man would include his habits, ideas, and in general his past in the sense of all that he has irrevocably become. However, in contrast to the fixity, the determinacy of what has already come into being, consciousness remains free, spontaneous, and creative. In fact, Sartre has argued, consciousness is to free that, whatever the influences from ones' past might be, one is nonetheless able to transcend these influences, at least by way of rebellion, when choosing and acting in the present and towards a future.

Carver & Scheier (1991) suggest a dynamic and flexible organization of the self in which data from all levels of functioning are continuously processed and evaluated. According to Stuss' (1991) model, when the systems are operating harmoniously, people experience themselves as coherent and consistent. The content of the self–concept, and therefore the experience of self, is malleable (McGuire, McGuire & Cheever, 1986, Markus & Wurf, 1987; McGuire & Mcguire, 1988; Hinkley & Andersen, 1996). Markus and Kunda (1986) presented evidence supporting a dynamic model of the self-concept through demonstrating that the accessibility of self-features is responsive to situationally induced motivations. These findings led Markus and her colleagues to develop the notion of a "working self-concept" that consists of an individual's set of currently active self-features (Markus & Wurf, 1987). The working self-concept provides an analog to working memory; it holds only a subset of ones stored self-information and, thereby, can explain malleability of the self-concept through alterations in the contents of the active subset.

Edmund Husserl (1931) asserted that the very fact of knowledge presupposes the existence of what he calls a transcendental ego. By virtue of his methodological procedure, which he calls phenomenological reduction, Husserl is able to distinguish between various perspectives on the self. To consider the self as the sum of bodily and physical characteristics is to deal with a psychophysical self. If one further abstracts from bodily characteristics, he may consider the self solely in terms of psychic manifestations, as, for example, thoughts, desires, wishes, memories, and so on. Underlying even this psychic self there is an ultimate subjective source of all such manifestations. This underlying subjectivity is the transcendental ego. Contrary to the theory of Kant, this transcendental ego is not merely hypothetical. It is subjective itself, without which no knowledge could have any structure or form, whether it is the knowledge of the "world" or knowledge of those physical or psychic phenomena that is referred to as the self. Indeed, it is this radical principle of subjectivity that "constitutes" all knowledge by ordering data into objects. He argues the very fact of objectification presupposes the subjectivity thus objectified (Byrne & Maziarz, 1969).

William James (1890, 1892) dealt with the nature of the self in ways that have had enduring influence on contemporary psychology. James' most helpful distinction was between 'the self as known', or the 'me', the 'empirical ego' and 'the self as knower', or the 'I', the 'pure ego'. This distinction was helpful, because it enabled psychologists to concentrate on the 'me', the self that is known, a simpler entity to explore than the self as knower is. James' discussion of the 'me', and its constituent parts, the material me, the social me, and the spiritual me, and in particular his treatment of self-esteem and the multiplicity of social selves, remain highly influential. James considers that personal identity and unity are properties of the empirical self. He disagrees with three varieties of a contrasting, "pure ego" theory—theories that consider identity and unity not as functions of the empirical self. These are theories of the soul, defined as immaterial substance; (for example, the un-extended mental substance postulated by Descartes); the associationist theory, which treats identity and unity as unexplained, emergent properties of associated collections of ideas; and the transcendental ego (especially Kant's) theory, in which identity and unity are innate properties of mind.

Gordon Allport (1943) reviews eight senses of ego (or self—he uses the two terms interchangeably). Greenwald and Pratkanis, (1984) present the following summary of Allport's eight senses of ego: (1) Ego as knower designates the experiencing agent, corresponding to the philosophers' "pure ego", and to the functions that James attributes to the spiritual portion of the empirical self. (2) Ego as object of knowledge is the bodily self, which is a part of James' material self. (3) Ego as primitive selfishness corresponds to James' material self-seeking. (4) Ego as dominance drive refers to "that portion of the personality that demands status and recognition", corresponding to James' social self-seeking. (5) Ego as a passive organization of mental processes was Allport's acknowledgement of Freud's concept of ego, a neutral arbitrator among the conflicting forces of id, superego, and environment. (6) Ego as a fighter for ends corresponds to James' spiritual self-seeking, and to the dynamic view of ego in psychoanalytic thinking. (7) Ego as a behavioral system designated by the Gestalt-psychological conception of a central region of personality, found in the framework of Koffka (1935) and Lewin (1936). (8) Ego as the subjective organization of culture refers to the self as a residue of socialization experience, a system of social values.

The Organismic Self

Gabriel Marcel (1949) was one of the first to address the problem of embodiment. According to him, it is still man the embodied self, who is doing the objectifying and who, as a result, can in no way find or establish a retreat away from his body. In order to arrive at the problem of embodiment, Marcel distinguishes first and second reflection. In the former, "there is no intelligible retreat in which I could establish myself outside of or apart from my body" (Zaner, 1964). Marcel maintains that the fundamental datum of philosophy is that I am embodied spirit, a body-self. He states that the classical dualism between matter and mind, as originally posed by Descartes, simply does not exist in man or for man. A second view of human embodiment is that which is contained in the philosophy of Maurice Merleau-Ponty, (1962, 1963). He proposes that, "though my body may be regarded as an "object" when investigated scientifically or when approached by others, my body-for-me is that expressive unity that I know through performance and activity. The body as an instrument of knowledge is more active than passive. The body is a point of view on the world; it is a subject, a source of meaning, and cannot, at least for the self, function as an object. In fact, the body is the very possibility or background for my having a world at all; and, at the same time, it is by means of the body that I project myself upon the world". Jean-Paul Sartre's (1956) theory of the body involves three aspects: my body-for-itself, is a point of view from which it is not possible for me to escape; my body-for-the-other, is a point of view when the other makes a pure object of me by his "look", thereby negating my subjectivity; and my body-as-the-body-of-the-other, is a point of view when I grasp the fact of my being when I am viewed by another. Byrne & Maziarz, (1969) thus conclude, that the theme of embodiment serves to demythologize any theory that would over accentuate mans' spirit, soul, and reason, to the detriment, neglect, or denial of his "bodiliness".

Contemporary thinkers from varied fields of the biological sciences have theorized the origins of the self within the cellular structure. As Ryan (1991) states, "psychology is, before all else, a life science. The inescapable and basic fact is that humans must count themselves among organisms" (p. 208). The self is viewed in organismic theories as both a point of contact between organism and world, and a structure that exhibits a continual tendency towards a mastery, synthesis, and integration. Williams (1970), Blasi, (1976), and Unger (1991) endorse a physical view of personal identity. In using this meaning of the 'self', Ryan (1991) refers to a vital core, from which one springs forth in development.

According to Ryan (1991), "two directions represent the most basic and important intrinsic, organizational strivings of personality and of self. First is the elaboration and extension of ones' capacities and interests and their integration, or reciprocal assimilation, into a unified structure that is coherent and self-regulating. Maturana & Varella (1975) use the term 'auto poietic' (self-creating) to describe this characteristic of organisms. A second direction concerns the striving for cohesion and integration of the individual within a social matrix. The principle of organization extends beyond the individual and concerns the unity among and between persons on which the continuity of all being depends. This is deeply ingrained in human nature" (p. 209). Psychological needs, corresponds to this aspect of organization, whereas biological needs correspond to the former.

According to DeCharms (1968), intrinsic motivation-- doing an activity for 'its own sake'--is present from infancy as evidenced in the spontaneous and active strivings for effects and responsiveness in ones' environment. This also suggests that from infancy there is present the nascent core of the self. The roots of the self, that is, are pre-reflexive, an idea well recognized by dynamic theorists, e.g. Stern (1985), Winnicott (1988). In this conceptualization, the self is no mere social construction or looking glass reflection. It is a natural endowment of the organism. What becomes identified or understood, as the self is that vital aspect of the human animal characterized by interest, curiosity and striving. The self is thus the psychological manifestation and extension of the organization properties common to all living things. The use of the term 'self' pertains to a referent deeper than the outer faeade of a person, to that vital core or origin implicated in the organismic conceptualization (Ryan, 1991).

The Genetic Self

In understanding the idea of 'organismic self', we refer to molecular biology. Richard Dawkins (1989, 1995, 1998) has effectively proposed the concept of a "genetic self". According to him, our genetic system is the universal system of all life on the planet. "There is no spirit-driven life force, no throbbing, heaving, protoplasmic, mystic jelly. Life is just bytes and bytes and bytes of digital information. Genes are pure information—information that can be encoded, re-coded, and decoded, without any degradation or change of meaning" (1995, p. 22). "Genes do not only make copies of themselves, which flow on down the generations, they actually spend their times in bodies, and they influence the shape and behavior of the successive bodies in which they find themselves. Bodies are important too" (1995, p. 22). The true utility function of life is DNA survival. This utility function seldom turns out to be the greatest good for the greatest number. The utility function betrays its origins in an uncoordinated scramble for selfish gain. Genes maximize their selfish welfare at their level, by programming unselfish cooperation, or even self-sacrifice, by the organism at its level. They cooperate specifically in the enterprise of building individual bodies. However, it is an anarchistic, 'each gene for itself' kind of cooperation. Group welfare is always a fortuitous consequence, not a primary drive. This is the meaning of the 'selfish gene'. In this sense, there is a non-linguistic, biochemical sense of self at the genetic level, where each cell organizes itself towards the primary goal of life, survival.

The Immune Self

Integrated with the genetic self is Francisco Varela's (1997) proposal of an 'Immune self' or the 'Body's self'. He calls the structure and function of the immune system, the 'second brain'. The interaction between the mind, the nervous system, and the immune system provides a physiological basis for the influence of emotions on health. The study of the responsive tuning between the nervous system and the immune system is called psychoneuroimmunology. The organs for the immune system are dispersed throughout the body. They include the thymus and bone marrow, the sources from which the system is constantly renewed; the spleen; and the lymphatic system. The cells that constitute the immune system are called lymphocytes or white blood cells. They are circulating all the time, unlike the fixed neurons of the nervous system. Just as the function of the nervous system takes on a cognitive identity, a sense of self, with its own memories, ideas, and tendencies, the body also has an identity or self with similar cognitive properties such as memory, learning, and expectations. The reaction of the body to a virus against which one has been vaccinated, is an instance of the 'body's self' responding to past 'memory', is a case in point. This identity functions through the immune system. The immune system allows us to have a bodily existence. If the functioning of the immune system is interrupted, the body starts to disintegrate. The body recognizes every part of its' self, rejecting or reacting against any foreign particles. This affirmation of a systems identity, which is not a defensive reaction but a positive construction, is a kind of self-assertion. This is what constitutes our "self" on the molecular and cellular level (including genetic determinants and "self" markers"). Just as the human brain, where capacities such as memory or a sense of self are emergent properties of all neurons, in the immune system there is an emergent capacity to maintain the body, and to have a history with it, to have a self. As an emergent property, it is something that arises but does not exist anywhere. From the point of view of psychoneuroimmunology, the body would also have an identity that is conceptually designated, but does not exist anywhere. The bodily identity is in the complex of interactions. The fact is that the body has wisdom to its own existence that entails regulation. "All that wisdom happens without my linguistically conscious self knowing it, yet at the same time it is me in some important sense" (Varela, 1997, p. 63).

The Neural Self

Stuss (1991) and Brown (1999), through extensive literature review in neurology, conclude that the psychological construct of self is related directly to brain functioning. The key processes are awareness (of self), monitoring (of the self's condition), and integrating experience across time (into the self). Antonio Damasio, (1994, 1999), stresses that "the biological forerunner for the sense of self is found in the ensemble of brain devices that continuously and non-consciously maintain the body-state within the narrow range and relative stability required for survival". Linking feelings and emotions inextricably with the sense of self, he calls the state of activity within this ensemble the "proto-self", the non-conscious forerunner for the levels of self which appear in our minds as the conscious protagonists of consciousness: core self and autobiographical self. In this section, we look at Damasios' thesis on the rise of the sense of self. Basing his thesis on extensive review of patients suffering from a wide variety of neurological conditions, he arrived at the biological root of consciousness, which forms the basis for a sense of self.

According to Damasio (1999), the neurological and neuropsychological evidence for consciousness reveals five facts:

The first fact is that some aspects of the processes of consciousness can be related to the operation of specific brain regions and systems.

The second fact is that consciousness and wakefulness, as well as consciousness and low-level attention can be separated.

The third and perhaps most revealing fact is that consciousness and emotion are not separable. It is usually the case that when consciousness is impaired so is emotion.

The fourth fact is that consciousness is not a monolith. It can be separated into simple and complex kinds. The simplest kind, core consciousness, provides the organism with a sense of self about one moment—now and about one place—here.

Core consciousness does not illuminate the future, and the only past it is vaguely aware of is that which occurred the instant before. The complex kind of consciousness—extended consciousness, and of which there are many levels and grades, provides the organism with an elaborate sense of self—an identity and a person, and places that person at a point of time in individual historical time. Neurological diseases reveal that impairments of extended consciousness allow core consciousness to remain unscathed. By contrast, impairments that begin at the level of core consciousness demolish the entire edifice of consciousness: extended consciousness collapses as well. The sense of self that emerges in core consciousness is the core self, a transient entity, ceaselessly re-created for each and every object with which the brain interacts. The autobiographical self depends on systematized memories of situations in which core consciousness was involved.

A fifth fact, language, reason, memory, attention and working memory are not required for core consciousness.

Damasio (1999) explains, "Our sense of self is a state of the organism, the result of cells, tissues, and organs to systems, operating in a certain manner and interacting in a certain way, within certain parameters" (p. 145). He distinguishes between three interdependent selves based on the level of our conscious awareness of them—the Proto self, Core self, and Autobiographical self.

The Proto-self is an interconnected and temporarily coherent collection of neural patterns, which represent the state of the organism, moment by moment, at multiple levels of the brain. We are *not* conscious of the proto-self. The sense of self is the first answer to a question the organism never posed. To who do the ongoing mental patterns now unfolding, belong? The answer is they belong to the organism, as represented by the proto-self. The simplest form in which the wordless knowledge emerges mentally is the feeling of knowing. It is the feeling that accompanies the making of any kind of image—visual, auditory, tactile, visceral—within our living organisms. The apparent self emerges as a feeling of feeling. The proto-self has no powers of perception and holds no knowledge. It does not occur in one place only, and it emerges dynamically and continuously out of multifarious interacting signals that span varied order of the nervous system. It is not an interpreter of anything. It is a reference point at each point in which it is. Damasio hypothesizes that the core consciousness depends most critically on the activity of a number of phylogenetically old brain structures, beginning in the brain stem, in the reticular nuclei structures, the hypothalamus, basal forebrain, and ending with the somatosensory and cingulate cortices. The interaction among the structures in this set up supports the creation of the proto-self. The neural pattern which underlies core consciousness for an object—the sense of self in the act of knowing a particular thing—is thus a large scale neural pattern involving activity in two interrelated sets of structures: the set whose cross regional activity generates the representation of the object. The evidence for this rests in patients with brain stem damage, resulting in coma or persistent vegetative states, which compromise the foundations of the proto-self (Damasio, 1999).

The *Core self* resides in the second-order nonverbal account that occurs whenever an object modifies the proto-self. The core self can be triggered by any object. The mechanism of production of core self undergoes minimal change across a lifetime. We are conscious of the core self. According to this hypothesis, structures deep within the brain, the superior colliculi-structures in the posterior region of the midbrain known as the tectum, the entire region of the cingulate cortex, the thalamus and some prefrontal cortices play a role in consciousness. Evidences of a loss of core self is observed in patients during the process of an absence seizure, epileptic automatisms, akinetic mutism following a stroke (lack of movement and speech), and in some patients in the advanced stages of Alzheimer's disease. In such states, most evidently observable in absence seizures where a clear demarcation can be made between the loss and subsequent regaining of consciousness, there would have been no sense of self. No identifiable person with a past and an anticipated future—specifically no core consciousness and no extended consciousness, hence, no core self and no autobiographical self (Damasio, 1999).

The *Autobiographical self* is a manifestation of extended consciousness, and is based on autobiographical memory, which is constituted by implicit memories of multiple instances of individual experience of the past and of the anticipated future. The invariant aspects of an individual's biography form the basis for autobiographical memory. Sets of memories, which describe identity and person can be reactivated as a neural pattern and made explicit as images whenever needed. Each reactivated memory operates as a "something-to-be-known" and generates its own pulse of core consciousness. The result is the autobiographical self of which we are conscious. It hinges on the consistent reactivation and display of selected sets of autobiographical memories. In core consciousness, the sense of self arises in the consistent, reiterated display of some of our own personal memories, *the objects of our personal past*, those that can easily substantiate our identity, moment by moment and our personhood. It occurs only in organisms endowed with a substantial memory capacity and reasoning ability, but does not require language. It develops under the shadow of an inherited biology. The rules and principles guiding its behavior, is developed under the control of its cultural environment. Damasio proposes that the neuroanatomical basis for the extended consciousness or autobiographical self is based on convergence zones located in the temporal and the frontal higher cortices, as well as in subcortical nuclei such as those in the amygdala. The coordinated activation of this multi-site network is paced by the thalamic nuclei, while the holding of components of memory for extended periods requires the support of prefrontal cortices involved in working memory. In patients with conditions such as transient global amnesia, stages of Alzheimer's disease, anosognosia (denial of a loss of function as in stroke victims who report nothing the matter with them), defects in working memory due to extensive frontal lobe damage, extended consciousness is compromised, although they retain core consciousness. There is loss of the autobiographical self (Damasio, 1999).

The Social Self

Immanuel Kant (1724–1804) considered all our concepts, even that of self, as meaningful only in relation to the world. Heidegger (1962), rejected Cartesian rationalism by insisting that a man finds himself not in his own isolated thoughts but in the world. Freud's concept of the ego, and various extensions, modifications and revisions of the ego remain central in a great deal of work on the self. His theory is in a certain sense relational in character. Both Freud and his followers recognized that the development of the ego is due not to the individual alone but to the individual as he relates to reality, to his parents, and to society as a whole.

The sociologist Charles Horton Cooley (1902) made a major contribution by proposing that the self-conception grew out of social interaction. As children develop, they acquire the capacity to reflect on how other people view them. They would imagine others' views, and although their perceptions might not be accurate, they were nevertheless important. Specifically, Cooley proposed that children develop a "looking glass self", a reflected appraisal based on others' imagined appraisal. In subsequent years, other sociologists in the symbolic interactionist tradition, notably G. H. Mead (1934), expanded the idea of reflected appraisal. He demonstrated the power of combining philosophical, psychological, and sociological perspectives. This remains a central idea in theorizing about the self.

In line with Cooley and Mead, Erikson (1968) proposed that people form an ego-identity on the basis of how others perceive them and how they perceive themselves in comparison to others that are relevant to them. Sullivan (1953) was another psychodynamic theorist who emphasized that ones' sense of self is affected by responses of others. Rogers (1951) proposed that the self-concept could be formed based on social expectations and may actually conflict with the drives of the organism and impede self-actualization. Thus, the self-concept is an image of a socially approved or ideal self that may thwart the organism's natural strivings.

Theoretical approaches to the self in current social psychology emphasize processes of social comparison, external feedback, and ones' public appearance as providing the primary basis for self-concept and identity. Of interest in the contrast between the looking glass self as typically conceptualized and the organismic self is their seemingly antithetical nature (Eichenbaum & Orbach, 1983; Strauss & Ryan, 1987; Ryan, 1991).

Harré (1995) highlights the important features of social constructionist theories. 'The ontology presupposed in discursive psychology takes persons to be originating centers of activity. Since they are ontologically elementary, they have no internal psychological complexity. A second important feature is the thesis that cognitive processes are properties of discourses, and thus they have their primary mode of being in interpersonal interactions. Persons are singularities and each has its unique attributes. Singularity of personhood is tied up with singularity of embodiment, deeply involved in the sense of self. In a similar manner, the discursive thesis that emotional displays are embodied expressions of judgments also brings the fact of embodiment to the center of psychological theory'.

In support of social constructionism, Shotter (1995) indicates the linguistic or normative nature of people's everyday social relations to each other. Disagreeing with the social constructionist thesis Fisher (1995a) argued that reductions of mind and body to social process disallow a causal basis for self and its autonomously generated origins. Further, Fisher (1995b) reasserts that including biological needs and assimilative functions of the self is necessary for agency and potentiality.

Burkitt (1994) analyzed the attempts of a variety of 20th-century social theorists to develop a conception of the self as a "social differences" construction, largely in opposition to what those theorists took to be the predominant implicit conception of the person in their own Western European and North American societies. In these constructionist accounts, the subjects of such societies—self-contained, isolated, unique, expressive individuals—were portrayed as no more than the discursive products of the dominant linguistic textual practices of their communities. Such theorists exemplified a major theme of the human sciences: the demonstration of the essential arbitrariness underlying the appearance of the naturalness of social arrangements, and through such a demonstration the establishment of the liberating potential of human science analysis. For Burkitt, this potential is fatally undermined by two weaknesses: an overly cognitive understanding of self and the corresponding neglect of its corporeality; and an underdeveloped sense of social context, a concept which for many social constructionists has remained an utterly necessary but largely unelaborated category.

Harré's (1991) social constructionist theory of self rests fundamentally on a distinction between the public fact of personal identity and the private fact of an individual's sense of identity. Harré claims that the public fact is a social matter. It is grounded in the concept of person as a publicly identifiable being with a characteristic combination of language skills and moral qualities, which mostly have to do with responsibility. The private fact of an individual's sense of identity concerns a particular way of organizing perception, thought, feelings, memories, and so on. He further claims that the concept of a "person" is culturally dependent. The basic social constructionist thesis is that this private sense of individual identity is made available to the members of a culture through the (mistaken) myth that the self is real. In sum, Harrés' thesis involves the claim that the self and its internal states, as well as the sense of personal identity are social phenomenon; to understand them properly we must attend to the social contexts in which the individuals find themselves. These phenomena are culture-relative.

In traditional Western psychological theories of development, the "self" has long been viewed as the primary reality and unit of study. Although most theorists have struggled with the issue of reification of the self, all have succumbed, to some degree, to the powerful pull to de-contextualize, abstract, and spatialize this concept. Sullivan (1953) took a major step away from the instinct-drive model, as did Horney (1926/1967) and Thompson (1941). In addition, Sullivan placed the development of the self directly within the interpersonal realm. In Eriksons (1963) ego identity schema, identity is early predicated on establishment of autonomy. Intimacy is established later, only after identity is consolidated. As such, the basic relationality of development is lost in much of this model. Most recently, Kohut (1984) has emphasized the ongoing need for relationships throughout life. His concept of the "self object" pertains to the importance of others in shaping our self-image and maintaining self-esteem. This theory too is built on a model of drives, with others used as objects to perform some function for a self that still remains intrinsically and ideally separate, if at best empathetically connected.

Trevarthan (1979) has pointed to a "primary intersubjectivity" in human development, which is innate and unfolding. Klein (1976) posited the existence of "we" identities in the development of a concept of self, an "aspect of ones' self construed as a necessary part of a unit transcending ones' autonomous actions". A contextual—relation view of self also has much in common with the earlier work of the symbolic interactionists (Baldwin, 1897/1968; Cooley, 1902/1968; Mead, 1925/1968), typified by Mead's idea that "selves exist only in relation to other selves" (Jordan, 1987).

In the past decade, an important impetus for shifting to a different paradigm of "the self" has come from feminist psychologists who have been increasingly vocal and articulate about their dissatisfaction with existing models of female development and the 'female self'. Miller (1976), Chodorow (1978), and Gilligan (1982) are the most notable of the new wave of women challenging existing conceptualizations of women's development and personal organization. Chodorow (1978) reexamined object relations theory and found that traditional theory failed to acknowledge the importance of the early and longer lasting bond between the girl and her mother. This bond leads to a different experience of boundaries and identity than what the boy, as objectified other, experiences with mother. Gilligan's (1982) ideas, about the nature of female development, derived from her awareness that prevailing theories of moral development were not applicable to women but were used in such a way that women consistently appeared as defective or deficient moral selves. An important truth being omitted was the power of the ethic of care taking and relationship in women's lives. What all these theorists allude to, and seek to begin to correct in psychological theory, reflects an old tradition expressed in Aristotle's statement that "the female is a female by virtue of a certain lack of qualities. We should regard the female nature as afflicted with a natural defectiveness".

Foreman (1978) argues that the focus of the self "from the outside" is a particularly strong force in the cultural subordination of women. By existing as "being for others", she argues, women define and regulate their behavior through projected external lenses. This can be related to the preoccupation with body, diet, and appearance, that appear to objectify a womans' worth and reflects a loss of more autonomous self-definitions (Eichenbaum & Orbach, 1983; Strauss & Ryan, 1987).

An alternative conceptualization of the self is the perspective of the "interacting" sense of self (Kaplan, 1984; Stiver, 1984; Surrey, 1985; Gergen, 1995) that "separate self" theory overlooks. This is sometimes called "self in relation" or "relational self", (Jordan, 1984, 1985, 1987; Surrey, 1985; Jordan & Surrey, 1986) or "being in relation" (Miller, 1984). The relational theory of self emphasizes the contextual, approximate, responsive, and process factors in experience. In short, it emphasizes relationship and connection. Rather than a primary perspective based on the formed and contained self, this model stresses the importance of the inter-subjective, relational, emergent nature of human experience. While there is still a "felt sense of self", which is acknowledged by this point of view, it is a "self inseparable from a dynamic interaction" (an "interacting self", Miller, 1984). From this inter-subjective perspective, the movement of relating, of mutual initiative and responsiveness, are the ongoing central organizing dynamics in women's (but probably all people's) lives. This goes beyond saying that ones' being is continuously formed in connection with others and is inextricably tied to relational movement. The primary feature, rather than structure marked by separateness and autonomy, is increasing empathic responsiveness in the context of interpersonal mutuality. The other's subjective experience becomes, as ones' own; this is at the heart of "relational being"(Jordan, 1989, 1991).

Not just at the level of goals, values, and beliefs do women experience a sense of connected self but at the very concrete and compelling level of feelings and body experience (Jordan, 1991). The way one conceptualizes ones' "place" in the world broadly affects interpretive, meaning-making, value-generating activity. The nature of relatedness, the nature of boundary concept shapes the openness to new experience and the quality of revelations about inner experience that occur between people. If "self" is conceived as separate, alone, "in control", personally achieving and mastering nature, others may tend to be perceived as potential competitors, dangerous intruders, or objects to be used for the self's enhancement. A system that defines the self as separate and hierarchically measurable is usually marked in Western cultures by power based dominance patterns. In such systems, the self-boundary serves as a protection from the impinging surroundings and the need for connection with, relatedness to, and contact with others is subjugated to the need to protect the separate self (Belenky, Clinchy, Goldberger, & Tarule, 1986).

Safety in a power-based society seems to demand solid boundaries; self-disclosure is carefully monitored, lest knowledge about the inner experience be used against one. As caricatured in this way, this actually prescribes much of the socialization of Western males. It should be no surprise to find important differences between mens' and womens' experiences of boundaries, contributing to vastly different experiences of "self with other" or the "interacting sense of self". As Gilligan (1982) notes, women "define themselves in the context of human relationships". For men, what is crucial is "separation as it defines and empowers the self". Women feel most themselves, most safe, most alive in connection, men in separation (Pollack & Gilligan, 1982). These two very different approaches to organizing "self with other" experience also have far-reaching effects on every aspect of our lives, including the theories of self and science that we construct. Psychological theories of self, an especially value-laden notion of the ideally functioning self, in turn broadly affects our experiences of ourselves, and they are saturated with gender bias (Jordan, 1987, 1991).

The Private/True Self

Theorists have also taken positions which insist that one must go beyond the polarity between self and society to develop ones' own, true or "authentic self". Fromm (1964) stressed that a person can fulfill himself only to the extent that he overcomes social pressures in order to realize that sum-total of his potentialities, which he calls the persons' "true self". Jung (1939) described the self as an archetype that becomes over the course of development the center of the personality. Its function is to draw the person to experiences that actualize or individuate unconscious potentials, and to integrate these unconscious tendencies in the personality with their conscious opposites. Thus, it strives during the entire life cycle, toward the completion of the whole personality (Strauss & Goethals, 1991). Other labels have also been applied in the literature:

the 'real self' (Horney, 1950; Rogers, 1951), the 'autonomous self' (Van Kamm, 1966), the 'true or spontaneous self' (Winnicott, 1986), the 'authentic self' (Wild, 1965), or the 'transparent self' (Jourard, 1964).

Fenigstein, Scheier, & Buss (1975) define the public self as consisting of observable self-produced stimuli, such as physique, clothing, grooming, facial expression and speech; the private self consists of self-produced stimuli that are not publicly observable, such as internal bodily sensations emotional feelings, thoughts and self-evaluations. Public and private self-consciousness is interpreted as predispositions to attend to public and private aspects of the self, respectively. In contrast, ego task analysis makes evaluative orientation toward other versus inner audiences central to the public versus private contrast. Greenwald (1982) integrated the social and private self in his meanings of ego-involvement. According to him, ego-involvement had three meanings; (1) concerns about public impression, or evaluation by others, similar to evaluation apprehension, need for approval; (2) concern about private self-evaluation, similar to need for achievement; (3) personal importance, linkage to central values. Greenwald related the first two senses of ego-involvement to concepts of public and private self-awareness/self-consciousness (Buss, 1980; Fenigstein, Scheier, & Buss, 1975; Scheier & Carver, 1981), and set them in a framework for analyzing person-situation interactions, ego task analysis. Greenwald & Breckler (1985), used ego-task analysis to identify four facets of the self that may be said to be engaged in ego tasks. These four facets (or sub-selves) are: (1) *The diffuse self*--a pre-self, a condition of not distinguishing sharply between self and others, with behavior hedonically guided toward positive affective states. (2) *The public self*--is sensitive to the evaluations of others and seeks to win the approval of significant audiences. Developmentally the public self depends upon achievement or a cognitive discrimination between the self and others, and an ability to attend to those aspects of ones' behavior that are also noticed by others. The ego task of the public self can be described as social accreditation, i.e., earning credit in exchange for relationships with others. However, another important aspect of the public self's task is to internalize the evaluative standards of significant others. (3) This self-definition aspect of the public self's task can lead to development of *the private self*. By providing an inner audience for behavior, the private self permits self-evaluation to proceed in the absence of others. (4) As a further developmental step, the goals of groups with which the person is identified (reference groups) become internalized, yielding the *collective self*. The collective self's task is also an achievement task, contributing toward a reference group's attainment of its goals (Greenwald & Pratkanis, 1984).

Bergmann (1991) distinguishes between "the true self" and "the false self". The "true self" is created from the pattern of identifications with our experiences. These unconsciously formed patterns create psychological structures that constitute what we call "the self", and depending on their effects, either a "true self" or a "false self". Bergmann claims that if these patterns of identifications create a true self, then the experience that results will be one of freedom—"a natural flow, neither cramped nor forced, a shift away from the need to control, to compensate and to correct, and toward the exuberance of actions and words at last taking shape unite effortlessly, as if by themselves". False selves impede this experience. This false sense can be thrust upon us and often, it is one that does not fit. Our cultural institutions tell us what we should be. This has a profound influence on how we see ourselves.

Neisser (1991) presents an integrated view of the different perspectives on self. He identifies five different sources of self-knowledge. He claims that the five distinct mechanisms that give rise to this knowledge constitute five distinct selves. Not only are you real, there are five of you. He identifies "the ecological self", the self that allows the organism to distinguish itself from its environment. The "interpersonal self" according to Neisser, is established by species-specific signals of rapport and communication, such as the way human infants respond to the facial expressions of their mothers. In addition to these two selves, Neisser also distinguishes three others. The "extended self", constructed based on memory and the anticipation relations. The "private self", constructed on the basis of the organism's recognition that the organisms conscious experiences are exclusively its own; and the "conceptual self", constructed on the basis of the organisms theories about itself—its "self-concepts". The reason Neisser thinks these five forms of information in effect create five different selves is that they are also distinct from each other in both structure and origin. They "differ in their developmental histories, in the accuracy with which we can know them, in the pathologies to which they are subject, and generally in what they contribute to human experience".

The Emotions in Contemporary Psychology

At first glance, there is nothing distinctively human about emotions since it is clear that so many non-human creatures have emotions in abundance. As one moves up the evolutionary scale, the following features appear to become prominent: the ability to process more complex stimulus patterns in the environment, the simultaneous existence of a multitude of motivational tendencies, a highly flexible behavioral repertoire, and social interaction as the basis of social organization. Emotions have become connected to the complex ideas, values, and principles, and judgments that only humans can have, and in that connection lies our legitimate sense that human emotion is special (Scherer, 1994b; Damasio, 1999).

Perspectives on Emotions

There are different viewpoints regarding the definition of emotions. Ekman, (1994) emphasizes the evolutionary and individual characteristics of emotions. He describes eight shared characteristics of emotions: presence in other primates, a universal signal, automatic appraisal, commonalities in antecedent events, quick onset, brief duration, unbidden occurrence, and a distinctive physiology. In addition to these shared characteristics, of particular importance at the individual/ontological level is when emotions appear developmentally, how they regulate the way in which we think, and the subjective experience of emotion. As Ekman states, "each emotion is not a single affective state but a family of related states. Each member of an emotion family shares the eight characteristics described. These shared characteristics within a family differ between emotion families, distinguishing one family from another. Each family can be considered to constitute a theme and variations. The theme is composed of the characteristics unique to that family, the variations on that theme are the product of individual differences, and differences in the specific occasion in which an emotion occurs. The themes are the product of evolution, while the variations reflect learning" (Ekman, 1994, p. 19).

Levenson (1994) defines emotions as "short-lived psychological—physiological phenomena that represent efficient modes of adaptation to changing environmental demands. They serve to establish our position vis-à-vis our environment, pulling us toward certain people, objects, actions, and ideas, and pushing us away from others. Emotions also serve as a repository for innate and learned influences, possessing certain invariant features along with others that show considerable variations across individuals, groups, and cultures".

According to Damasio (1999), "the human impact of the causes of emotions, refined and not so refined and of all the shades of emotions they induce, subtle and not so subtle, depends on the feelings engendered by those emotions. It is through feelings, which are inwardly directed and private that emotions, which are outwardly directed and public, begin their impact on the mind. But, the full and lasting impact of feelings requires consciousness, because only along with the advent of a sense of self, do feelings become known to the individual having them. Consciousness must be present if feelings are to influence the subject having them beyond the immediate here and now. The significance of this fact, that the ultimate consequences of human emotion and feeling pivot on consciousness, has not been properly appreciated" (p. 36).

He adopts an unorthodox view in combining self, consciousness, feeling, and emotion. "We know that we have an emotion when the sense of a feeling self is created in our minds. Until there is the sense of a feeling self, in both evolutionary terms as well as in a developing individual, there exist well-orchestrated responses, which constitute an emotion, and ensuing brain representations, which constitute a feeling. But we only know that we feel an emotion when we sense that emotion is sensed as happening in our organism" (p. 279). Damasio, (1999) proposes that the term feeling should be reserved for the private, mental experience of an emotion, while the term emotion should be used to designate the collection of responses, many of which are publicly observable.

He further distinguishes between "feelings" and "background feelings". "Background feelings" arise from background emotions, and these emotions, although more internally than externally directed, are observable to others in myriad ways: body postures, the speed and design of our movements, and even the tone of our voices and the prosody in our speech as we communicate thoughts that may have little to do with the background emotion. Prominent background feelings include: fatigue, energy, excitability, wellness, sickness, tension, relaxation, surging, dragging, stability, instability, balance, imbalance, harmony, discord. The relation between background feelings and drives and motivations is intimate: drives express themselves directly in background emotions and we eventually become aware of their existence by means of background feelings (Damasio, 1999).

The relation between background feelings and moods is also close. Moods are made up of modulated and sustained background feelings as well as modulated and sustained feelings of primary emotions--sadness, in the case of depression. Finally, the relation between background feelings and consciousness is just as close: background feelings and core consciousness are so closely tied that they are not easily separable. It is probably correct to say that background feelings are a faithful index of momentary parameters of inner organism states (Damasio, 1999).

Highlighting the biological basis of emotions, Damasio, (1994) defines emotions as "the combination of a *mental evaluative process*, simple or complex, with *dispositional responses to that process*, mostly *toward the body proper*, resulting in an emotional body state, but also *toward the brain itself*, resulting in additional mental changes" (, p. 139).

Averill (1994c) emphasizes emotions at an individual level. He highlights three meanings of emotions used in psychological theory namely emotional syndromes, emotional states, and emotional reactions. "An emotional syndrome is what we mean when we speak of anger, fear, love, grief, and so on, in the abstract. An emotional state is a relatively short-term reversible (episodic) disposition to respond in a manner representative of the corresponding emotional syndrome. An emotional reaction is the actual (and highly variable) set of responses manifested by an individual when in an emotional state" (p. 265).

Ellsworth (1994a) tends towards a view of emotions as a process rather than a set of entities. There are universal antecedents to human emotions insofar as there are universal human needs and goals. He emphasizes that, human beings are all of the same species sharing the same biological makeup. Ledoux (1994) further states that, emotional experience is initially an output of emotional-processing systems, not an integral part of the system that activates and processes emotional information. However, once emotional experiences occur, they come to exert important influences on subsequent emotional processing. It is important to keep this dual role of emotional experience in mind.

Theoretical Issues in Emotions

To emphasize the universality of emotions, Lazarus, (1993, 1994) states that there is a substantial biological influence in the emotion process, which leads to universals that should be found across divergent cultures. In his view, "some aspects of the emotion process are innate, and others are influenced by cultural values and individual differences in personality and the resulting coping process" (Lazarus, 1994, p. 171). Frijda (1994b) states that there are a number of stimuli to which humans are innately affectively sensitive; these stimuli are in themselves capable of eliciting affect. According to Hupka, Lenton, & Hutchinson (1999), what is universal is not only the ability to be emotional in the cultural setting's of ones' society but also, the perception of which emotion-arousing situations are worth encoding. Scherer, Wallbott, & Summerfield (1986), Scherer, Wallbott, Matsumoto, & Kudoh (1988), Lazarus & Smith (1988), Heider (1991), Scherer & Wallbott (1994), Scherer (1994c), present supporting evidence for the universality and cultural specificity of emotion elicitation.

As Scherer (1994a) states, "all organisms, at all stages of ontogenetic development, encounter blocks to need satisfaction or goal achievement at least some of the time. Thus, frustration in a very general sense is universal and ubiquitous. Equally universal are the two major reaction patterns—fight and flight. Consequently, it is not surprising that the emotional states that often elicit these behaviors—anger and fear, respectively—seem universal and present in many species" (p. 28).

Öhman, Flykt, & Lundqvist (2000) recently concluded, the evolutionary-functional perspective on the psychology of emotion shifts the emphasis from the unique phenomenology of human feeling to action tendencies and response patterns that we share with fellow inhabitants of the animal kingdom. Rather than conceptualizing emotion as a central feeling state more or less imperfectly mirrored in verbal reports, physiological responses, and expressive behavior, the evolutionary perspective views emotion as complex responses that include several partly independent components.

Are there basic emotions? For Panksepp (1994a, 1994b), the term basic refers to the unfolding of genetic potentials, emphasizing that genes are "dynamically responsive (to specific environmental influences) information stores". For Ekman (1994), Johnson-Laird & Oatley (1992), Tooby & Cosmides (1990), Öhman (1986), Zajonc (1985), all emotions are basic, all are relevant to deal with fundamental life tasks, and there are themes and variations due to learning influence. They use the term basic to emphasize the role of evolution and universal human predicaments in shaping both the unique and common features that emotions display. Thus, emotions evolved for their adaptive value with fundamental life tasks. Plutchik (1980) and Oatley & Johnson-Laird (1987), among others, have argued that basic emotions should also be defined at the most elementary level—that is, as those emotions which are no longer divisible into more elementary emotions.

Averill (1994a), Scherer (1994a), Shweder (1994) say the answer to the question "are there basic emotions?" should be "no". According to Averill, "being basic is a property of our concepts, not of emotions per se" (Averill, 1994a, p. 7). Simply because an emotional concept is basic within some classification scheme, it does not follow that the corresponding emotion is somehow more fundamental than other emotions. Although recognizing that basic emotions should be universal among the human species, they should be observable in rudimentary form in nonhuman primates, and so forth. He argues that the amount that biology contributes to our emotions is minimal. Scherer's theoretical stance is that it is the elements found in emotions that are universal, not the gestalts or patterns. Shweder acknowledges that all people have feelings, but not that all people interpret any of their feelings as emotions.

'Peripheral' and 'central, deep and shallow, inner and outer, have meanings other than only the description of physical space. Because of this interest in value, distinction, position, a view of emotion as quality also appears. Kühn (1947) hypothesizes that emotion performs the function of 'bridging the gap' between intellect and instinctual life. Heiss (1956) speaks of emotion as a mediator between inner and outer. Gerard (1951) and Lersch (1952) refer to emotion as a qualitative inner experience. Lersch holds that what we might call in general 'feeling life' signifies not only objective values, but also signifies the values of our own inner selves. Wenger (1950) conceives emotion as an activity that is always going on as a part of our experience. Thus, ascetic practices aim at the eradication of all emotions since emotion means attachment to life (Hillman, 1992).

For Freud, and Jung, emotions are 'ultimate, real existents, psychic forces or tendencies, independent of consciousness', so that 'the search for the essence of emotion leads necessarily to the question of the unconscious, or better said, of unconscious psychic forces'.

Ledoux (1994), Clore, (1994b), Damasio (1994, 1999) are explicit in stating that emotions cannot be non-conscious, i.e. they are conscious states. Ledoux (1994) however states that, "While non-conscious emotions do not exist, conscious emotional states are produced by unconscious processes" (p. 291). This is simply a statement about emotional consciousness that is often made about consciousness in general--that the content of consciousness is determined by processes that are themselves not accessible to consciousness (Jackendoff, 1987; Kihlstorm, 1987; Johnson-Laird, 1988; Lashley, 1956).

Some theorists bring in the idea that emotion is grounded (located) in the existential situation. Thus, emotion is the resultant of socially determined forces, which make up a situation. It is a reflection of social mans' adjustment to social milieu and it forms part of the conditioning process itself, informing the individual of the success or failure of his adjustment. In a review of some basic concepts in this field, Wittkower & Cleghorn (1954) summarize the various ways in which the term 'situation' is used. It is used to denote social environment (Landis, 1935), socio-historical conditions (London, 1950), geographical or physical location (Köhler, 1930), the immediate present (Lewin, 1935), socio-cultural patterns (Halliday & Mead), as regressions from maturation (Margolin), as environmental stimuli (Wolff, 1945), as a field of communications (Ruesch). Furthermore, the concept of situation plays a dominant role in theories of psychosomatic medicine, as in Selye's (1950) stress theory, where correlations are made between life-situations and emotional syndromes (Hillman, 1992).

Emotions are also viewed as an aspect, accompaniment, or result of something else. Hillman (1992) summarizes these as accompaniments and not causes (Pillsbury, 1928), as something secondary (Daly King), an epiphenomenona (Masserman, 1946), an after-effect (Malmud, 1927), as clues to the instinctive impulses (McDougall, 1937), as the 'felt aspect' of a drive or motive (Rivers, 1923; Sullivan, 1955). Malmud (1927) sees emotions as an accompaniment not of parts of the personality, but of the whole personality in its attitude at any given moment.

The modern view of conflict as an essential criterion of emotions is credited to John Dewey (1894). In the following theories, conflict becomes the essential criterion for emotion. Smith (1922) and Drever (1917) refer all emotion to the single concept of conflict. These theories take a view of man, which hardly allows him emotion. It becomes semi-pathological (Janet, 1931), destructive (Luria, 1932), substitutive (Tuttle, 1940), inappropriate (Drever, 1917), disharmonious (Paulhan, 1930). As a sign of human frailty, it is best rid of. It implies that the right state of man is an animal state without problems and conflicts. If there is an emotion at all, it must only represent harmony and appear as joy (Hillman, 1992).

Thus, disorder becomes a recurrent implication in these theories and forms a dominant hypothesis for other theorists. Wolff (1945), Kantor (1924) and Young (1943) view emotions as disorders. Howard (1928) and Carr (1928) add that this disorder makes emotion meaningless. Howard (1928) concludes that emotions "..have absolutely no value at all, but represent a defect in human nature" (p. 147). The disorder view uses a moral and ontological model, the foundations of which lie deep in antiquity. The Church Fathers identified emotion (desire) with the fall, and hence with evil and irrationality. Descuret (1860) presents a clear example of a theory of emotion built on this model. For him, emotion (passion) arises out of desire, which arises from 'need', which in turn signifies emptiness. Theories of emotion which depend on such key concepts as 'abreaction', 'social adaptation', 'well-adjusted', 'autonomic balance', 'homeostasis', 'compensatory feedback' imply an ideal condition of harmonious order and are only understandable on the moral model of perfection. The third variety of disorder theory accepts emotion as disorder, but it gives a positive and meaningful interpretation by finding reason and usefulness in it (Bergson, 1928). Strasser (1956), however, concludes that although emotion is irrational, it is nevertheless conditioned by reason. Sartre (1948) and Scheler (1967), however, look upon emotion as a necessary but inadequate solution to the problems that come up in the course of a lifetime. It does not resolve one single problem; but it enables one to endure the problem even though it has not been resolved. It is wider in scope than is reason as it is operative before and independently of reason. They tend to view affectivity as a mode of contact with the world that is immediate and hence more revealing than reason (Hillman, 1992, Byrne and Maziarz, 1969).

The Biological Basis of Emotions

Theorists have championed the role of the body in the causation of emotions. Shifting focus from the visceral, vascular, and glandular changes, contemporary theorists follow the lead of William James. He proposed that during an emotion the brain causes the body to change, and that the feeling of emotion is the result of perceiving the body's change. As Damasio (1994) states "not only must the mind move from a non-physical cogitum to the realm of biological tissue, but it must also be related to a whole organism possessed of integrated body proper and brain and fully interactive with a physical and social environment" (p. 252). As Panksepp, (1994a) states, "to believe that such brain systems, conserved throughout mammalian evolution, no longer move the human mind, is to plead a privileged metaphysical status for the human condition" (p. 22).

For an emotion to be an emotion there must be some bodily demonstration--and this holds true for those rare and saintly states of beatitude, not just for the turmoil's of fright, rage, or lust. When hope, boredom, or gladness does not transfuse the body, we have only feelings, sensations, or attitudes, we do not have emotion (Hillman, 1992). Damasio (1994) further states that, "the processes of emotion and feeling are part and parcel of the neural machinery for biological regulation, whose core is constituted by homeostatic controls, drives, and instincts" (p. 84). Brain and body are also interconnected chemically, by substances such as hormones and peptides.

Kolb and Taylor (2000) delineate the assumptions made in support of the neuronal basis of emotions: Behavioral states, including mind states, correspond to brain states. Emotions are not a unitary construct but rather are a multidimensional one. Different emotionally relevant behaviors are controlled by dissociable neural circuits. It is useful to dissociate brain-behavior relationships involved in the production of emotional behavior from those involved in the perception of emotions in others as well as the perception of emotionally relevant stimuli. An analysis of the neural control of facial expression provides a window on at least some of the neural systems involved in emotion. It is likely that fundamentally different neural circuits control categories of emotions, such as fear, than are emotions such as happiness. In addition, brain-behavior relationships can only be understood in the context of the neural pathways of emotional behavior in other animals, especially mammals.

Different emotions are produced by different brain systems. The essence of the available findings can be summarized as follows. First, the brain induces emotions from a remarkably small number of brain sites. Most of them are located below the cerebral cortex and are known as subcortical. The main subcortical sites are in the brain stem region, hypothalamus, and basal forebrain. Another important subcortical site is the amygdala. Aggleton and Young (2000), in their extensive literature review on the function of the amygdala in emotions, state that new lines of research are leading to a reappraisal of amygdala function in humans and other primates, and these suggests a similarity rather than a divergence of function across species. The results reviewed suggest that the amygdala has an especially important role in the identification of and reaction to negative (aversive) stimuli, (Ledoux, 2000). The findings help to reinforce the overall view that this structure is involved in a constellation of events related to stimulus-affective associations. Second, these sites are involved in processing different emotions to varying degrees. Third, some of these sites are involved in the recognition of stimuli, which signify certain emotions (Damasio, 1999).

Functions of Emotions

For Sartre (1948), Adler (1928), Britan (1931), Price (1953) and Dejean (1933), emotion has a functional purpose, which is a key to understanding it. It intends a specific object, goal, or end-result. In short, there is reason in emotion. According to Averill (1994b), "any given emotion can have a multiplicity of functions depending on the aspect of the emotion under consideration the nature of the consequences being considered (e.g. short term v/s long term), and whether the point of reference is the individual, species or society" (p. 102). Woodger (1956) and McGill (1954) think the split and conflict between emotion and reason is unnecessary. They seek to find reason *in* emotion, not to find the reason *of* emotion as do Adler, Sartre, Britan, and Dejean. MacMurray (1935) argues that "reason reveals itself in emotion by its objectivity, by the way it corresponds to and apprehends reality". "Our emotional life is us in a way our intellectual life cannot be; in that it alone contains the motives from which our conduct springs" (pp. 49–50).

According to Hillman (1992), "a principle intention of emotion is to connect our animal nature with the world in which it is embedded" (p. xii). Stein & Trabasso (1992), Ekman (1994) and Frijda (1994a) adhere to the Darwinian functionalist position, in that emotions serve an adaptive purpose. Frijda (1994a) proposes that just as all language does not fulfill its purpose of communication, so too, all emotion need not fulfill a functional purpose.

Clore (1994a) states that, "the primary function of emotion is to provide information". Emotions guide ones' attention to things that are relevant to goals and concerns of the individual. Such processes ensure that what appears most important is attended to first (Simon, 1967). They serve as an appraisal system for evaluating events that are relevant to the individual's well-being or concerns to the cognitive and action systems (Frijda 1994a). Emotions are further viewed as inner, non-verbal communications (Knapp, 1957) that serve as indicators of our motives (McDougall 1948). Thus, they are "complex narrative structures that permit us to express our feelings" (Shweder, 1994). Intrapersonal and interpersonal communication and expression is the functional purpose of emotions (Rapaort, 1950; Knapp, 1957; Saul, 1951; Frijda, 1994a; Clore, 1994b; Levenson, 1999).

Damasio (1994) showed that emotional processes are required for certain types of decision-making to occur. Other researchers indicate that "emotional intelligence", a particular type of socially oriented cognition (Salovey and Mayer, 1989) may be an important predictor of success in the real world independent of traditional, purely cognitive intelligence (Goleman, 1995). These findings are consistent with growing evidence that greater refinement and organizational complexity of emotion and cognition go hand in hand (Lane and Shwartz, 1987; Sommers and Scioli, 1986).

Reid (1923) emphasizes that emotions cognize real fact[2]. These real facts are in the social world and not only in subjective ideas and images within the personal psyche of the perceiver. This view accepts as normal that which is presented by emotion, including situations evoking hatred, fear, and depression. The concept of normalcy then becomes based on importance, on meaning, on value and not on normative data. This concept permits the person to adapt to his view of normal reality, which tells the truth about his world.

Moreover, emotions have social consequences (Fischer, 1991; Frijda, 1994a). Frijda and Mesquita (1994) add that norms exist with regard to having or not having particular emotions; to having or not having particular emotions in particular situations; and to showing or not showing the expression of particular emotions in either general or particular circumstances. Such norms can be assumed to be of both social and individual origin. These forms of significance can be assumed to depend both upon cultural emotion scripts (Fischer, 1991) and upon individual history and standards. The two may be at variance with one another. Also, individual norms and self-standards may cover emotions or emotion manifestations that cultural emotionology is silent about.

Emotions can be considered as processes that serve to monitor and safeguard the individual's concerns. Thus, protection of the self indicates their function (Scherer, 1984; Frijda, 1986; Ortony, Clore, & Collins, 1988; Lazarus, 1991; Frijda & Mesquita, 1994).

Socio-Cultural Basis of Emotions

Although the genetic and physiological basis of emotions is similar in all human beings, talk about emotions may vary because of cultural scripting and individual history. Talk about emotions and the beliefs that underlie them are separate issues from the physiology of emotions (Damasio, 1994; Lazarus, 1994; Hupka, et al, 1996).

Lutz (1988) takes an extreme functionalist position in stating that emotions are social in nature or, "anything but natural". The components may be combined and accorded their divergent functions and forms through social and cultural processes by which individuals try to accomplish, collectively and personally, a form of adaptation and adjustment to their own immediate socio-cultural, semiotic environment. Through this pursuit of adaptation and adjustment to ones' cultural and social environment, the component processes are organized and enabled to become emotions (Kitayama & Markus, 1994).

Lazarus (1994) identifies five basic propositions regarding biological universals with cultural sources of variability. Proposition 1: is central to all cognitive approaches in presuming that all complex creatures capable of learning--especially mammals--are characterized by the fundamental biological property of constantly evaluating what is happening with respect to their well-being. Proposition 2: takes as its premise that the appraised significance of what is happening involves a particular kind of relational meaning. Proposition 3: is that the connection between relational meaning and each emotion is innate, a characteristic of the species. Proposition 4: states that, coping changes emotions by changing the appraisals on which emotions rest. Proposition 5: which is an ontogenetic principle, is that variability in the emotion process arises from the divergent ways in which person-environment relationships are appraised.

Shweder (1993, 1994), Mesquita (1993), Frijda & Mesquita (1994) and Markus, Kitayama, & Vandenbos (1996) emphasize the mutual interactions of culture and emotion, and the relevance of cultural factors in the identification of emotions. Although there is a psychobiological basis for emotions (Lazarus, 1994), there might well be genuine cross-cultural differences in the extent to which primary evaluations of, say, loss, actually result in the "emotionalization" of experience at all. On this account, the emotional response is not a foregone conclusion of biology. The majority of the events that elicit emotions do so through their associated meanings, as grasped by the individual and as defined by the culture or the history of the individual.

Clore & Ortony, (2000) postulate three kinds of value structures underlying perceptions of goodness and badness: goals, standards, and attitudes. Different sources of value give ise to different kinds of affective reactions. (At times) goals are the source. Some emotions are based on standards rather than goals. Other emotions are based on attitudes or tastes. They further state that, "in any given situation the emotions experienced should vary as ones' focus shifts among the outcomes, actions, and objects involved, so that the same event might make one feel many different emotions in a short space of time".

Markus & Kitayama (1994) state that, "variation in normative social behavior provides a window on the interdependence between emotion and culture. Such variation implies that affective reactions, including what types of feeling states are commonly experienced and elaborated, as well as how, and under what conditions these states are experienced, may vary substantially" (p. 91).

Cognitive Appraisal and Emotions

"Emotion is a result of appraisal" is the mainstay of Lazarus's theory (1993). He grounds his principle by suggesting that "we are constructed in such a way that certain appraisal patterns and their core relational themes will lead to certain emotional reactions". And that, "once the appraisals have been made, the emotional response is a foregone conclusion, a consequence of biology". The psychobiological principle addresses universals in the process of emotional arousal, and the psychosocial principle, addresses variability and its causation. Lazarus analyzes emotions as a cognitive system. Cognitive appraisal is an evaluation of the significance of what is happening in the world for personal well-being. Whereas the emotional events that elicit emotions and the significance of emotions may differ appreciably from one culture to another, the elements of appraisal appear to be highly similar (Ellsworth, 1994b; Frijda & Mesquita 1994). Thus, events that are culturally coded as terrorist attacks or shameful behaviors are indubitably bad; events coded as actions of freedom fighters are indubitably good (Fisk, 1991). Concepts such as these are represented by affective schemas. Fiske (1982), Zajonc (1985), and Öhman (1986) subsequently developed a position of appraisals: automatic appraisal does not simply and solely operate on what is given biologically, dealing only with stimulus events that exactly fit what is given. Individual differences in our experience allow for enormous variations in the specifics of what calls forth emotion that are attributable to personality, family, and culture. And yet what calls forth an emotion is not totally malleable, there are some commonalities.

According to Trabasso & Stein (1993), situations in which emotions arise are appraised and reappraised, and this monitoring leads to the formulation of ways of coping with the problems that evoked the emotions, as well as with the problems that the emotions themselves cause. Emotions are thus defined as part of a dynamic process, sensitive to and changing with the environmental circumstances in which they occur.

Emotions and the Individual

Even more than the striking differences that have been observed between cultures, is the important role of individual differences within a single culture (Scherer, 1994a). As Averill (1994d) states, "each person writes the script of his emotional stories, based on his or her own past experiences, present circumstances, and future aspirations. However, an individual is not free to write just any story. It is society, more than personal biography that determines the types of subject-object relations that help constitute the emotions. More specifically, the personal-biographical subjectivity is a particularization of a social-historical subjectivity. In this sense, an emotional syndrome can be conceived abstractly as kind of social role that must be interpreted by the individual in order to be experienced. A person feels emotional just to the extent that he or she becomes engrossed in an emotional role, like a deep actor who experiences the part he or she is playing" (p. 385).

To summarize, an interdisciplinary approach has provided contemporary psychology with a holistic perspective on self and emotions. The self is no longer perceived in metaphysical terms. "It is not only the separation between brain and mind that is mythical: the separation between mind and body is just as fictional. The mind is embodied, in the full sense of the term, not just embrained" (Damasio, 1994). The self is a fact of our existence: a perceptually recreated neurobiological state. Feelings and emotions form an intrinsic, inseparable aspect of this sense of self.

An emotion is recognized as happening when our sense of self is created in our minds. Our emotions too find their base in the functioning of the brain and body. Evidence in the form of absence of a felt sense of self combined with absence of emotion is observed in patients with epileptic automatisms, absence seizures, akinetic mutism, advanced stages of Alzheimer's disease, and in states of coma. A decentralized, flexible, and pluralistic concept of self has emerged. The self is a dynamic knower, with many aspects to its identity. Although perceived as a "fictional character in a story told by the brain" (Dennet, 1991), this 'character' is our reality. Its distinctiveness is influenced by the socio-cultural surroundings in which it finds its self.

Although the self is an individual entity, it exists in relation to other selves. Thus, 'relationality' or 'being in relation' is its nature. The self, through emotion cognize facts in the environment, relevant for the well-being of the individual. Reason and emotions are intrinsically linked as seen by the way it corresponds and apprehends reality. They provide information to the self, guiding our attention to things that are relevant to the self. They are intrapersonal and interpersonal communications of the self, influencing the self and social relations. The aspects of social stimuli attended to by the self, and mode of emotional expression, is learnt by cultural scripting, and individual history.

NOTES

1. Most philosophers have been reactionary in nature to existing norms of human nature/behavior. Their teachings have been more ethical and moral, rather than metaphysical. The metaphysical/religious aspect has been more a fortuitous/incidental outcome of their contemplation on the savage nature of humanity. This can be seen in the teachings of Zoraster, Jesus, Mohammed, Mahavira, Buddha, and the more contemporary Hindu thinkers.
2. This would form the entire basis for our argument against the 'ideal' as expressed in all philosophies—emotions, in other words the self—the true self—(as emotions are an expression of the self) present the true picture of reality. The religio-philosophical aim of shunning emotions is, in effect, a means of escaping reality, as cognized by the self. 'I' recognize the 'reality' as it exists in the temporal world, 'I' feel or react to it, and 'I' experience or express an emotion to it. The search for the ideal thus becomes a search to escape this perceived reality. Escapism thus becomes the hallmark of our social behavior. Buddhism is in fact based entirely on this. In fact, all religions that speak of an ideal reality existing outside the realm of observed reality have these means and methods to escape from the 'normal' 'natural' (negatives) of the world. The illusion of "ideal" is what is created, and this creation causes the descent of man. (As in search for the ideal, he enters into a vicious circle of trying to achieve an illusive goal, and in the process adheres more to his essential nature). Whereas reality becomes his bête-noire, as he is constantly trying to escape it. This is reflected in mans' heart-rending eternal question, "what is happiness and where is the key to happiness?"

9

Understanding the Colors

In the preceding chapters an over view of concepts on self and emotions as elucidated in different religious belief systems and in contemporary interdisciplinary fields of psychology was presented. What is irrefutably evident is the range of perspectives present in the repertoire of our creative and linguistic capacities.

For the "true believer" in any belief system, other perspectives may seem like figments of imagination, half truths, and absolute fiction. For the skeptics, these perspectives viewed together may provide validation for their stand on the erroneousness or relativity of our belief systems. For the scientist within us, viewed with reason, these perspectives enable us to have a glimpse of humanity stripped off his belief systems. To see Man as Man—Man the animal, Man as a limb on the phylogenetic tree. Nevertheless, they provide us with a range of choice from which to select a belief system of our own, if we choose to exercise our freedom of thought and will. Contrarily, it provides us a constricting view of the world if, for whatever reason, we choose not to exercise our freedom.

Each aspect of the philosophies merits a comparative analysis as they have a bearing on our understanding of our conceptualizations about ourselves. A detailed analysis would be voluminous; I therefore restrict this discussion to the concepts under study.

The perspectives presented here are not that of a theologian or philosopher. As Khwaja (1977) states, "the theologian explores new meanings of traditional concepts in a spirit of defensive reverence to tradition." The philosopher reflects on the nature of our existence, and speculates on evolving an ideal. As psychologists, we seek to face up theology and philosophy, with our lived reality, reason, and science, and see how they influence our lives.

I do not stand on judgment on the genesis or validity of the belief systems reviewed. Rather, I accept them as part of our lived reality or *vyavharika satya*, and study their influence and impact on the life of individuals and society. Being nonjudgmental does not imply that we do not question our belief systems. If we consider them eternal and universal, why then are there differences in their concepts? Is it because they have grown from mans cognitive abilities, social exigencies, and personal emotional idiosyncrasies? In viewing ourselves as different socio-cultural products, do we disregard our shared evolutionary history?

The philosophies of Zoroaster, Mohammed, and Nanak are strikingly different from the rest. They are primarily directed at the individual to develop a moral self, group welfare being the goal; in other words, development of individualism within a group context. Here the influence of the context within which these systems grew is evident, in that the prophet/seers were responding to the chaos in their social environment. Their personal sensitivities recognized the "bad" in man, and gave rise to a philosophy emphasizing·the learning and development of the "good". Bliss or heaven is a fortuitous outcome. In contrast, the philosophies of Gautama and Mahavira are individualistic, arising from their individual angst, leading to personal salvation as the goal of life. As they were from princely backgrounds, excesses in their daily lives can be assumed. Gautama's ignorance of the realities of life is well known, in his discovery of poverty, disease, old age, and death. An intense emotional reaction gave rise to a conclusion that life is suffering, and that one needs to end this suffering. Thus, attaining *moksha* or *nirvana* is the goal. The origins of Hindu philosophy are unknown but one can speculate that it too grew in some such manner.

In this concluding chapter, I bring to fore the universality of our species, and the uniqueness of each individual within it. Unlike the creationist perspective, our universality is there for us to see in the shared prehistory of our species and our common biological basis. To address our uniqueness I look at our religious belief systems, and their influence on the formation of our distinctive personality. I compare the systems with contemporary knowledge, to address the issue of 'self' and 'emotions'. Further, I address the validity and relevancy of archaic beliefs in the formation and continued development in our present identity and behaviors.

The Biological Self

Like John Locke, I accept as obvious that the self truly exists. The moot point however, is our interpretation of the self. This forms the basis of our identity as individuals and as a society. As we have seen in the preceding chapters, there are numerous perspectives. According to Rhys David (1936/1978), with reference to the Vedas, we are so forgetful of the nascent stage of the concepts, that we overlook the fervor, and tend to look at these old sayings as conveying truths already old and well established. Truths that are an expansion of an all-inclusive wisdom.

A striking difference emerges in the perception of man in systems originating in the Indian subcontinent and those from the Middle East. Zoroastrianism and Islam accept man as man, and thus the principles of their belief system revolve around dealing with man as he is. Sikhism, the most recent belief system defers from the others of Indian origin in that it emphasizes the reality of man and his existence, within the larger framework of life. Buddhism and Jainism, being primarily atheistic, and ethical systems, accept man as man, although its philosophy veers him away from the state of his natural being. However, Buddhism denies the existence of the self, as the self is not identified with the body. In contrast, with its concept of the supreme self, Hindu philosophy perceives man, in his embodied state, as an illusion of the senses, created by the egos' false identification with the body. Although recognizing man as given in common experience, the Jaina does not accept him in this state, by perceiving his nature as antithetical to an ideal state, and thus needing to be transcended. This perception of man-as-man versus man-as-illusion, guides the further consideration of the biological self.

To what can we attribute this difference? Being in a thriving agricultural community, with relatively stable environmental conditions, the seers and sages of ancient India, may not have had to face up with the adversity of nature's fury, thus enabling them to conceive of a higher order of existence. Sikhism was born at a relatively stable time, in cosmopolitan environs. Guru Nanak was exposed to a wide array of contrasting beliefs which he probably evaluated and then arrived at his own humanistic concepts. The other systems grew in mountainous regions and stark, violent desert conditions. The instinct for survival was constantly tested. Thus, it should seem appropriate that man, as he is, is the focus. The reflection of this is evident in their conception of the after-life. Zoroastrianism and Islam speak of an after-life, with all that man desires, an ideal existence for him. This is a promise to provide man all that he has lacked in his sparse surroundings. Hinduism, Buddhism, and Jainism speak of an ideal that merges him with eternal bliss. An ideal, that rises above the excesses of the corporeal world.

Erikson (1968, 1982) begins his theorizing with the explicit statement of the following basic assumption: "man is, at one and the same time, part of a somatic order of things, as well as a personal and social one". The somatic order is said to involve the "body self" in which biological processes operate to bring about a hierarchical organization of organ systems.

In the words of Damasio (1994), "from an evolutionary perspective, if there had been no body, there would have been no brain (and consciousness, emotions, reason, and higher consciousness). The simple organisms with just body and behavior but no brain or mind are still here, and are in fact far more numerous than humans by several orders of magnitude" (p. 90).

In contrast to Hindu, Buddhist, and Jaina thought, in Zoroastrian, Islamic, and Sikh philosophy there is no clash between materialism and spirituality. They both have a role to play in man's life. However, there is a dichotomy between Islamic philosophy and practice, which views the two as antithetical to the goal of man. This however, differs according to the interpretation of the philosophy and dogmatism of the believer.

Man forms an integral part of Zoroastrian theological mythology, in his role in the fight against evil. Hence, its entire philosophy is centered on man, as he exists. Aside from this aspect, Zoroaster's thoughts were his emotional reaction, to the strife and bloodletting that formed a part of society then. A sense of helplessness, despair, pain, emanating from the sensitivities of an individual gave rise to a system that strived to enhance in man his proclivity to think about his actions, and improve them for his personal welfare and the welfare of his world. The instinctual needs of man, the importance of his body and its needs, the acceptance of pleasure and pain, the choice to experience his emotions, be they joy, anger, fear, grief, as a natural condition, are a part of Zoroastrian thought. It considers the biological self and the emotions as a natural condition.

Islam too grew from Mohammed's emotional reactions to social exigencies, as had existed at the time of Zoroaster. Islam too accepts man in his embodied state, his instincts and emotions as a part of the natural order. Islam says, the present physical is but a step in the process of life, the importance of the present not being denied at all.

Sikhism too developed from Guru Nanak's experience in two contradictory philosophies. The poet-philosopher that he was, arrived at his truth of the reality of man in his embodied state, with his instinctual and emotional needs. In the acceptance of the biological self, none of these systems accept the doctrine of the original sin. Thus, asceticism does not form a part of these systems.

Christianity too maintained the idea of man as a psychophysical organism, regarding the body as an essential constituent of human personality. However, due to the rise of an ascetical attitude within the church, the body came to be despised and regarded as the prison of the soul during the period of earthly life. The doctrine of original sin helped to supply part of the reason for this situation.

In contrast, as Hinduism sees the biological self as the "not-self", it does not regard the body as a relevant part of the being, but rather the part that produces the ills that put him in an enduring cycle of life and death. According to it, the self has a body, but the body is not the self. This misconstrual constitutes the primeval illusion (*māyā*) and is the prime cause of human suffering. Hindu philosophy considers the body and the sense of self that emerges with it, as a false identification of the ego with an illusion that lures us away from the supreme self. This tie leads to the suffering of the cycle of birth and death. The primeval illusion (*māyā*) has always masked the single reality hence people suffer from the same error of mistaking their true self with body, mind, and ego. Nevertheless, as the body forms a part of our reality, however illusory, Hindu thought deals with it extensively in its system of Ayurveda and yoga. However, yoga or psychophysical exercises are used as a means to transcend the body and attain *moksha* or supreme bliss. Thus, the conceptual split between the true self (the supreme self) and the empirical self (the embodied self) forms the primary differentiation in the conceptualization of the biological self in Hindu thought. Hindu thought recognizes the emotions as emanating from the body. This is expressed in various texts such as the *Mahābhārata, Bhagvad Gita,* Ayurveda system, the *Nātyaśāstra,* where the experiential descriptions of the emotions are extensively illustrated.

The Jaina emphasizes the causal interrelation between self and body, although the relation between them is external.

However, although the self is the constituent cause of emotions, the emotions do not originate in the body, but rather are "*karman matter*" attracted to the body. Although recognizing man as man, with his senses and emotionality, Buddhism and Jainism do not accept the biological self, further they negate it. Like Hinduism, they consider the existence of the body as due mainly to attachment, and the egos false identification with it. They consider it as the source of all suffering.

In Buddhism too, we find an inherent contradiction, for as much as it is based on a here-and-now principle, and recognizes the pain associated with life, the philosophy aims at evading these facts of life. When it states that birth, life, and death are the cause of mans suffering, it does not unconditionally accept life, in all its colors. It looks for an ideal state of existence. Existence in ignorance is suffering, and the clinging to a false individuality, as something real and permanent, is the root of this ignorance. Buddha declares that only life as we know it, and as we live it in ignorance, is painful.

Hinduism, Buddhism, and Jainism negate the vital core— the body. The progress in the biological sciences, have brought back into focus the organism, or the body, as the essential element, of our existence. Without the body, there would be no self. If we try to think of what this "no-self" is, it turns out to be an abstraction of our thought.

Although our conception of the biological self is wide and all-inclusive, sexuality, an instinctual expression of the biological self merits attention, as it is a focus in all the systems, in acceptance or rejection, and it influences how women are perceived. Northrup (1998, p. 112) has written on our cultural inheritance vis-à-vis our perception of our body. Although writing mainly from the western perspective, her observations cut across the East-West boundaries. All the belief systems reviewed negate our innate sensuality. They give girls and women the message that their bodies, their lives, and their femaleness demand an apology. Like the Judeo-Christian cosmology, that informs Western civilization that the female body and female sexuality are the personification of Eve, responsible for the downfall of mankind, the Eastern traditions too view the female as responsible for luring men away from their true goal of achieving eternal bliss, godhood, heaven, or supreme bliss. The menstrual cycle and the female body were seen as sacred until five thousand years ago[1]. Yet, throughout much of Western and Eastern written history, and in religious codes, the menstrual cycle has been associated with shame and degradation, with women's "dark, uncontrollable nature". The taboo associated with menstrual cycle has continued to this day. Instead of celebrating it as a positive aspect of our female being, our culture teaches us that we should not acknowledge our cycles; rather consider them as being a "curse." Humans are the only primates whose sexual desire and functioning are not necessarily related to the reproductive cycle. Our culture associates sexuality with genitalia, even though the expression of sexuality involves much more than that. Sexuality is an organic, normal, physical, and emotional function of human life. Paradoxically the men of Indian society too have not escaped from the misconceptions regarding the body and its instinctual needs. For men too perceive their functions as abnormalities, seeping them of their vital strength, intellect, and wisdom, causing grave anxiety in their discovery of their sensuality and sexuality. This is commonly perceived in the myths associated with normal sexual function. Thus, the life principle itself is negated.

Sikhism does not consider woman and her menstrual cycles as evil or unclean. Although Islam and Sikhism accept the biological self, in its social strictures and customs the woman and her body are negated. However, this negation appears to be more from a psychosocial perspective, as it is considered the prime factor that distracts man. Hence, the need to conceal it, lest it influence the man. Zoroastrianism too considers her cycles as being in the highest possible degree impure. As Sethna (1984) states in her review of mental health issues of Parsi women, "sometimes guilt is expressed by women about having defiled a prayer book or picture of Zoroaster by touching these when menstruating; this guilt has occasionally assumed delusional proportions". This observation may well be valid across women from all religions.

The conceptual framework of our belief systems, with the exception of Sikhism, is still pre-Darwinian, pre-genome. Consequently, a tension exists between science and our belief systems in the mind of the educated and the informed. The implications of this are seen in perceptions of what construes natural behavior and emotionality. The consequences of which are obvious on self-construal. Our sexuality is merely one aspect of our sensuality. Sensuality extends to other domains expressing our rhythmic flow with our surroundings. The individual thus lives in a world of dualities—the real world of his body and the abstraction of his belief system. Conflict arising between the two, are either dealt with anxiety or with a clear demarcation between the two. Thus living in a schizoid world of the real and the ideal, or unreal.

Conflict between individual pursuit for eternal bliss and denial of the biological self permeate in to social interactions, eventually our private self, and our intimate life. The Vedic perspective underlines the need to rise above nature in order to gain insight into the structure of reality. Does rising above nature imply discounting nature?

Ironically, the systems that advocate denouncement of the biological self emphasize the same in its social value systems. The pronounced need for a male heir (present in all systems), to facilitate the passage to heaven, forces man to address his biological self. The social fallout of this governs the skewed gender status and discriminations prevalent within society.

Contemporary interdisciplinary field of psychology has adequately emphasized the role of the content of our thoughts on our body and emotions, and its consequent effect on mental health and well-being. Our body is as much a source of our emotions as our cognitive appraisal of them and our

Understanding the Colors

environment. Hinduism, Buddhism, and Jainism advocate the negativity of our emotions and thereby a denial of their value. It is not the emotion that causes the problem, rather, it is our inability to understand, accept, and express the emotion, and respond to the situation in a healthy and adaptive fashion. Thus, denial, repression, and suppression of our emotionality adversely affect our body and sense of self, leading to mental and physical health problems. Thus, the sensitivity of our belief system to our body has a vital role to play in our considering our body as our comfort zone, rather than a zone of personal strife.

The Social Self

Our symbolic world influences our perception of the "real" world. However, a "commonsense" approach needs to be adopted in understanding these. The social self is the second tier of the self. It comprises the persona of the individual. The roles he plays based on his status within the group, and the internalized norms that dictate his behavior, eventually translates into the identity that he assigns himself. There are two aspects of the social self: the Collective self, and the Projected self.

As specified in the introductory chapter, the collective self develops from the acquired norms, and is learnt behavior. It is acquired through the acculturation process, representing the typical cognitive and emotional styles, prescribed norms of behavior and beliefs of the culture and subculture. It encompasses internalized roles, group goals, and is largely "other" defined. The projected self is based on the collective self that commands the individual to abide by the percepts of the collective self, in order to maintain his association with the group. It varies with the role that the individual is playing within a group. It is the 'persona' or the functional or representational behavior of an individual in social interactions. Within this domain lie the social ideals that were described in the earlier chapters.

In synthesizing the percepts of our belief systems with this psychosocial construct, it is imperative to bear in mind the discussion on the biological self. An aspect to be borne in mind is the schism between what a belief system states, the interpretation of it, the understanding of it, and the extent to which it is imparted to the laity. Thus we may find that aspects, of a system that find the approval of a section of society may be emphasized, or the beliefs may be followed without understanding their true meaning and rationale.

Zoroastrianism, Buddhism, Islam, and Sikhism are predominantly systems of ethical and moral behavior, laying emphasis on the development of the moral conscience. Their philosophy emerging from their prophets' angst with the then existing social reality. They developed out of a moral revolt against the ruling class i.e., from the oppressed against the powerful, and the inequalities of life. Hence their emphasis on moderation and goodness. Thus, the common man is urged to be good, discount as virtueless or evil that which is not good, and urged to live a moderate life, although enjoying the pleasures of a worldly existence.

Zoroastrianism and Sikhism emphasize the role of man in society. It is his duty to live in society, and look after his own and the welfare of others. Every individual has a moral right to the wealth and education of society. Man has the right of choice and a free will based on an objective and ethical structure. As the Parsees and Sikhs in Indian society and the world over, are in a minority, they prefer to maintain their distinctive ethnic and religious identity. As the Parsees have no restrictions on learning and education in all spheres, they have assimilated the world culture. As they are a non-aggressive community, valuing life and its pleasures, they have been able to maintain themselves apart from the larger communal strife that is a part of contemporary India. Although influenced by the larger attitude towards women, the Parsi women too exercise their freedom of choice.

Zoroastrianism is the only system that gives due importance to the child. The child is as much a part of their society as any other member. It is the bounden duty of a parent to inculcate within the child the basic principles of developing good thoughts, good words, and good deeds.

The social self of the Sikhs is largely influenced by Hindu cultural norms, as members of the Sikh community have arisen from the Indian Hindu/Muslim stock. Thus, cultural traditions and norms of behavior are perpetuated. This further adds to the fear of the Sikh community of being engulfed by the larger Hindu community. Hence, they strive to maintain their identity by emphasizing the external features of their community.

As Zoroastrianism and Sikhism advocate self-expression against self-repression, there is no inbred guilt regarding their behavior. Developing a personal conscience is a basic philosophy of these systems. Ironically, their need to maintain their ethnic and religious identity has proved to be contradictory to their philosophy and needs of their theology. Thus, the freedom of life, emotions, and will is laid down in defense of maintaining their distinctive identity. This forms their group or collective self.

Although Zoroastrianism, Islam, and Sikhism share similar perspectives on man, the social self of the Muslim in India is far more complex than that of the others. It is influenced by two factors, the belief system, and their status within the nation. In addition, there is a marked contradiction between philosophy and practice of Islam.

The meaning of "Muslim" is 'state of submission to one true God—*Allah*. According to Islam man is to conduct himself in accordance with the laws of his own being, and in harmony with the laws governing the rest of creation. The social strictures command self-discipline and self-control in an individuals' behavior. Truthfulness, reliability, respect for others, honesty, fairness, and justice are requirements of an individual in Islamic society. He is encouraged to be compassionate, pure, modest, and decent. The dignity and honor of women are strongly stressed. He is encouraged to be forgiving, but also maintains the right to retaliation. He is expected to live a fruitful life in the world, providing for himself and his family the necessities of life. Enjoyment in moderation is also a part of being a Muslim. Indiscipline, lying, injustice, killing, except in self-defense, revenge, tyranny, and oppression, stealing, irresponsibility, and excesses of any kind are strongly prohibited in Islam. Free mixing between the sexes outside of marriage is strictly prohibited.

However, there is a schism between the scriptures and their interpretations. These interpretations vary according to the interpreter and the political belief system within which they are practiced. Although Islam is democratic in spirit, Islamic society has not been able to usher in true democracy. The interpretations of Islamic social laws are relatively liberal in some societies than in others. This variance is found even within the same nation. The sub-sects have their own areas of emphasis that are strictly imposed on its followers.

The unity within the Islamic world rests in its principle that all humans belong to the family of *Allah*, thus there is no social hierarchical system governing their society. Although, the Mullahs and the Maulvis considered as being the interpreters of the Books, are accorded a higher status. This status takes on the form of an autocracy, where the common Muslim is denied his natural endowment of freedom of choice and judgment. Although the *Quran* and the Prophet do not claim that the *Sunnah* and the *Quran* is not the end of knowledge, implying the need for acquiring more knowledge, Islamic society adheres to a contrary view. The restriction to acquire knowledge is applied to women in all spheres of their lives. Thus, although equality and justice form an integral part of the belief system, in practice, women are denied this. Although this principle is extended to a marital relationship, in reality, freedom and equality are not part of women's lives.

The social injunctions further influence the perception of women and the biological self. Although the belief system recognizes and accepts the biological self, at the level of the social self, the biological self is negated. Women are socialized

Understanding the Colors

into fearing their bodies as that which invites sexual harassment or unfair treatment.

Although the source of the women's strength lies in their religious faith, few are able to recite the *Quran* in Arabic, a language that they do not know, and freely admit their ignorance of Islamic tenets and traditions. Few of them know what is exactly contained in the *Quran*. Their faith consists of following codes set forth by the clergy and simple moral code which makes them feel pious: cleanliness of the body and purity of mind, respect for the aged, remembering *Allah* often, saying *namaz*, and keeping the ritual fast of the *rozas*. In Kakar's (1996) analysis, a womans' religious beliefs contribute to her feeling of integration with the community and to a personal well-being that comes from an approving conscience. Yet, the belief system keeps the women imprisoned in a 'false consciousness', forming the schism between the social, and private self. The faith makes women accept their inferior status in relation to men who are deemed to be physically, mentally, and spiritually superior. From this perspective, the men of Islamic society too are governed by these injunctions and rules of behavior that influence their identity as individual Muslims within society. This, in fact, holds true for the majority believers of *any* system.

In India, an added component to the Muslim collective self is the communal aspect which has played a major role in the self perception of Muslims and the Hindu perception of the Muslim, which further influences his collective self. The constant battle of a 'them' versus 'us', although sharing the same national roots with the Hindu, creates a sense of alienation within the Muslim. Hence, the heightened identification with their faith infuses the Muslim with a sense of belonging to a shared historical past, with other Islamic states. The manifestation of this is observed in the increase in the external codes of identity and behaviors that provide the distinguishing 'cultural identification mark'. Further, zealousness may be adopted in order to maintain or highlight this identity, thereby increasing the identification with the collective self. This has an effect on the projected self, which strives to live by the norms of the collective self. These factors add to his aggression, as both their status and their group are in a volatile communal relation. In addition, individual experiences in strife with other communities enhance their aggressive responses. Thus, his emotions become an expression of the conflict within himself and with his environment.

Kakar (1996) has analyzed the components of the Muslims self-image, and his image from the perspective of a Hindu community. "The two components of the Pardi (a Hindu sub-caste) image of Muslims are the powerful and the animal like Muslim. Shared alike by men and women, the image of the Muslim's power seems to be more pronounced in men. This image of Muslim power is in relation to the Hindus' lack of it, due to their internal divisions" (p. 287). As Kakar states, the Hindu's image of Muslim animality is composed of the perceived ferocity, rampant sexuality, and demand for instant gratification of the male and a dirtiness, which is less a matter of bodily cleanliness and more of an inner pollution because of the consumption of forbidden foods (i.e., foods forbidden to the Hindu). The Hindu considers himself as 'morally *dharmic*', as they treat all women as mothers and sisters. The Muslim animality also lies in a heedless pursuit of pleasure without any regard for the concerns and obligations which make one human. Everything they do is for enjoyment. For the Hindu, a civilized moral self must renounce the Muslim animality as expressed in the males' perceived aggressiveness and sexual licentiousness. This perception has an impact on the relation between the two communities. From the Hindu perspective, the Muslim must be kept at a distance because that animality is too near their lived reality. In my analysis, the source of the conflict between the two can be traced to the divergent conception of man in the two belief systems. For the collective self is not only influenced by ones' own belief system, but also that of another that expresses a belief contrary to ones' own.

Describing the Hindu social self presents a big challenge. It has to be viewed from the perspective of its larger philosophy, social norms, and the differences that exist within the various sub-cultures that are a part of Hindu society. The primary challenge in Hindu thought arises in reconciling its concept of self with our lived reality. Hinduism negates the latter, thereby causing a primary schism between the belief system and the lived reality--a reality that is experienced by all and not just an abstraction or experience of a few 'enlightened' individuals. Our lived reality is our truth. The Hindu is steeped in a belief system that emphasizes the former as the true reality. Concepts of rebirth, *karma*, *moksha*, are a part of contemporary common language. In addition, contemporary sects of Hinduism, its various gurus, and schools of thought propound perspectives of the *Vedas* and *Upanishads* as the *only* truth of life. Thus, the Hindu lives in a dual mindset of another unknown 'true reality' and the known 'false reality'. Simultaneously, Hindu social norms immerse him within the boundaries of this 'false reality', compelling him to abide by its conventions. To reconcile to this dichotomy, the Hindu bifurcates his world in to the *adhyatmik* or spiritual and the *dharmic* or Hindu way of life.

The family, social customs, the myths and fables, influence the acquisition of cultural concepts and ideals. The mass media, particularly the movies and television, form a major role in popularizing and maintaining these themes. Thus, the individual attempts to live within both these worlds at the same time. However, there is a conflict between the two. This conflict is resolved from the scriptures itself, which prohibit him from doubting and questioning what is stated in them. Thus, at one level he is governed by laws of human nature, at another, this nature is constricted by social norms.

For instance, this is evident in the permission granted him to express his emotionality. At the outset, there is a negation of emotions, as they are considered as mental perversions. Restrictions of expressing emotions are more for men than for women. However, anger and aggression, which are strongly denounced by the belief system, are socially permitted as signs of "manliness". This is evident in the lack of condemnation of violence in society, and against women and children. Although the reason for the violence lies elsewhere, socially, as an emotion, it is not strongly condemned, as is the mutual expression of love. Ironically, the permission to acknowledge love is accepted only when expressed towards a god or a god man.

Although the concept of man varies between Islam, Sikhism, and Hinduism, Buddhism and Jainism, its social norms share similarities that influence the social self of the individual within the belief system. Like Islam, the others too command a strict adherence to its social rules of conduct. As these customs are of long standing and have become a way of life, they do not require a reference to its texts to ascertain their validity. For the individual, they are unquestionable. They share a similar interdependent social norm as opposed to an individualistic one, emphasizing the need for relationality. However, their concept of relationality is not individualistic but is group oriented. They both emphasize segregation between the sexes in social interaction, emphasizing a 'we' identity with respect to their subgroups. Thus, the individual exists *only* in relation to others. This is more apparent for women whose identity is over-shadowed by the parental family, which for them is a temporary home, and the husband's family, where they exist as outsiders. Thus, the strong relational bonds within which they ostensibly live are also restrictive and limited.

Although relationality or being in relation is emphasized, communication is not. There are rules of communication between family members, including parent and child, which are to be adhered to. Thus, the interdependence appears to be at a group level rather than between individuals. Socially prohibited from developing strong communicative relationships, the individual may well find comfort in an abstraction, which finds social approval.

Understanding the Colors

The social self of the Hindu is further governed by the various social ideals, the *Rama* ideal, the *Sita* ideal, the *Sati Savitri* ideal, that colors their social expectations. (*Sati Savitri* offered herself to *Yama*, the god of death, in return for the life of her husband). An extreme example of the Rama and Sita ideal is seen in a recent report (PTI, 2002), of a woman having to prove her chastity by undergoing the "*agni pariksha*" (fire test) by holding hot iron rods in her hands. (Sita had to prove her chastity by walking on fire, at the command of her husband Lord Rama)[2]. This ideal is pervasive in its other forms. This, influences the projected self of the individual, who strives to achieve or at least project this ideal. The social ideal, the *Rama* ideal, for men emphasizes deference and allegiance to the parents and for women to the husband, in preference to any other relationships, including her parents. For women, it emphasizes subservience to men. This further brings out a dichotomy in Hindu social thought, which on the one hand emphasizes bonding, and on the other discourages communication and developing a relationship. This adds to the dissonance between the social and private self, as relationality or being "in relation" is a need of the individual.

The social self of the individual is further influenced by the status of his group within society, and his status within the group. This has a tremendous impact on his individuality as it influences how others perceive him and his perception of himself. This increases the scope for prejudiced interactions, as an individual is addressed as a member of his caste, subcaste, and gender rather than on personal merit or demerit. The impact of this extends to all spheres, his life condition, relationships, and the opportunities that he can avail of. The influence on his sense of self is unfathomable as the philosophy binds him within a structure that is hereditary, unalterable, and contradictorily, where he plays a role in his destiny due to his actions or *karma*. Whereas the philosophical thought emphasizes the freedom of the soul, the social thought emphasizes constriction of the self.

Although maintaining a distinctive religio-cultural philosophy, the Jaina in Indian society is influenced by the Hindu social norms. Further, as the Jaina comes from all regional groups within the Indian sub-continent, it encompasses within its fold the varied social norms, that are common across the Indian spectrum. By contrast, the social self of the Buddhist or the neo-Buddhist in Indian society presents a peculiar challenge. However, this has a greater socio-political than a religio-philosophical reason. The tribals and schedule castes embraced Buddhism at the behest of Dr. Ambedkar, in reaction to the non-egalitarian divisions within Hindu society. In order to give them a status outside the constricting caste system, they were urged to embrace Buddhism, which propagates an egalitarian, casteless society. In the absence of sufficient data, I hypothesize that the tenets of Buddhism do not play a role in their personal and social development. It would appear that they are governed by their distinctive tribal and caste customs and norms. Due to their primary hierarchy in the larger Hindu caste based society, their social self is influenced by the constant conflict, prejudices, and discrimination against them through time. In such circumstances, it would be difficult to practice Buddhist principles of *ahimsa* and compassion. Moreover, the question arises as to how much of Buddhist principles are taught to them in the absence of a larger Buddhist base in India. Even in a Buddhist nation such as Sri Lanka, the on-going strife precludes the practice of Buddhist thought. For an individual who is *born* into a particular faith, as opposed to one who has studied the principles and *adopted* them as his chosen path, the social environment plays a far greater role in the formation of his social self. Thus, in the social sphere the influence of the larger Hindu social thought is far greater than that of Buddhist principles.

Although sharing similar belief systems, the linguistic and regional community to which the individual belongs further influences the Indian social self. Each community within the Indian fabric possesses distinctive characteristics that differentiate them from others.

Thus, in systems that do not accept man as man, and emphasize a higher, other reality, the individual has to deal with a dichotomy between the belief system and the lived reality.

In agreement with Kant, Cooley (1902, 1968), Mead (1925/1968, 1934), Erikson (1963, 1968, 1982), Shotter (1995), Harré (1991, 1995), and others, social constructionism plays a dominant role in our concept of self and our self-concept. Including the biological self in the total definition of the self, addresses Fisher's (1995a, 1995b) arguments opposing the reductions of mind and body to social processes. Both these aspects form an essential part of the whole.

As much as there are social differences in the construction of the self, there are social similarities that diffuse these differences. Harré's (1991) distinction between the public fact of personal identity (and an individual's sense of personal identity) and his claim that the concept of a "person" is culturally dependent, is evident in our review of the concept of self in different belief systems. As much as they are different, a common thread of human nature passes through them.

The Private Self

Hidden behind the mask of the social self, is the private self or the true self. It is the individual within. It is that aspect reflecting the hopes, dreams, and fantasies of an individual, hidden from external view, accessible only to the individual's consciousness, dealing with matters in the personal-emotional sphere, matters of day-to-day life, away from the glare of society. Matters as mundane as personal choice of food, to the profound, as his experience of existence, and his world. A personal interpretation of the world he lives in, of himself, and his life. His hopes to meet the adversities of daily life to his existential angst--whatever level that his sophistication of thought leads him to. His very own personal self, his "personhood". An element of his self, eclipsed by the shadows of his social self.

Sikhism is the only belief system that refers to a "real self" of the individual. The real self is evolved through the dialogue that it has within itself, which is referred to in Sikhism as the inner voice, voice of conscience or the voice of God within us. Self-examination is the basic requirement of the real self. From this self-examination emerges the moral self, which is central to Sikh philosophy.

Zoroastrianism, to an extent recognizes this aspect of the individual in its concepts of *Urvan* (the willing self), recognizing the duality in man's nature, and in the freedom of will and thought that it assigns to man. For it is from these principles that the private self is realized.

The schism between the belief system, biological self, and social self has its greatest impact on the private self. Further, as the principles of the belief systems for the biological and social self are constricting in nature, I hypothesize that the private self is most in dissonance with the social self. It is here that the individuals needs, desires, freedom of will and thought is curbed. The private self finds its expression in the emotions, conducting a dialogue between the different facets of the self. Our self-talk keeps us in touch with our feeling self--our body, and our social self--our environment. This constant interaction between the body and the verbalized private self gives an indication of the status of the individual. For at every point the individual is assessing the "feel good" factor in his environment. Much of the self-talk is devoid of the censorship that one imposes on oneself when talking externally. In this sense, then, the private self exercises freedom of thought. However, this freedom may be illusory, as guilt and repression are common when the bounds of what is permissible are crossed even in the shadows of the mind. Thus, self-censorship by an internalized external conscience induces him to shy away from his "true self".

As an individuals belief and value system determines much of his personality, and, as we have seen, there is considerable dichotomy between social beliefs, human nature, and personal needs, a concomitant discord is a part of the self. This further leads to aspects such as self-deception, self-alienation, self-image discrepancy, issues of self-esteem etc. Combined with the biological self, these contribute to our sense of well–being.

The private self emerges in a woman's stifled protest against subservience, even though she accepts the suppression commanded by the belief system. Although she may be a 'true believer', her private self comes to the fore to maintain her individuality, and survival. The private self is either a victim or a subjugated willing partner of its belief systems.

In exercising his freedom of will and finding his "true self", the individual may find himself isolated from society. In choosing to establish his own identity, perforce he needs to flow against the tide of social norms. This position too involves a certain degree of conflict within the individual and with society. The extent to which the individual is able to fuse his social self with his private self determines his sense of satisfaction and well–being. This fusion is not only in terms of accepting the social self or beliefs as ones' own, but also in accepting the difference between the social and private self, accepting the façade that stands in front of his true self.

Thus, an individual is able to maintain a balance between the two spheres, and in the absence of major dissonance between the two, experience a sense of well-being. However, in the presence of major dissonance between the two spheres the individual needs to identify his feelings and emotions that are translating his intimate self to himself. Thenceforth, to recognize and accept the differences, and evolve a position that permits him the least discomfort. Self-realization thus involves the integration of our biological, social, and private sense of self.

Out of this emerges the true self of the individual, that which is "I". At this point I raise the question, is the true self lost in the quagmire of the social self? Although a part of a collectivistic, interdependent society, does the individual rest without his personhood? The answers to these questions may not be amenable to any form of empirical investigation. The investigator would need to wade through the defenses of the social self and social conditioning to even get a glimpse of this self.

Human Nature

Morality is relative, as are cultural taboos. It is learnt behavior. Ethical principles propounded by a belief system aim to develop an ideal society. As involved students of human behavior, we need to look at ourselves as we are, without the coloring of morality. For it is only then that we can understand our selves as a species.

What then is human nature? The paradox of human nature is that it is as simplistic as it is complex. Any attempt at describing it is bound to do injustice to the panorama of images that it can evoke. At best, an overview of it can be presented within the scope of this study. Very concisely, our emotional ability is the essence of our nature, aside from our characteristic cognitive abilities. Without taking an extreme reductionist position, I present the essence of our nature.

A good starting point to explore our nature is to look at our belief systems. They provide implicit and explicit evidence regarding human nature as it has existed since the distant past. Irrespective of the geographical or cultural region, a common thread of fear, anger, violence, greed, abuse, oppression, and such are consistently observed through the ages. These behaviors have been denounced by our belief systems. No belief system has been able to rid man of "evil", rather they have aided it, ironically in its own name. An implication of this observation is that these form an inherent characteristic of our species. These behaviors have always existed in man. We have always lived in a "*kali yug*", where power, greed, violence, and oppression have been a part of the social order. Sociobiologists have pointed out our genetic predisposition for violence, which is significantly stronger in males, because of their different genetic makeup (Hamberg, 1971; MacCoby & Jacklin, 1975; Goldberg, 1979).

This, then, *is* the nature of man. Our mythologies are replete with the battle of good versus evil. Evil, represented as the abhorrent aspects of our nature, projected on the personal, social, or political opponent of a group. Very simplistically, a battle between love and hate, power, survival and death. Hate as a manifestation of fear, anger, greed, and such. Love as a manifestation of safety and contentment. Power as a means to survival.

The need for survival is an instinct. As Dawkins (1989) has proposed in his concept of the "selfish gene", this survival instinct emerges at the cellular level, where each cell strives to organize his environment in a manner that ensures its survival. As he states, "cooperation between the cells is a fortuitous outcome of this process". Guru Nanak called the life instinct *sanjog* (union). This instinctual need is translated in our experience of fear. Emergent from this is our fear of death. Fear for our survival, at a biological and psychological level. As our cognitive, linguistic, and creative abilities developed, we as a species developed our concept of immortality to cope with this fear. Our philosophers prophets and seers translated this instinctual fear, in their elaborate propositions on life after death, in the form of a heaven or a supreme soul or eternal bliss. Fear is seen universally in our species and across species.

This feeling of our biological self is translated into our emotional experience of fear. This further expands into the psychological fears of our private self and the social fears of our social self. In defense of this, arise our emotional reaction of anger and its concomitant behavioral manifestation as aggression, violence, at the threat to our existence, as individuals or as a group. Frustrations in our environment, threaten the survival of our self, bringing forth our emotional reaction of anger. In our collectivistic society, our individual identity is intrinsically linked to our group identity. Any threat to the survival of the group necessarily brings forth a fear of personal existence. Thus, we observe greater occurrences of mass violence in protection of a belief system.

The nascent stage of thought of our belief systems, addressed this fear by presenting us with idealized states of being. A conceptual shift is required to inculcate within man an acceptance of his mortality. However, the force of our belief systems prevents this, aiming to achieve equilibrium in a life hereafter. This is translated even in our concept of mental health. As Frankl (1984) states, "... it is a dangerous misconception of mental hygiene to assume that what man needs in the first place is equilibrium or, as it is called in biology, 'homeostasis', i.e., a tensionless state" (p. 127).

The need for power is another driving force in our nature. In Khwaja's (1977) analysis, power, whether existent by law or without it, implies the ability to coerce others into submission through physical strength or through control over the environment or the decision making process. The will to power is not suppressed in animals that fight without any sense of disapproval by others or by themselves. However, among man while the struggle for existence is acknowledged and approved, the struggle for power is not approved, although it is extensively pursued.

Nevertheless, the will to power, still is the pivot for group and interpersonal interactions. Power, in whichever manner or extent it is displayed, sustains our sense of self. Here we interpret power not only as a negative force, but also as a positive affect. Either the need arises as a compensatory affect to maintain a sense of self-worth, or it arises out of a positive sense of self. As a compensatory affect, power, fear, and aggression are intrinsically linked. Negativistic power, more often than not, is expressed in aggression--verbal or non-verbal, mild or violent. The ramifications of this need are seen in all spheres of group, interpersonal, and individual life. Irrespective of the belief system, this need is implicitly emphasized in our social norms. The most pernicious being the one held over children, women, and other oppressed classes.

All our belief systems advocate the suppression of women in some form or the other. Thus, being a persecutor and being a victim becomes an integral part of our nature. They express in some form or the other a fear of female sexuality. To what can we attribute this fear? What role do our belief systems play in the development of this fear? In Freudian analysis, it is the mother-whore dichotomy. Or, as in Kakar's (1996) analysis, in its Hindu version, the mother-whore-partner-in-ritual trichotomy. Alternatively, does it arise from a fear of loneliness, or, a need for power, and possession manifesting as jealousy? Is it simply the male's fear of his errant uncontrollable libido, projected on to the woman? Does it imply a fear of loss of freedom for man, being tied into the bonds of relationality and child-bearing responsibility that is a natural legacy for women? Is this fear translated into an elaborate philosophical system, that promises an ideal state of existence, which is unattainable for man if he were to be entrapped in the sensual, material life of women? Or is it simply a lack of understanding of and identification with the female body and its processes that has given rise to the aversion and awe? If child-bearing was the natural norm for both the genders--women *and* men, would our philosopher (and belief systems) have taken a turn towards asceticism and negation of our lived reality? The answer can lie anywhere in a wide spectrum of possible reasons.

Our socio-religious norms of sexual behavior are responsible for negating an instinctual need, our biological self that man has not been able to surmount. Thereby, creating guilt regarding sexuality, and generating the consequences of a suppressed and repressed need. The implications of this are far greater than they seem, as they influence the status of the female in society (as she is the conduit for arousing his passions), her freedom of will, choice, thought, and action. Her right to accept her self.

Whether reared in an interdependent or independent cultural milieu, man's primal search is for happiness and contentment. It is a need expressed by every individual. Being in a relationship is an instinctive need, the loss of which is expressed in the intense emotion of grief or fear. For a child reared in isolation, survival itself is at stake. Bonding and belonging are expressed as love and are essential for our sense of well-being, self-worth, our sense of self. From this emerges our emotion of happiness. In the words of the Dalai Lama (1999), "when we are born, we are free from all ideology and religion which come later, but we are not free from the need for human affection" (p. 25).

The consequences of the lack of happiness pervade the biological, social, and private self. However, in the Indian collectivistic society, social norms discourage individual relationships. The expression of independent relational love is denounced as being alien and against our cultural ethos. However, finding acceptance when expressed to an abstract, unknown being.

Our self and emotions have been variously negated. Despite condemnation by our moral and ethical doctrines, we follow our nature, although with the burden of retribution not only in an afterlife or in rebirth, but also in our social lives, at times with disastrous consequences. Are our belief systems responsible for creating a schism between the various facets of our self, further influencing our collective lives as a species?

Truth, As I See It

In this exposition of various perspectives on self and emotions, I have attempted to integrate philosophy and personal identity, within the background of contemporary knowledge of the dynamics of being human.

Following the lead of John Dewey (1894), Lazarus (1993, 1994), Damasio (1994, 1999), Neisser (1991), Harré (1991, 1995), and others, I put forth an integrationist position in the study of human behavior, a synthesis between reductive analysis and functional analysis. I put forth the view of species holism, psycho-cultural relativism, and individual atomism.

In contrast to the Hindu philosophies, I take a pragmatic position, that ours is not an observer-dependent reality. A world exists out there, regardless of whether we happen to perceive or measure it. This viewpoint finds its echoes in the Jaina concept of knowledge that accepts the existence of an objective reality, beyond and beside consciousness, and apprehended in perception. Zoroastrianism, Islam, and Sikhism accept the reality of the existent world. As Sperry (1995) states, "after laborious excavation of a giant ammonite or large dinosaur femur from a known geologic formation of some hundred million years past, one retains little patience with conjectures that these or their world did not exist until our observation". As the ancient Indian Lokayatas state, the *vyavaharika satya* (the truth of practical life) is the only truth.

Our species and our mind did not spring into existence fully formed. The entire edifice of the creationist stories of some of our belief systems, crumbles to the ground, with the weight of evidence garnered by evolutionary biologists, genetic scientists, cognitive archaeologists. This has far reaching consequences as it impacts the philosophical and social percepts of our belief systems.

The emergence of our species, homo sapiens, is dated at 100,000 years ago. The oldest of the existing belief systems, Zoroastrianism and Hinduism, are dated at 4000—4500 years ago. Thus, a wide period is seen before their development. In the intervening periods, numerous other beliefs have influenced the individual and been considered as "absolute truth".

Our belief systems are a creation of our cognitive and linguistic capacities, as much as they are a creation of our emotions, perception, and experience. This review of Hindu,

Buddhist, Jaina, Zoroastrian, and Islamic philosophies starkly brings into focus the differences existent in "absolute truth". In the absence of evidence, these "absolute truths" are perspectives of nascent thought. Despite contrary evidence, religious belief systems do not acknowledge errors in their beliefs. Conventional fields of science acknowledge errors in their perceptions, and present evidence in support of their truths.

As Carl Sagan (1995) remarked, "How is it that hardly any major religion has looked at science and concluded, 'this is better than we thought! The Universe is much bigger than our prophets said, grander, more subtle, more elegant? Instead they say, 'No, no, no! My god is a little god, and I want him to stay that way.' A religion, old or new, that stressed the magnificence of the Universe as revealed by modern science might be able to draw forth reserves of reverence and awe hardly tapped by the conventional faiths".

The whole spectrum of our emotions and behaviors, virtues and vices, whether in acceptance or condemnation, are seen in each of our belief systems. Thus, the single most common factor that binds our belief systems is our human nature.

Territoriality may well have been the cause for earlier battles between groups, but now the cause is primarily the belief system that rules our lives. Ironically, religion has not served its purpose of inculcating morality, but it has given a new, potent, reason for man to express his innate aggressive and fearful nature.

The biological self brings forth into existence our consciousness and cognitive capabilities. It lays the blueprint for the emergence of the self and its expression in emotions. In its absence, the self, consciousness and higher consciousness, ceases to exist. The biological sciences and the field of neuropsychology provide ample evidence in its support. This is "I".

Our personal identity is a product of social construction. However, I partially reject my hypothesis on one count:

Although our belief systems have influenced our values, beliefs, and social structure, it has failed to influence our nature as an animal species. For although influenced—profoundly at that— by the social self, the private and the biological self function on their own account. Man is still working in conjunction with his instincts and his internal self, still subject to an emotional life. Man is an instinctual rational emotive being. This is "me".

Our conception of our self is viewed on a historical continuum. As individuals, we view ourselves linked to our past. To achieve maturity, it becomes imperative to extricate ourselves from our past, to enable us to live in the present and look forward to a freer existence. This is our personal growth. As a society too, we need to extricate ourselves from our past, and look forward to a renewed existence. This would be a ancient society's growth. To extricate oneself from the past does not mean denial of the past. Rather, it is an understanding of the past, the context within which the concepts of our past were developed. The freedom thus gained, is not freedom from all suffering, for pain is as much a part of life, as is joy and rage. The freedom is from bondage to nascent ideas.

With the evidence from conventional scientific knowledge, the question arises, are our guiding philosophies misleading? Do they draw us away from the essence of our personhood in the hope of a utopian, blissful existence? The violence in historical and contemporary world need compel us to look beyond narrow boundaries, to develop a tradition of universalism. Coon (2000) uses the concept of "secularization" to label a cultural shift from mainly theological explanations of the workings of the universe to mainly naturalistic ones. Thus, in our strife ridden times a paradigm shift in our perception of the self as a "secular soul" in a "secular natural world" may be essential. "Secularism" or "universalism" not based on any theological or philosophical percepts, but that based on the truism of man as a unified animal species, sharing the same biological foundation. This is our "self" devoid of the colors of a faith.

NOTES

1. Northrup C. (1998) "*Women's Bodies, Women's Wisdom*". Bantam Books, p. 112. In her notes on this chapter (p. 840), she states, "for further information, see Riane Eisler, *The Chalice and the Blade: Our History, Our Future* (Harper San Francisco, 1988), and Marija Gimbutas, *Godesses and Gods of Old Europe, 7000 to 3500 B. C.* (Berkeley and Los Angeles: University of California Press, 1982). The degradation of women's wisdom took place gradually. By the time European settlers arrived in what would become the United States, native tribes were mixed in their approach to women. Some degraded them and their bodily processes, setting them apart in shame, while others revered women's wisdom." Although writing from a western perspective, much of what she says regarding "our cultural inheritance" for women, are features that we can identify with from an eastern perspective.
2. Draupadi, the central woman character of the epic *Mahabharata*, portrayed as a strong, assertive, and self-willed individual, does not find a place amongst the ideal Indian women.

References

Adler, A. (1928). Feelings and emotions from the standpoint of individual psychology. In Reymert, M. (Ed.) *Feelings and emotions—The Wittenberg Symposium.* Clark University.

Aggleton, J.P. & Young, A.W. (2000). The enigma of the amygdala: On its contribution to human emotion. In Lane, R.D. & Nadel, L. (Eds.), *Cognitive neuroscience of emotion.* New York: Oxford University Press.

Allen, G. (1931). *The evolution of the idea of god.* The Thinker's Library, No. 18, London: Watts & Co.

Allport, G.W. (1943). The ego in contemporary psychology. *Psychological Review,* 50, 451–478.

Ambedkar, B.R. (1973). *The Buddha and his dharma.* Siddharth Publication, Bombay.

Ambedkar. B.R. (1987). The ancient regime: The state of the Aryan society. In *Dr Babasaheb Ambedkar: Writings and speeches.* Vol. 3. Compiled by Vasant Moon. Edn. Dept. Govt. of Maharashtra.

Averill, J.R. (1980). A constructivist view of emotions. In R. Plutchik & H. KellerMan (Eds.), *Theories of emotion.* New York: Plenum.

Averill, J.R. (1991). Emotions are episodic dispositions, cognitive schemas, and transitory social roles: Steps towards an integrated theory of emotion. In D. Ozer, J.M. Healy, Jr., & A. J. Stewart (Eds.), *Perspectives in personality.* (Vol. 3a). London: Jessica Kingsley.

Averill, J.R. (1994a). In the eyes of the beholder. In Paul Ekman & Richard J. Davidson (Eds.) *The nature of emotion: Fundamental questions.* New York: Oxford University Press.

Averill, J.R. (1994b). Emotions are many splendored things. In Paul Ekman & Richard J. Davidson (Eds.) *The nature of emotion: Fundamental questions.* New York: Oxford University Press.

Averill, J.R. (1994c). Emotions unbecoming and becoming. In Paul Ekman & Richard J. Davidson (Eds.) *The nature of emotion: Fundamental questions.* New York: Oxford University Press.

Averill, J.R. (1994d). I feel therefore I am—I think. In Paul Ekman & Richard J. Davidson (Eds.) *The nature of emotion: Fundamental questions.* New York: Oxford University Press.

Baldwin, J. (1968). The self-conscious person. In C. Gordon & K. Gergen (Eds.), *The self in social interaction.* New York: John Wiley and Sons. (Original work published 1897).

Baumgardner, S.R. & Rappoport, L. (1996). Culture and self in post-modern perspective. *Humanistic Psychology,* 24(1), 116–139.

Belenky, M., Clinchy, B., Goldberger, N., & Tarule, J. (1986). *Women's way of knowing: The development of self, voice, and mind.* New York: Basic Books.

Bergmann, F. (1991). Freedom and the self. In Daniel Kolak and Raymond Martin (Eds.) (1991). *Self and identity: Contemporary philosophical issues.* New York: Macmillan Publishing Co.

Bergson, H. (1928). *Creative evolution.* London.

Bhaskar, B.J. (1972). *Jainism in Buddhist literature.* Alok Prakshan, Nagpur, India.

Bhole, R.R. (1991). Preface by Justice R.R. Bhole, 1973. In *The Buddha & his dharma,* by Dr. B.R. Ambedkar, 4th edition. Siddharth Publication, Bombay.

Blasi, A. (1976). The concept of development in personality theory. In J. Loevinger, *Ego development.* San Francisco: Jossey-Bass.

Bradley, D.G. (1963). *A guide to the worlds religions.* Englewood Cliefs, New Jersey: Prentice Hall.

Brandon, S.G.F. (1962). *Man and his destiny in the great religions*. Manchester University Press.

Britan, H.H. (1931). *The affective consciousness*. New York.

Brown, J.W. (1999). Neuropsychology and the self-concept. *Journal of Nervous and Mental Disease*, 187(3), 131–141.

Buhler, G. (1990). *Sacred books of the East—The laws of Manu*. Atlantic Publishers and Distributors, New Delhi.

Burkitt, I. (1994). The shifting concept of the self. *History of the human sciences*. 7(2) 7–28.

Buss, A.H. (1980). *Self-consciousness and social anxiety*. San Francisco: Freeman.

Byrne, E.F. & Maziarz, E.A. (1969). *Human being and being human: Mans' Philosophies of man*. New York: Meredith Corporation.

Campos, J., Campos, R.G., & Barrett, K.C. (1989). Emergent themes in the study if emotional development and emotion regulation. *Developmental Psychology*, 25, 394–402.

Carr, H. (1928). The differentia of an emotion. In Reymert, M. (Ed.) *Feelings and emotions—The Wittenberg Symposium*. Clark University.

Carver, C.S. & Scheier, M.F. (1991). self-regulation and the self. In J. Strauss & G.R. Goethals (Eds.). *The Self: interdisciplinary approaches*. New York: Springer-Verlag.

Chatterjee, J.M. (1934). *The ethical conceptions of the Gatha*. Jehangir B. Karani & Sons, Bombay.

Chattopadhyaya, D. (1976). *What is living and what is dead in Indian philosophy*. New Delhi: People's Publishing House.

Chaudhuri, N.C. (1979). *Hinduism— A religion to live by*. New Delhi B.I. Publications.

Chitkara, M.G. (1997). *Dr Ambedkar towards Buddhism*. New Delhi: APH Publishing Co.)

Chodorow, N. (1978). *The reproduction of mothering: Psychoanalysis and the sociology of gender*. Berkeley: University of California Press.

Chomsky, N. (1957). *Syntactic Structures*. Mouton.

Clore, G.C. & Ortony, A. (2000). Cognition in emotion: Always, sometimes, or never? In Lane, R. D. & Nadel, L. (Eds.), *Cognitive neuroscience of emotion*. New York: Oxford University Press.

Clore, G.C. (1994a). Why emotions are felt. In Paul Ekman & Richard J. Davidson (Eds.) *The nature of emotion: Fundamental questions*. New York: Oxford University Press.

Clore, G.C. (1994b). Why emotions are never unconscious. In Paul Ekman & Richard J. Davidson (Eds.) *The nature of emotion: Fundamental questions*. New York: Oxford University Press.

Colby, Chris. (1996–1997). *Introduction to Evolutionary Biology*, Version 2

Cooley, C.H. (1902). *Human nature and the social order*. New York: Scribner.

Cooley, C.H. (1968). The social self: on the meanings of "I". In C. Gordon & K. Gergen (eds.), *The self in social interaction*. New York: John Wiley and Sons. (Original work published in 1902).

Coon, D.J. (2000). Salvaging the self in a world without soul: William James' the principles of psychology. *History of Psychology*, 3(2), 83—103.

Cosmides, L. & Tooby, J. (1987). From evolution to behavior: evolutionary psychology as the missing link. In J. Dupré (Ed.), *The latest on the best: Essays on evolution and optimality*. Cambridge: Cambridge University Press.

Cosmides, L. & Tooby, J. (1992). Cognitive adaptations for social exchange. In J.H. Barkow, L. Cosmides, & J. Tooby (Eds.), *The adapted mind*. New York: Oxford University Press.

Cosmides, L. & Tooby, J. (1994). Origins of domain specificity: the evolution of functional organization. In L. A. Hirschfeld & S.A. Gelman (Eds.), *Mapping the mind: Domain specificity in cognition and culture*. Cambridge: Cambridge University Press.

References

Dalai Lama, (1999). *The Transformed mind: Reflection on truth, love, and happiness*. Renuka Singh (Ed.) Viking.
Damasio, A.R. (1999). *The feeling of what happens: body and emotion in the making of consciousness*. New York: Harcourt Brace.
Damasio, A.R. (1994). *Descartes' Error: Emotion, reason, and the human brain*. New York: Putnam Books.
David, R. (1936/1978). *The birth of Indian psychology and its development in Buddhism*. Delhi: Oriental Books Reprint Corporation.
Dawkins, R. (1989). *The selfish gene*. Oxford: Oxford University Press.
Dawkins, R. (1995). *River out of Eden*. London: Weidenfeld & Nicolson.
Dawkins, R. (1998). *Unweaving the rainbow*. Allen Lane: Penguin Press.
deCharms, R. (1968). *Personal Causation: The internal affective determinants of behavior*. New York: Academic Press.
Dejean, R. (1933). *L'Emotion*. Paris.
Dennet, D.C. (1991). The origins of selves. In Daniel Kolak and Raymond Martin (Eds.) (1991). *Self and identity: Contemporary philosophical issues*. New York: Macmillan Publishing Co.
Descuret, J.B.F. (1860). *La Médecine des passions*, 3rd Edition, Paris.
Dewey, J. (1894). The theory of emotion. *Psychological Review*, 1894, 1895.
Donald, M. (1991). *Origins of the modern mind*. Cambridge, MA: Harvard University Press.
Drever, J.A. (1917). *Instinct in man*. Cambridge.
Eagle, M.N. (1991). Psychoanalytic conceptions of the self. In J. Strauss & G.R. Goethals (Eds.). *The self: interdisciplinary approaches*. New York: Springer-Verlag.
Eichenbaum, L., & Orbach, S. (1983). *Understanding Women: A feminist and psychoanalytic approach*. New York: Basic Books.

Ekman, P. (1994) All emotions are basic. In Paul Ekman & Richard J. Davidson (Eds.) *The nature of emotion: Fundamental questions.* New York: Oxford University Press.

Ellsworth, P.C. (1994a). Some reasons to expect universal antecedents of emotion. In Paul Ekman & Richard J. Davidson (Eds.) *The nature of emotion: Fundamental questions.* New York: Oxford University Press.

Ellsworth, P.C. (1994b). Sense, culture, and sensibility. In S. Kitayama, & H.R. Markus. (1994). *Emotion and Culture: empirical studies of mutual influences.* Washington: American Psychological Association.

Engineer, A.A. (1985). *Islam and Muslims: A Critical Reassessment.* Jaipur: Printwell Publishers.

Engineer, A.A. (1992). *The Rights of Women in Islam.* Sterling Publishers Private Limited.

Engineer, A.A. (2001). *The Great Betrayal. What became of Islam's democratic vision?* The New Indian Express, March 24, 2001.

Erikson, E.H. (1963). *Childhood and society.* New York: W.W. Norton.

Erikson, E.H. (1968). *Identity, youth, and crisis.* New York: Norton.

Erikson, E.H. (1982). *The life cycle completed.* New York: Norton.

Fenigstein, A., Scheier, M.F., & Buss, A.H. (1975). Public and private self-consciousness: Assessment and theory. *Journal of Consulting and Clinical Psychology,* 43, 522–527.

Fernández-Armesto, F. (1998). *Truth: A history and guide for the perplexed.* Black Swan.

Fischer, A.H. (1991). *Emotion scripts. A study of the social and cognitive facets of emotions.* Leiden, the Netherlands: DSWO Press.

Fisher, A.H. (1995a). Whose right is it to define the self? *Theory and Psychology,* 5(3), Aug 323–352.

Fisher, A.H. (1995b). Empty sets of empty self: A response to comments on "Whose right is it to define the self?" *Theory and Psychology,* 5(3), Aug 391–400.

References

Fisk, R. (1991). *Pity the nation: Lebanon at war.* Oxford, England: Oxford University Press.

Fiske, S.T. (1982). Schema-triggered affect: Applications to social perception. In M.S. Clark & S.T. Fiske (Eds.), *Affect, and cognition: The 17th Annual Carnegie Symposium on Cognition.* Hillsdale, NJ: Erlbaum.

Fodor, J. (1983). *The modularity of mind.* Cambridge, MA: MIT Press.

Foreman, A. (1978). *Femininity as alienation.* Dallas, TX: Pluto Press.

Frankl, V.E. (1984. *Man's search for meaning.* New York: Washingto Square Press.

Frijda, N.H. & Mesquita, B. (1994). The social roles and functions of emotions. In S. Kitayama, & H.R. Markus. (1994). *Emotion and Culture: empirical studies of mutual influences.* Washington: American Psychological Association.

Frijda, N.H. (1986). *The emotions.* Cambridge, England: Cambridge University Press.

Frijda, N.H. (1994a). Emotions are functional, most of the time. In Paul Ekman & Richard J. Davidson (Eds.) *The nature of emotion: Fundamental questions.* New York: Oxford University Press.

Frijda, N.H. (1994b). Universal antecedents exist and are interesting. In Paul Ekman & Richard J. Davidson (Eds.) *The nature of emotion: Fundamental questions.* New York: Oxford University Press.

Fromm, E. (1964). *The heart of man.* New York: Harper Row.

Gard, R.A. (1962). *Buddhism.* New York: George Braziller.

Gerard. R.W. (1951). Discussion following 'The central mechanism of the emotions', by Spiegel, W. et. al., *American Journal of Psychiatry.*

Gergen, K.J. (1991). The social construction of self-knowledge. In Daniel Kolak and Raymond Martin (Eds.) (1991). *Self and identity: Contemporary philosophical issues.* New York: Macmillan Publishing Co.

Gergen, M. (1995). Postmodern, post-Cartesian positionings on the subject of psychology. *Theory and Psychology*, 5(3), Aug, 361–368.

Gilligan, C. (1982). *In a differing voice*. Cambridge: MA: Harvard University Press.

Goldberg, S. (1979). *Male dominance: The inevitability of patriarchy*. London: Sphere.

Goleman, D. (1995). *Emotional Intelligence*. New York: Bantam Books.

Greenfield, P.M. (1991). Language, tools, and brain: The ontogeny and phylogeny of hierarchically organized sequential behavior. *Behavioral and Brain Sciences*, 14, 531–595.

Greenwald, A.G. & Pratkanis, A.R. (1984). The self. In R.S. Wyer, Jr., & T.K. Srull (Eds.), *Handbook of social cognition*. (Vol. 3). Hillsdale, NJ: Lawrence Erlbaum.

Greenwald, A.G. (1982). Ego task analysis: An integration of research on ego-involvement and self-awareness. In A. Hastorf & A.M. Isen (Eds.), *Cognitive Social Psychology*. New York: Elsevier North Holland.

Greenwald, A.G., & Breckler, S.J. (1985). To whom is the self presented? In B.R. Schlenker (ed.), *The self and social life*. New York: McGraw-Hill.

Gupta, H.R. (1997). Guru Gobind Singh: Creation of the Khalsa. In Daljeet Singh & Kharak Singh (Eds.) *Sikhism: Its philosophy and history*. Institute of Sikh Studies, Chandigarh, India.

Gurumurty, S. (2000). Nursing Hatred. *The New Indian Express*, May 11, 2000. With refrences from: On the Abyss—Pakistan after the coup; and Beyond Faith, by V.S. Naipaul.

Halbfass, W. (1991). *Tradition and Reflection: Explorations in Indian Thought*. Delhi: Sri Satguru Publications. Indian Books Centre.

Hamberg, D. (1971). Psychobiological studies of aggressive behavior. *Nature*, 230, 19–23.

Handiqui, K.K. Yasastilaka, and Indian Culture. In Sangave, V.A., 1997, *Jaina Religion and Community*. Long Beach Publications.

Haneef, S. (1994). *What everyone should know about Islam.* Delhi: Adam Publishers and Distributors.

Harré, R. (1991). Personal being as empirical unity. In Daniel Kolak and Raymond Martin (Eds.) (1991). *Self and identity: Contemporary philosophical issues.* New York: Macmillan Publishing Co.

Harré, R. (1995). The necessity of personhood as embodied being. *Theory and Psychology,* 5(3), Aug, 369–373.

Hassnain, S. S. (1968). *Indian Muslims—Challenge and opportunity.* Lalvani Publishing House.

Haug, M. (1878). *Essays on the Sacred Language, Writings, and Religion of the Parsis'.* Kegan Paul, Trench, Trubner and Co. Ltd.

Heidegger, M. (1962). *Being and Time.* Transl. By John Macquarrie & Edward Robinson. London: Robinson Press.

Heider, K.G. (1991). *Landscapes of emotion: Mapping three cultures of emotion in Indonesia.* New York: Cambridge University Press.

Heiss, R. (1956). *Allgemeine Tiefenpsychologie.* Bern and Stuttgart.

Hillman, J. (1992). *Emotion: a comprehensive phenomenology of theories and their meaning for therapy.* Illinois: Northwestern University Press.

Hinkley, K., & Andersen, S.M. (1996). The working self-concept in transference: Significant-other activation and self-change. *Journal of Personality and Social Psychology,* 71, 1279–1295.

Hitti, P.K. (1956). *History of the Arabs.* New York.

Horney, K. (1950). *Neurosis and human growth.* New York: Norton.

Horney, K. (1967). The flight from womanhood. In H. Kelman (Ed.), *Feminine psychology.* New York: W. W. Norton. Original work published 1890).

Howard, D.T. (1928). A functional theory of the emotions. In Reymert, M. (Ed.), *Feelings and emotions—The Wittenberg Symposium.* Clark University.

Hupka, R.B., Lenton, A.P., & Hutchison, K.A. (1999). Universal development of emotion categories in natural language. *Journal of Personality and Social Psychology*, 77(2), 247–278.

Hupka, R.B., Zaleski, Z, Otto, J., Reidl, L., & Tarabrina, N.V. (1996). Anger, envy, fear, and jealousy as felt in the body: A five-nation study. *Cross-Cultural Research*, 30(3), 243–264.

Husserl, E. (1931). *Ideas: General introduction to pure Phenomenology.* Transl. By W.R. Boyce Gibson. New York: Macmillan.

Hutchinson, J.A. (1969). *Paths of faith.* New York: Mcgraw Hill.

Jackendoff, R. (1987). *Consciousness and the computational mind.* Cambridge: Bradford Books, MIT Press.

Jacobi, H. (1975). Jainism. In Jain, A.K. (Ed.), *Lord Mahāvīra in the Eyes of Foreigners'* New Delhi: Meena Bharati Publications Division.

Jain, J.C. (1947). *Life in Ancient India, as depicted in Jaina Canons.* Bombay.

James, W. (1890). *Principles of Psychology.* New York: Holt.

James, W. (1892). *Psychology: Briefer course.* New York: Holt.

Janet, P. (1931). *L'Etat mental des hystériques.* Paris.

Johnson-Laird, P.N. & Oatley, K. (1992). Basic emotions, rationality, and folk theory. *Cognition and Emotion*, 6, 201–223.

Johnson-Laird, P.N. (1988). *The computer and the mind: An introduction to cognitive science.* Cambridge: Harvard University Press.

Jordan, J. & Surrey, J. (1986). The self-in-relation: Empathy and the mother-daughter relationship. In T. Bernay and D. Cantor. *The psychology of today's woman: New psychoanalytic visions.* New York: Analytic Press.

Jordan, J. (1984). *Empathy and self-boundaries.* Work in Progress, No. 16. Wellesley, MA: Stone Center Working Paper Series.

Jordan, J. (1985). *The meaning of mutuality.* Work in Progress, No. 23. Wellesley, MA: Stone Center Working Paper Series.

Jordan, J. (1987). *Clarity in connection: Empathic knowing, desire, and sexuality.* Work in Progress, No. 29. Wellesley, MA: Stone Center Working Paper Series.

Jordan, J. (1989). *Relational development: Therapeutic implications of empathy and shame.* Work in Progress, No. 39. Wellesley, MA: Stone Center Working Paper Series.

Jordan, J. (1991). The Relational self: Understanding women's development. In Strauss, J. & Goethals, G. R. (Eds.) (1991). *The Self: Interdisciplinary Approaches.* New York: Springer-Verlag Inc.

Jourard, S. (1964). *The transparent self.* New York: Van Nostrand.

Jung, C.G. (1939). *The integration of personality.* New York: Farrar and Rinehart.

Kakar, S. (1981). *The Inner World.* Oxford University Press.

Kakar, S. (1996a). *Intimate relations. The Indian Psyche.* Viking: Penguin Books.

Kakar, S. (1996b). *The colors of violence.* The Indian Psyche. Viking: Penguin Books.

Kantor, J.R. (1924). *Principles of psychology.* New York.

Kaplan, A. (1984). *The "self-in-relation": Implications for depression in women.* Work in Progress, No. 14. Wellesley, MA: Stone Center Working Paper Series.

Karmiloff-Smith, A. (1992). *Beyond modularity: A developmental perspective on cognitive science.* Cambridge MA: MIT Press.

Kaur, U.J. (1990). *Sikh religion and economic development.* New Delhi: National Book Organization.

Khwaja, J. (1977). *Quest for Islam.* Allied Publishers Private Ltd.

Kihlstrom, J.F. (1987). The Cognitive Unconscious. *Science,* 237, 1445–1452.

Kitayama, S. & Markus, H.R. (1994). *Emotion and Culture: empirical studies of mutual influences.* Washington: American Psychological Association.

Klein, M. (1976). *Psychoanalytic theory: An explanation of essentials*. New York: International Universities Press.

Knapp, P.H. (1957). Conscious and unconscious affects: A preliminary approach to concepts and methods of study. Research in Affects (*Psychiatric Research Reports*, 8, 1957).

Koffka, K. (1935). *Principles of Gestalt psychology*. New York: Harcourt.

Köhler, W. (1930). *Gestalt Psychology*. London.

Kohut, H. (1984). *How does analysis cure?* Chicago: University of Chicago Press.

Kolb, B. & Taylor, L. (2000). Facial expression, emotion, and hemispheric organization. In Lane, R. D. & Nadel, L. (Eds.), *Cognitive neuroscience of emotion*. New York: Oxford University Press.

Kriyananda Swami (1975). *Translation of nine principal Upanishads*. Bihar School of Yoga.

Kühn, H. (1947). *Die bedeutung des fühlens für den erlebnisaufbau*. Der Nervenartz.

Kuppuswamy, B., (1990). *Elements of ancient Indian psychology*. Konark Publishers Pvt. Ltd.

Landis, C. (1935). Emotion. *Psychology*. N. Y.: Boring, Langfeld & Weld.

Lane, R.D. & Schwartz, G.E. (1987). Levels of emotional awareness: a cognitive developmental theory and its application in psychopathology. *American Journal of Psychiatry*, 144, 133–143.

Lashley, K. (1956). Cerebral organization and behavior. In H. Solomon, S. Cobb, & W. Penfield (Eds.), *The brain and human behavior*. Baltimore: Williams and Wilkins.

Latif, S.A. (1960). *Bases of Islamic Culture*. Hyderabad, India: The Institute of Indo-Middle East Cultural Studies.

Lazarus, R.S. & Smith, C.A. (1988). Knowledge and appraisal in the cognition-emotion relationship. *Cognition and Emotion*, 2, 281–300.

Lazarus, R.S. (1991). *Emotion and adaptation*. New York: Oxford University Press.

References

Lazarus, R.S. (1993). Lazarus rise. *Psychological Inquiry*, 4(4), 343–357.

Lazarus, R.S. (1994). Universal antecedents of emotions. In Paul Ekman & Richard J. Davidson (Eds.) *The nature of emotion: Fundamental questions.* New York: Oxford University Press.

Leakey, R. (1994). *The origin of human kind.* New York: Basic Books.

Ledoux, J.E. (1994). Emotional processing, but not emotions, can occur unconsciously. In Paul Ekman & Richard J. Davidson (Eds.) *The nature of emotion: Fundamental questions.* New York: Oxford University Press.

Ledoux, J.E. (2000). Cognitive-emotional interactions: Listen to the brain. In Lane, R.D. & Nadel, L. (Eds.), *Cognitive neuroscience of emotion.* New York: Oxford University Press.

Lersch, P. (1952). *Aufbau der person.* München.

Levenson, R.W. (1994). Human emotion: A functional view. In Paul Ekman & Richard J. Davidson (Eds.) *The nature of emotion: Fundamental questions.* New York: Oxford University Press.

Levenson, R.W. (1999). The intrapersonal functions of emotions. *Cognition and Emotion.* 13 (95), 481–504.

Levy, R. (1965). *The social structure of Islam.* Cambridge University Press.

Lewin, K. (1935). *A dynamic theory of personality.* N. Y.

Lewin, K. (1936). *Principles of topological psychology.* New York: McGraw-Hill.

London, I. (1950). Theory of emotions in Soviet dialectic psychology. In M. Reymert (Ed.). *Feelings and emotions: The Moosebeart Symposium.* New York.

Luria, A.R. (1932). *The nature of human conflicts, or emotion, conflict, and will.* New York.

Lutz, C. (1988). *Unnatural emotions: Everyday sentiments on a Micronesian atoll land their challenges to western theory.* Chicago: Chicago University Press.

MacCoby, E. & Jacklin, C. (1975). *The psychology of sex differences.* Stanford CA: Stanford University Press.

MacMurray, J. (1935). *Reason and emotion.* London.

Malmud, R.S. (1927). Poetry and the emotions. *Journal of Abnormal Psychology,* 1927–28.

Mansukhani, G.S. (1968). Introduction. In Harbans Singh (1968) *The message of Sikhism.* Delhi: Gurdwara Prabhandak Committee.

Mansukhani, G.S. (1977). *Introduction to Sikhism.* New Delhi: Hemkunt Press.

Maqsood, R.W. (1998). *Living Islam.* India: Goodword Books.

Marcel, G. (1949). *Being and having.* Transl. By Katherine Farrer, London: Dacre.

Margulis, L., & Sagaan, D. (1986). *Microcosmos: Four billion years of microbial evolution.* New York: Simon & Schuster.

Markus, H.R. & Kitayama, S. (1994). The social construction of self and emotion: Implications for social behavior. In S. Kitayama, & H.R. Markus. (1994). *Emotion and Culture: empirical studies of mutual influences.* Washington: American Psychological Association.

Markus, H.R. & Kunda, Z. (1986). Stability and malleability of the self-concept. *Journal of Personality and Social Psychology,* 51, 858–866.

Markus, H.R. & Wurf, E. (1987). The dynamic self-concept: A social psychological perspective. *Annual Review of Psychology,* 38, 299–337.

Markus, H.R., Kitayama, S., & Vandenbos, G.R. (1996). The mutual interactions of culture and emotion. *Psychiatric Services,* 47(3), 225–226.

Masserman, J.H. (1946). *Principles of dynamic psychiatry.* Philadelphia.

Maturana, H.R., & Varella, F. (1975). *Autopoietic systems.* (Report BCL 9.4). Urbana, IL: University of Illinois.

McCrone, J. (1991). *The ape that spoke: Language and the evolution of the human mind.* New York: Morrow.

McDougall, W. (1937). Organization of the affective life. *Acta Psychologia.*

References

McDougall, W. (1948). *An outline of psychology*, (12th Edn.), London.

McGill, V. (1954). *Emotions and reason*. Springfield, Ill.

McGuire, W.J., & McGuire, C.V. (1988). Content and process in the experience of self. In L. Berkowitz (Ed.), *Advances in experimental psychology* (Vol. 21). New York: Academic Press.

McGuire, W.J., McGuire, C.V., & Cheever, J. (1986). The self in society: Effects of social contexts on the sense of self. *British Journal of Social Psychology*, 25, 259–270.

McLeod, W.H. (1976). *Guru Nanak and the Sikh religion*. New Delhi: Oxford University Press.

McLeod, W.H. (1996). *The evolution of the Sikh community*. New Delhi: Oxford University Press.

Mead, G.H. (1934). *Mind, self, and society*. Chicago: Chicago University Press.

Mead, G.H. (1968/1925). The genesis of the self. In C. Gordon & K. Gergen (Eds.), *The self in social interaction*. New York: John Wiley and Sons.

Mehta, M.L. (1969). *Jaina Culture*. Varanasi: P. V. Research Institute, Jainashram.

Merleau-Ponty, M. (1962). *Phenomenology of Perception*. Transl. By Colin Smith. London: Routledge.

Merleau-Ponty, M. (1963). *The Structure of Behavior*. Transl. By Alden L. Fisher. Boston: Beacon Press.

Mesquita, B. (1993). *Cultural variations in emotions: A comparative study of Dutch, Surinamese, and Turkish people in the Netherlands*. Unpublished doctoral dissertation, University of Amsterdam, The Netherlands.

Miller, J.B. (1976). *Toward a new psychology of women*. Boston: Beacon Press.

Miller, J.B. (1984). *The development of women's sense of self*. Work in Progress, No. 12. Wellesley, MA: Stone Center Working Paper Series.

Mistree, K.P. (1998). *Zoroastrianism: An Ethnic Perspective*. Mumbai: Zoroastrian Studies.

Mithen, S. (1996). *The pre-history of the mind*. London: Thames & Hudson Ltd.
Monier, Willams. (1877). Hinduism. Quoted in Chaudhuri, Nirad C. (1979). *Hinduism– A religion to live by*. New Delhi: B.I. Publications.
Morgan, Kenneth W. (Ed.). (1953). *The Religion of the Hindus*. New York: The Ronald Press Company.
Muller, F.M. & Palmer. E.H. (1880 / 1996). *The Sacred books of the East Vo. VI, The Quran*. Delhi: Low Price Publications.
Navroji, D.M. (1928). *The Moral and ethical teachings of Zarathustra*. The University of Bombay.
Neisser, U. (1991). Five kinds of self-knowledge. In Daniel Kolak and Raymond Martin (Eds.) (1991). *Self and identity: Contemporary philosophical issues*. New York: Macmillan Publishing Co.
Northrup, C. (1998). *Women's bodies, women's wisdom*. New York: Bantam Books.
Oakley, K. (1951). Cf. Leakey, R. (1994). *The origin of human kind*. New York: Basic Books.
Oatley, K. & Johnson-Laird P. (1987). Towards a cognitive theory of emotion. *Cognition and Emotion*, 1, 51–58.
Öhman, A. (1986). Face the beast and face the fear: Animal and social fears as prototypes for evolutionary analyses of emotion. *Psychophysiology*, 23, 123–145.
Öhman, A., Flykt, A., & Lundqvist, D. (2000). Unconscious emotion: evolutionary perspectives, psychophysiological data, and neuropsychological mechanisms. In Lane, R.D. & Nadel, L. (Eds.), *Cognitive neuroscience of emotion*. New York: Oxford University Press.
Olton, D.S. (1984) Comparative analysis of episodic memory. *Behavioral and Brain Sciences* 7:250–251.
Ortony, A., & Turner, T.J. (1990). What's basic about basic emotions? *Psychological Review*, 97, 315–331.
Ortony, A., Clore, G., & Collins, A. (1988). *The cognitive structure of emotions*. Cambridge, England: Cambridge University Press.

References

Padmarajiah, Y.J. (1963). *A Comparative study of the Jaina Theories of Reality and Knowledge.* Delhi: Motilal Banarsidass.
Panksepp, J. (1994a). The basics of basic emotions. In Paul Ekman & Richard J. Davidson (Eds.) *The nature of emotion: Fundamental questions.* New York: Oxford University Press.
Panksepp, J. (1994b). Evolution constructed the potential for subjective experience within the neurodynamics of the mammalian brain. In Paul Ekman & Richard J. Davidson (Eds.) *The nature of emotion: Fundamental questions.* New York: Oxford University Press.
Paranjpe, A.C. (1998). *Self and identity in modern psychology and Indian thought.* New York: Plenum Press.
Parihar, R. (2001). Death Defying—An increasing number of Jainas are deciding when they want to die. *India Today,* April 2, 2001.
Paulhan, F. (1930). *The laws of feeling.* London.
Pillsbury, W.B. (1928). The utility of emotions. In Reymert, M. (Ed.) *Feelings and emotions—The Wittenberg Symposium.* Clark University.
Plutchik, P. (1980). *Emotion: A psychobioevolutionary synthesis.* New York: Harper & Row.
Pollak, S. & Gilligan, C. (1982). Images of violence in thematic apperception test stories. *Journal of Personality and Social Psychology,* 42, (1), 159–167.
Prabhavananda, S. (1978). *Spritual Heritage of India.*
Press Trust of India, (2002). 'Agni Pariksha' over chastity. *Indian Express,* July 7, 2002, pg. 9.
Price, H.H. (1953). *Thinking and experience.* London.
Pruthi, R. & Sharma, B.R. (Ed.). (1995). *Buddhism, Jainism and Women.* New Delhi: Anmol Publications.
Qutub, M. (1964). *Islam—The Misunderstood Religion.* Delhi: The Board of Islamic Publications.
Raju, P.T. (1995). The concept of man in Indian thought. In Radhakrishanan, S, and Raju, P.T. (Eds.) *The concept of man: A study in comparative philosophy.* New Delhi: Harper Collins.

Rapaport, D. (1950). *Emotions and memory.* New York.
Reid, L.A. (1923). Instinct, emotion, and the higher life. *British Journal of Psychology,* 191–2, 225.
Renou, L. (1961). *Hinduism.* New York: George Braziller.
Ridley, M. (1999). *Genome.* London: Fourth Estate Ltd.
Rivers, W.H.R. (1923). *Conflict and dream.* London.
Rogers, C.R. (1951). *Client-centered therapy: its current practice, implications, and theory.* Boston: Houghton.
Rosaldo, M.Z. (1984). Towards an anthropology of self and feeling. In R.A. Shweder & R.A. LeVine (Ed.), *Culture theory: Essays on mind, self, and emotion.* Cambridge, England: Cambridge University Press.
Rouhani, S. (1989). Molecular genetics and the pattern of human evolution. In Paul Mellars & Christopher Stringer (Eds.), *The human revolution: Behavioral and biological perspectives on the origins of modern humans.* Edinburgh: Edinburgh University Press.
Roy, K. (1966), *The concept of self.* Firma K.L. Mukhopadhyay, Calcutta.
Ryan, R.M. (1991). The nature of the self in Autonomy and Relatedness. In Strauss, J. & Goethals, G. R. (Eds.) (1991). *The Self: Interdisciplinary Approaches.* New York: Springer-Verlag Inc.
Sagan, C. (1995). *Pale blue dot.* London: Headline.
Saksena, S.K. (1944). *Nature of consciousness in Indian philosophy.* Banaras: Nand Kishore and Bros.
Salovey, P. & Mayer, J. D. (1989). Emotional Intelligence. *Imagination, Cognition, and Personality,* 9, 185–211.
Sangani, K.C. (1997). Ethical Doctrines in Jainism, In Sangave, Vilas. (1997). *Jaina religion and community.* Long Beach Publications.
Sangave, V. (1997). *Jaina religion and community.* Long Beach Publications.
Sartre, J.P. (1948). *The emotions: Outline of a theory.* Transl. By Bernard Frechtman. New York: Philosophical.
Sartre, J.P. (1956). *Being and nothingness: An Essay on phenomenological ontology.* Transl. By Hazel E. Barnes, New York: Philosophical.

Saul, L.J. (1951). *Bases of human behavior.* Philadelphia.
Scheier, M.F., & Carver, C.S. (1981). Public and private aspects of the self. In l. Wheeler (Ed.), *Review of personality and social psychology* (Vol. 2). Beverly Hills, CA: Sage.
Scheler, M. (1967). Towards a stratification of the emotional life. In Nathaniel Lawrence & Daniel O'Connor (Eds.) *Readings in existential phenomenology.* Englewood Cliffs, NB. J.: Prentice-Hall.
Scherer, K.R. (1984). Emotion as a mulitcomponent process: A model and some cross-cultural data. In P. Shaver (Ed.), *Review of personality and social psychology* (Vol. 5). Beverly Hills, CA: Sage.
Scherer, K.R. (1994a). Toward a concept of "modal emotions". In Paul Ekman & Richard J. Davidson (Eds.) *The nature of emotion: Fundamental questions.* New York: Oxford University Press.
Scherer, K.R. (1994b). Emotion serves to de-couple stimulus and response. In Paul Ekman & Richard J. Davidson (Eds.) *The nature of emotion: Fundamental questions.* New York: Oxford University Press.
Scherer, K.R. (1994c). Evidence for both universality and cultural specificity of emotion elicitation. In Paul Ekman & Richard J. Davidson (Eds.) *The nature of emotion: Fundamental questions.* New York: Oxford University Press.
Scherer, K.R., & Wallbott, H.G. (1994). Evidence for universality and cultural variation of differential emotion response patterning. *Journal of Personality and social Psychology,* 66, 310–328.
Scherer, K.R., Wallbott, H.G., & Summerfield, A.B. (Eds.). (1986). *Experiencing emotion: A cross-cultural study.* Cambridge: Cambridge University Press.
Scherer, K.R., Wallbott, H.G., Matsumoto, D., & Kudoh, T. (1988). Emotional experience in cultural context: A comparison between Europe, Japan, and the USA. In K.R. Scherer (Ed.), *Facets of emotion: Recent research.* Hilldale, NJ: Lawrence Erlbaum.

Schubring, W. (1962). *The Doctrine of the Jainas*. Delhi: Motilal Banarsidass.

Selye, H. (1950). *Stress*. Montreal.

Sen, K.M. (1961). *Hinduism*. Pelican Books.

Sethna, K.J. (1984). The Psychology and Psychopathology of Parsis'. In DeSousa, A. & DeSousa, D.A. (Eds.) *Psychiatry in India*. Bombay: Bhalani Book Depot.

Shaykh, N. (1964). The Perfumed Garden, tr. Sir Richard Burton (New York, 1964), cf. Vernal L. Bullough, *The subordinate sex—A history of attitudes towards women* (Chicago, 1974).

Shotter, J. (1995). A "show" of agency is enough. *Theory and Psychology*, 5(3), Aug, 383–390.

Shweder, R.A. (1993). Everything you ever wanted to know about cognitive appraisal theory without being conscious of it. *Psychological Inquiry*, 4(4), 322–326.

Shweder, R.A. (1994). "You're not sick, you're just in love": Emotion as an interpretive system. In Paul Ekman & Richard J. Davidson (Eds.) *The nature of emotion: Fundamental questions*. New York: Oxford University Press.

Simon, H.A. (1967). Motivational and emotional controls of cognition. *Psychological Review*, 74, 29–39.

Singh, Dalip. (1979). *Sikhism: A modern and psychological perspective*. New Delhi: Bahri Publications Pvt. Ltd.

Singh, Daljeet (1997a). Sikhism: Basic elements. In Daljeet Singh & Kharak Singh (Eds.) *Sikhism: Its philosophy and history*. Chandigarh, India: Institute of Sikh Studies.

Singh, Daljeet. (1997b). The gurus live their ideology. In Daljeet Singh & Kharak Singh (Eds.) *Sikhism: Its philosophy and history*. Chandigarh, India: Institute of Sikh Studies.

Singh, Daljeet. (1997c). Naam in Sikhism. In Daljeet Singh & Kharak Singh (Eds.) *Sikhism: Its philosophy and history*. Chandigarh, India: Institute of Sikh Studies.

Singh, Daljeet. (1997d). Sikh theory of evolution: Haumain and problem of hermeneutics. In Daljeet Singh & Kharak Singh (Eds.) *Sikhism: Its philosophy and history*. Chandigarh, India: Institute of Sikh Studies.

Singh, Daljeet. (1997e). The Sikh worldview. In Daljeet Singh & Kharak Singh (Eds.) *Sikhism: Its philosophy and history.* Institute of Sikh Studies,

Singh, Harbans. (1997). Guru Granth Sāhib—Guru eternal for Sikhs. In Daljeet Singh & Kharak Singh (Eds.) *Sikhism: Its philosophy and history.* Chandigarh, India: Institute of Sikh Studies.

Singh, I. (1969). *Philosophy of Guru Nanak: A comparative study.* New Delhi: Ranjit Publishing House.

Singh, I.J. (1997). *Sikhs and Sikhism: A view with a bias.* New Delhi: Manohar Publishers.

Singh, K. (1976). *The Sikhs today.* New Delhi: Sangam Books, Orient Longman Ltd.

Singh, Kapur. (1997). The Sikh thought. In Daljeet Singh & Kharak Singh (Eds.) *Sikhism: Its philosophy and history.* Institute of Sikh Studies,

Singh, W, (1981). *Philosophy of Sikh religion.* New Delhi: Ess Ess Publications.

Sinha, J. (1961). *Indian Psychology, Volume II Emotion and Will.* New Delhi: Motilal Banarsidass.

Smart, N. (1976). *The religious experience of mankind.* New York: Charles Scribner's Sons.

Smith, W.W. (1922). *The measurement of emotion.* London.

Snelling, J. (1987). *The Buddhist Handbook; A complete guide to Buddhist teaching and Practice.* Rider Publications.

Sommers, S. & Sciolo, A. (1986). Emotional range and value orientation: towards a cognitive of emotionality. *Journal of Personality and Social Psychology,* 5, 417–422.

Sperber, D. (1994). The modularity of thought and the epidemology of representations. In L.A. Hirschfeld & S.A. Gelman (Eds.), *Mapping the mind: Domain specificity in cognition and culture.* Cambridge: Cambridge University Press.

Sperry, R.W. (1995). The riddle of consciousness and the changing scientific worldview. *Journal of Humanistic Psychology,* 35(2), 7–33.

Stein, N.L. & Trabasso, T. (1992). The organization of emotional experience: Creating links among emotion, thinking, language, and intentional action. *Cognition and Emotion*, 6, 225–244.

Stern, D. (1985). *The interpersonal world of the infant: A view from psychoanalysis and developmental psychology*. New York: Basic Books.

Stiver, I. (1984). The meanings of "dependency" in female-male relationships. Work in Progress, No. 11. Wellesley, MA: Stone Center Working Paper Series.

Strasser, S. (1956). *Das gemüt*. Utrecht, Antwerpen & Freiburg.

Strauss, J. & Goethals, G.R. (Eds.), (1991). *The self: interdisciplinary approaches*. New York: Springer-Verlag.

Strauss, J. & Ryan, R.M. (1987). Autonomy disturbances in subtypes of anorexia nervosa. *Journal of Abnormal Psychology*, 96, 254–258.

Stringer, C. (1990). The emergence of modern humans. *Scientific American*. Dec. 1990, 98–104.

Stuss, D.T. (1991). Self, awareness, and the frontal lobes: A neuropsychological perspective. In J. Strauss & G.R. Goethals (Eds.). *The self: interdisciplinary approaches*. New York: Springer-Verlag.

Sullivan, H.S. (1953). *The interpersonal theory of personality*. New York: W. W. Norton.

Sullivan, H.S. (1955). *The interpersonal theory of psychiatry*. London.

Surrey, J. (1985). *Self-in-relation: A theory of women's development*. Work in Progress, No. 13. Wellesley, MA: Stone Center Working Paper Series.

Thompson, C. (1941). Cultural processes in the psychology of women. *Psychiatry*, 4, 331–339.

Tigunait, R.P. (1983). *Seven systems of Indian Philosophy*. The Himalayan International Institute of Yoga science and Philosophy of the U.S.A., Honesdale, Pennsylvania.

Titus, M.T. (1959). *Islam in India and Pakistan*. Calcutta: YMCA Publishing House.

Tiwari, K.N. (1983). *Comparative Religion*. Motilal Banarsidass Indological Publishers and Booksellers.

Tooby, J. & Cosmides, L. (1990). The past explains the present: Emotional adaptations and the structure of ancestral environment. *Ethology and Sociobiology*, 11, 375–424.

Trabasso, T. & Stein, N.L. (1993). How doe we represent both emotional experience and meaning?" *Psychological Inquiry*, 4(4), 326–333.

Trevarthan, C. (1979). Communication and cooperation in early infancy: A description of primary intersubjectivity. In J. M. Bullower (Ed.), *Before speech: The beginning of interpersonal communication*. New York: Cambridge University Press.

Tuttle, H.S. (1940). Emotion as substitute response. *Journal of General Psychology*.

Unger, P. (1991). The Physical View. In Kolak, D & Martin, R. (Eds.) (1991) *Self and identity—contemporary philosophical issues*. New York: Macmillan Publishing Co.

Van Kamm, A. (1966). *The art of existential counseling: A new perspective in psychotherapy*. Wilkes-Barre, PA: Dimension.

Varela, F. (1997). The Body's self. In Daniel Goleman (Ed.), *Healing emotions*. Boston: Shambhala.

Wadia, S.N. (1923). *The message of Mohammed*. London and Toronto: Dent and Sons, Ltd.

Watt, M.W. (1990). *Mohammed: Prophet and Statesman*. Oxford University Press.

Wenger, M. (1950). Emotions as visceral action: an extension of Lange's theory. In M. Reymert (Ed.). *Feelings and emotions: The Mooseheart Symposium*. New York.

West, E.W. & Muller, F.M. (1995a). *The sacred books of the East. Pahlavi Texts*. Vol. V, Part I. Delhi: Low Price Publications.

West, E.W. & Muller, F.M. (1995b). *The sacred books of the East. Pahlavi Texts*. Vol. V, Part III. Delhi: Low Price Publications.

Wild, J. (1965). Authentic experience: A new approach to "Value Theory". In J.M. Edie (Ed.), *An invitation to phenomenology: Studies in the philosophy of experience.* Chicago: Quadrangle.

Williams, B. (1970). The self and the future. *Philosophical Review,* 79, 161–180.

Williams, J.A. (Ed.) (1961). *Islam.* George Braziller, New York.

Willis, C. (1994). *The runaway brain.* London: Harper Collins.

Wilson, A.C. & Cann, R.L. (1992). The recent African genesis of humans. *Scientific America,* April 1992, pp. 68–73.

Wing-tsit, C., Ismal'il R., Kitagawa, J., Raju, P.T. (1969). *The great Asian religions: An anthology.* New York: Macmillan.

Winnicott, D.W. (1986). *The motivational processes and the facilitating environment: Studies in the theory of emotional development.* New York: International Universities Press.

Winnicott, D.W. (1988). *Human nature.* New York: Schocken.

Winternitz, M.A. (1933). *History of Indian literature.* Vol. II, University of Calcutta.

Wittkower, E.D. & Cleghorn, R.A. (1954). *Recent developments in psychosomatic medicine.* London.

Wolff, C. (1945). *The psychology of gesture.* London.

Woodger, J.H. (1956). *Physics, psychology, and medicine.* Cambridge.

Young, P.T. (1943). *Emotion in man and animal.* New York.

Zaehner, R.C. (1956). *The teachings of the Magi: A Compendium of Zoroastrian beliefs.* London: George Allen and Unwin Ltd.

Zajonc, R.B. (1985). Emotion and facial efference: A theory reclaimed. *Science,* 228, 15–21.

Zakaria, R. (1991). *Muhammad and the Quran.* Penguin Books.

Zaner, R.M. (1964). *The problem of embodiment.* The Hague: Martinu Nijhoff.

Zimmer, H. (1975). Jainism: A study. In Jain, A.K. *Lord Mahavira in the Eyes of Foreigners.* New Delhi: Meena Bharati Publications Division.

Subject Index

ahamkara, 51, 53, 57
   Sikhism, 209
ahimsa, 82, 274
   Jainism, 100, 108, 110, 125, 129
anger, 280
   Jainism, 116
   Hinduism, 58-60
   Islam, 171, 173
   Sikhism, 209
   Zoroastrianism, 143, 153
asceticism, 94, 261
   Islam, 170
   Sikhism, 191, 198, 207, 209
   Zoroastrianism, 145
Associationist theory, 219,
atheism, 258
   Jainism, 99
atman, 47, 50, 53, 58, 65, 74
   Avesta, 132, 133, 136
   Ayurveda, 261

Bhagavad Gita, 40-43, 49, 52, 67, 122, 261
bhakti, Sikhism, 183
Bible, 173
brotherhood, Sikhism, 208
buddhi, 51, 53

Carvakas, 39, 63, 90
celibacy
   Jainism, 126,
   Zoroastrianism, 147
children, Zoroastrianism, 150
Christianity, 133, 261, 208
conflict theory, 245

consciousness, 91, 104, 225, 240
   core -, 225, 227
   extended -, 226, 228
   Islam, 168, 171
   Sikhism, 200
creative freedom, Sikhism, 205, 206

death, Buddhism, 93
   Islam, 168, 171
death, life after -, Islam, 162, 164
determinism, 78
   Islam, 169, 176, 177
   Sikhism, 197
dharma, 68-70
   Buddhism, 79, 81
   Hinduism, 49
   Jainism, 98
dualism, Zoroastrianism, 135, 147

ego, concept of -, 220
ego, Sikhism, (*see* haumain), 194, 196, 201, 203
emotions, 25, 26, 225, 238, 240, 278, 282
   basic -, 243
   biological -, 241, 246-48, 251
   Buddhism, 91, 264
   culture, 33
   cognitive appraisal, 252-253
   disorder, 245
   evolution, 238
   evolutionary function, 242
   functions, 248-50
   Hinduism, 30-32, 57-60, 72-74, 264, 271
   intelligence, 249

Jainism, 104, 107, 110-112, 116-119, 126, 264
process, 241
religion and, 260
Sikhism, 208, 210, 260, 267
social -, 244
sociocultural basis, 250-252
Zoroastrianism, 145, 153, 260, 267
equality, Islam, 180
Sikhism, 188
evil, 266, 278, 279
Islam, 169, 170, 176
Jainism, 107
Sikhism, 192, 204, 206, 209
Zoroastrianism, 137-139, 141, 143, 147, 149, 152, 153
evolution theory, Sikhism, 212
evolution, 22, 23
creative -, 146,
language, 25
evolutionary psychology, 24, 25

fatalism, Islam, 176
fate, Islam, 169
fear, 127, 279
Buddhism, 93
Hinduism, 60
Islam, 171
Sikhism, 209
Zoroastrianism, 153
feelings, 225, 240
Buddhism, 93
feminist psychology, 232-235
free will, 277
Islam, 175-176
Sikhism, 192
Zoroastrianism, 150
freedom, 237
Buddhism, 84
creative -, Sikhism, 205, 206
Islam, 166, 167, 174, 177, 179
Sikhism, 188, 201, 214
grief, Islam, 171

gunas, 45, 52, 53, 57, 59, 67-69
Guru Granth Sahib, 183, 188, 189

Hadith, 160, 161, 165, 179, 180
halal, 163, 169
haram, 163, 167, 169
hate, Islam, 173
haumain, 201, 205, 209
heaven, Zoroastrianism, 140, 144
hell, Zoroastrianism, 140
human nature, 278
Jainism, 126
Sikhism, 209
humanism, 79
Islam, 177
Sikhism, 199, 200

Ideal,
Rama -, 71, 273
Sati Savitri -, 273
Sita -, 70, 273
ideals,
Hinduism, 34
Sikhism, 206
idol worship, Islam, 155
immortality, 279
individualism, Sikhism, 211
instinct,
survival, 279
death, Sikhism, 208
Islam, 171
Jainism, 116-117, 126
life, Sikhism, 208
Sikhism, 209
Islam, 267-268

Jainism, 257, 274
jihad, 170
joy, Hinduism, 58, 60, 72
joy, Sikhism, 211, 212

Kabbah, 155
kamma, 83, 84
karma, 129, 271, 273, ,

Subject Index

Buddhism, 77, 78, 81, 83, 86, 87, 95
Hinduism, 47, 48, 67-70,
Jainism, 100, 101, 103, 105, 106, 109, 114, 116, 118, 126, 262
Sikhism, 197

Khalsa panth, 187, 190
kosha, 50

Lokayatas, 39, 63, 64, 283
love, 282
   Hinduism, 58, 60
   Islam, 171, 173
   Sikhism, 183, 197, 208, 210, 212
   Zoroastrianism, 153

Mahabharata, 41-43, 49, 53, 59, 70
man in
   Buddhism, 90
   Hinduism, 65
   Islam, 167, 171, 173, 182, 260
   nature of -, 168, 172, 173
   role of -, 160
man, nature of -, 215
man, pre-history, 22
man, Sikhism, 192, 260, 266
man, Zoroastrianism, 141, 142, 147, 260, 266
   role of -, 147
Manu Smriti, 49, 53-56, 70, 71, 115
materialism, 260
   Hinduism, 63
   Islam, 171
maya, 261
   Hinduism, 57, 61-63
   Sikhism, 195, 196
Mimamsa-Vedanta, 46, 103
moksha, 40, 74, 81, 129, 257, 261, 271
   Hinduism, 47, 48, 70
   Jainism, 100, 107, 120, 121
monotheism, Islam, 157, 158
   Sikhism, 192

Zoroastrianism, 135
moral conscience, 266
   Buddhism, 266
   Islam, 266
   Sikhism, 187, 193, 202, 266
   Zoroastrianism, 150, 153, 266
morality, 278, 280
   Islam, 161, 167
   Sikhism, 188, 195, 198
   Zoroastrianism, 133

Natyashastra, 261
nirvana, Buddhism, 80, 81, 89, 92, 96
   Jainism, 100, 101
   Sikhism, 200, 201
Nyaya-Vaisesika, 44, 103

original sin, 127
   Sikhism, 211
   Zoroastrianism, 152
power, 280
   Islam, 173
   Jainism, 126
prakriti, 45, 52
   Sikhism, 192
prana, 50
prayer, Islam, 163
purusha, 45, 65

Quran, 154, 158-168, 173, 174, 178-181, 268-269

Rama ideal, 71, 273
Ramayana, 53, 70-71
rationalism, 229
   Jainism, 122, 123
   Sikhism, 197, 203, 204
reality, 257
   Jainism, 105
reason, Sikhism, 210
   Zoroastrianism, 144
rebirth, Buddhism, 84
   Jainism, 121

reincarnation, Zoroastrianism, 142
relativity, 282
renunciation, Islam, 172
　Sikhism, 200
resurrection, Zoroastrianism, 140
revelation, Islam, 162, 175
　Sikhism, 184
　Zoroastrianism, 137
Rig Veda, 132

salvation, Islam, 171
　Sikhism, 201, 208, 257
Samkhya-Yoga, 45, 103
Self psychology, 217
self realization, 277
self, 26-28, 216
　authentic -, 235,
　autobiographical -, 226, 228,
　autonomous -, 236,
　biological -, 29, 30, 32, 152, 258, 260, 264, 266, 276, 277, 282, 284
　Buddhism, 89, 262
　Hinduism, 50, 60, 261, 273
　Islam, 167, 168, 171, 172, 268, 269
　Jainism, 109, 120, 126, 261, 262
　Sikhism, 202, 211, 276
　Zoroastrianism, 141, 276
　collective -, 29, 30, 237, 265
　concept of -, 218, 230, 275
　core -, 29, 225, 227
　ecological -, 237
　empirical -, 219
　false - (see self Hinduism-), 237
　female -, 233
　genetic -, 223
　Greek, 215
　immune -, 29, 223, 224
　looking glass -, 229
　material -, 220
　metaphysical -, 215
　moral -, Sikhism, 202, 203, 205, 211, 257
　neural -, 29, 225

　organismic -, 29, 220-222, 230
　private -, 32, 235, 236, 275, 277, 279, 282
　women, 277
　projected - , 29, 30, 265
　proto -, 226
　public -, 30, 236
　real -, 30, 236,
　relational -, 30, 229, 233, 272
　social -, 29, 30, 32, 229, 236, 265, 267, 272, 276, 278, 282,
　Hinduism, 53, 271, 273
　Islam, 174, 177
　Jainism, 110, 126
　Sikhism, 207, 211
　Zoroastrianism, 152
　spiritual -, 219
　true -, 30, 235, 237, 276, 277

　universal, 61
　Upanishad, 52
　willing -, 276,
　Zoroastrianism, 141, 152
selfish gene, 279
sexuality, 281
　Jainism, 127, 128
Sharia, 163, 166, 174, 181
sin, Zoroastrianism, 135, 139, 152
Sita ideal, 70, 273
Social Constructionist Theory, 26, 29, 217, 230, 231
soul, Islam, 167, 171
　Zoroastrianism, 142
spirituality, 93, 100, 260
　Sikhism, 192, 194, 197, 201, 208, 210, 212
　Zoroastrianism, 144
suffering, Islam, 169

universality, 258
Upanishads, 43, 47, 49, 52, 62, 73, 81, 102, 271
Urvan, (see Self, Willing -), Zoroastrianism, 143, 152, 276

Subject Index

varnashram dharma, Sikhism, 207
Vedas, 39-43, 173
violence, 279, 280
    Sikhism, 209

women, 128, 263, 281
    Arab society, 155
    Buddhism, 94
    Hinduism, 54-56, 71

Islam, 174, 181, 182, 268
Jainism, 114-116, 126
private self, 277
    Sikhism, 198, 213, 263
    Zoroastrianism, 148, 149, 150, 152, 263
work, Sikhism, 207
worldly life, 283
    Sikhism, 210, 212

Author Index

Adler, A. 248
Aggleton, J. P. 248
Allport, G. 220
Ambedkar, B. R. 78-84, 91-95
Andersen, S. M. 218
Averill, J. R. 241, 243, 248, 253
Baldwin, J. 29, 232
Barrett, K. C. 32
Baumgardner, S. R. 215
Belenky, M. 234
Bergmann, F. 30, 237
Bergson, H. 246
Bhaskar, B. J. 97-99, 119
Bhole, R. R. 79
Blasi, A. 29, 222
Bradley, D. G. 184
Brandon, S. G. F. 64, 90, 92, 94, 131-134, 146, 173, 174
Breckler, S. J. 236
Britan, H. H. 248
Brown, J. W. 29, 225
Buhler, G. 56-57
Burkitt, I. 29, 232
Buss, A. H. 30, 236
Byrne, E. F. 29, 216, 217, 219, 221, 246
Campos, J. 32
Campos, R.G. 32
Cann, R. L. 23
Carr, H. 245
Carver, C. S. 218, 236
Chatterjee, J. M. 145
Chattopadhyaya, D. 49, 62-64
Chaudhuri, N. C. 39, 42, 49
Cheever, J. 218

Chitkara, M. G. 79, 89
Chodorow, N. 233
Chomsky, N. 26
Cleghorn, R. A. 244
Clinchy, B. 234
Clore, G. 244, 249, 250, 252,
Colby, C. 23
Collins, A. 250
Cooley, C. H. 29, 229, 232, 275
Coon, D. J. 285
Cosmides, L. 24, 25, 243
Dalai Lama 93, 94, 282
Damasio, A. 26, 29, 225-229, 238-241, 244, 246-251, 254, 259, 282
David, R. 90, 97, 258
Dawkins, R. 22, 29, 223, 279
deCharms, R. 29, 222
Dejean, R. 248
Dennet, D. C. 216, 254
Descuret, J. B. F. 246
Dewey, J. 245, 282
Donald, M. 24
Drever, J. A. 245
Eagle, M. N. 217
Eichenbaum, L. 230, 233
Ekman, P. 238, 239, 243, 249
Ellsworth, P. C. 32, 241, 253
Engineer, A. A. 177, 180-182
Erikson, E. H. 29, 229, 232, 259, 275
Fenigstein, A. 30, 236
Fernández-Armesto, F. 34
Fischer, A. H. 29, 230, 275
Fisher, A. H. 29
Fisk, R. 253

Author Index

Fiske, S. T. 253
Flykt, A. 242
Fodor, J. 25
Foreman, A. 223
Frankl, V. E. 270
Frijda, N. H. 32, 242, 249-251, 253
Fromm, E. 30, 235
Gard, R. A. 79, 85, 86, 87, 94
Gerard. R. W. 244
Gergen, K. J. 30, 233
Gergen, M. 217
Gilligan, C. 30, 233, 235
Goethals, G. R. 216, 235
Goldberg, S. 279
Goldberger, N. 234
Goleman, D. 249
Greenfield, P. M. 25
Greenwald, A. G. 30, 220, 236, 237
Gupta, H. R. 191
Gurumurty, S. 179
Halbfass, W. 44, 65, 66, 68
Hamberg, D. 279
Handiqui, K. K. 116
Haneef, S. 158, 163-165, 167, 171
Harré, R. 29, 217, 230, 231, 275, 282
Hassnain, S. S. 166
Haug, M. 33-136, 138-140
Heidegger, M. 29, 229
Heider, K. G. 242
Heiss, R. 244
Hillman, J. 244-246, 249
Hinkley, K. 218
Hitti, P. K. 154
Horney, K. 30, 232, 236
Howard, D. T. 245
Hupka, R. B. 242, 251
Husserl, E. 216
Hutchinson, J. A. 242
Hutchison, K. A. 184
Ismal'il R. 184
Jackendoff, R. 244
Jacklin, C. 279
Jacobi, H. 102, 107
Jain. J. C. 116

James, W. 219, 220, 246
Janet, P. 245
Johnson-Laird P. 243
Jordan, J. 30, 232-236
Jourard, S. 30
Jung, C. G. 30, 235
Kakar, S. 61, 68, 69, 128, 270
Kantor, J. R. 245
Kaplan, A. 30, 233
Karmiloff-Smith, A. 25
Kaur, U. J. 197
Khwaja, J. 161, 162, 165, 170, 173, 174, 256, 280
Kihlstrom, J. F. 244
Kitagawa, J. 184
Kitayama, S. 26, 251, 252
Klein, M. 30, 232
Knapp, P. H. 249
Koffka, K. 220
Köhler, W. 245
Kohut, H. 30, 217, 232
Kolb, B. 247
Kriyananda, Sw. 52
Kühn, H. 244
Kunda, Z. 218
Kuppuswamy, B. 52, 56, 90, 93
Landis, C. 245
Lane, R. D. 250
Lashley, K. 244
Latif, S. A. 160, 162-166, 168-170
Lazarus, R. S. 175, 176, 242, 250-252, 282
Leakey, R. 22, 23, 26
Ledoux, J. E. 241, 244, 248
Lenton, A. P. 242
Lersch, P. 244
Levenson, R. W. 239, 249
Levy, R. 156, 157
Lewin, K. 220, 245
London, I. 245
Lundqvist, D. 242
Luria, A. R. 245
Lutz, C. 32, 251
MacCoby, E. 279

MacMurray, J. 249
Malmud, R. S. 245
Mansukhani, G. S. 184, 193, 209
Maqsood, R. W. 160-164, 167, 169, 171
Marcel, G. 29, 220
Margulis, L. 23
Markus, H. R. 26, 218, 251, 252
Masserman, J. H. 245
Maturana, H. R. 29, 222
Matsumoto, D. 242
Mayer, J. D. 249
Maziraz, E. A. 29, 216, 217, 219, 221, 246
McCrone, J. 22, 26
McDougall, W. 245, 249
McGill, V. 248
McGuire, C. V. 218
McGuire, W. J. 219
McLeod, W. H. 183-187, 190, 193, 194, 208
Mead, G. H. 29, 229, 232, 245, 275
Mehta, M. L. 102, 103, 106, 112
Merleau-Ponty, M. 29, 221
Mesquita, B. 250, 251, 253
Miller, J. B. 30, 233, 234
Mistree, K. P. 132, 136, 137, 140, 142-148, 152
Mithen, S. 22, 24-26
Monier, W. 42
Morgan, K. W. 40
Muller, F. M. 137, 145, 146, 150, 154, 156
Navroji, D. M. 132, 133, 140-144
Neisser, U. 29, 30, 237, 282
Northrup, C. 262
Oakley, K. 25
Oatley, K. 243
Öhman, A. 242, 243, 253
Olton, D. S. 24
Orbach, S. 230, 233
Ortony, A. 32, 250, 252
Otto, J. 242, 251
Padmarajiah, Y. J. 102, 105

Palmer, E. H. 154, 156
Panksepp, J. 243, 247
Paranjpe, A. C. 26
Parihar, R. 125
Paulhan, F. 245
Pillsbury, W. B. 245
Plutchik, P. 243
Pollak, S. 235
Prabhavananda, S. 54
Pratkanis, A. R. 30, 220, 237
Price, H. H. 248
Pruthi, R. 114-116, 120, 127
Qutub, M. 171
Raju, P. T. 75
Rapaport, D. 249
Rappoport, L. 215
Reid, L. A. 250
Reidl, L. 242, 251
Renou, L. 48, 49
Ridley, M. 22, 26
Rivers, W. H. R. 245
Rogers, C. R. 30, 236
Rosaldo, M. Z. 32
Rouhani, S. 23
Roy, K. 102, 104, 120, 216
Ryan, R. M. 29, 221, 222, 230, 233
Sagaan, D. 23
Sagan, C. 17, 284
Saksena, S. K. 61
Salovey, P. 249
Sangani, K.C. 111
Sangave, V. 99, 101, 111-116
Sartre, J. P. 29, 246, 248
Saul, L. J. 249
Scheier, M. F. 30, 218, 236
Scheler, M. 246
Scherer, K. R. 238, 242, 243, 250, 253
Schubring, W. 98, 99, 103, 105, 107, 109, 110, 118, 127
Schwartz, G. E. 250
Sciolo, A. 250
Selye, H. 245
Sen, K. M. 47
Sethna, K. J. 151, 152, 263

Author Index

Sharma, B. R. 114-116, 120, 127
Shaykh, N. 181
Shotter, J. 29, 230, 275
Shweder, R. A. 243, 249, 251
Simon, H. A. 249
Singh, Dalip. 188, 193-195, 202-206, 209-211
Singh, Daljeet 184, 186, 188, 189, 191-194, 198, 199, 202, 204-206, 208, 211
Singh, Harbans. 185, 188-190
Singh, I. J. 207, 212, 214
Singh, K. 184, 191, 192, 214
Singh, Kapur. 197
Singh, W. 189, 196-201, 206
Sinha, J. 53, 57-60, 92, 94, 104, 110, 116-119
Smart, N. 184
Smith, C. A. 242
Smith, W. W. 245
Snelling, J. 77, 81, 89, 91, 93, 94
Sommers, S. 250
Sperber, D. 25
Sperry, R. W. 283
Stein, N. L. 249, 253
Stern, D. 222
Stiver, I. 30, 233
Strasser, S. 246
Strauss, J. 216, 230, 233, 235
Stringer, C. 23
Stuss, D. T. 29, 218, 225
Sullivan, H. S. 30, 229, 232, 245
Summerfield, H. 242
Surrey, J. 30, 212, 214, 233
Tarule, J. 234
Taylor, L. 247
Thompson, C. 232
Tigunait, R. P. 45, 46, 50-52, 85-89

Titus, M. T. 179
Tiwari, K.N. 42, 48, 79, 89, 90, 100, 106-108, 132-135
Tooby, J. 24, 25, 243
Trabasso, T. 249, 253
Trevarthan, C. 30, 232
Turner, T. J. 32
Tuttle, H. S. 245
Unger, P. 29, 222
Van Kamm, A. 30, 236
Vandenbos, G. R. 251
Varela, F. 29, 223, 224
Varella, F. 29, 222
Wadia, S. N. 176
Wallbott, H. G. 242
Watt, M. W. 156
Wenger, M. 244
West, E. W. 137, 145, 146, 150
Wild, J. 30, 236
Williams, B. 29, 222
Williams, J. A. 157, 160, 177, 219
Willis, C. 25
Wilson, A. 23
Wing-tsit, C. 184
Winnicott, D. W. 30, 222, 236
Winternitz, M. A. 97, 116
Wittkower, E. D. 244
Wolff, C. 245
Woodger, J. H. 248
Wurf, F. 218
Young, A. W. 248
Young, P. T. 245
Zaehner, R. C. 133, 136, 137, 141, 147-149
Zajonc, R. B. 243, 253
Zakaria, R. 157-159
Zaner, R. M. 221
Zimmer, H. 121-123